AF290392

Dunkirk, D-Day,
Kohima and
The Death Railway

This book is dedicated to the memory of all who served in the Royal Norfolk Regiment during The Second World War.

'When you go home, tell them of us and say.
For your tomorrow. We gave our today.'

Dunkirk, D-Day, Kohima and The Death Railway

The Royal Norfolk Regiment in the Second World War

Neil R. Storey

PEN & SWORD HISTORY

AN IMPRINT OF PEN & SWORD BOOKS LTD.
YORKSHIRE – PHILADELPHIA

First published in Great Britain in 2026 by
PEN AND SWORD HISTORY
An imprint of
Pen & Sword Books Ltd
Yorkshire – Philadelphia

ISBN 978 1 03614 991 8

A CIP catalogue record for this book is available from the British Library.

Typeset in Times New Roman 11.5/15 by
SJmagic DESIGN SERVICES, India.
Printed and bound in the UK by CPI Group (UK) Ltd.

The Publisher's authorised representative in the EU for product safety is
Authorised Rep Compliance Ltd., Ground Floor, 71 Lower Baggot Street,
Dublin D02 P593, Ireland.
www.arccompliance.com

For a complete list of Pen & Sword titles please contact
PEN & SWORD BOOKS LIMITED
George House, Units 12 & 13, Beevor Street, Off Pontefract Road,
Barnsley, South Yorkshire, S71 1HN, England
E-mail: enquiries@pen-and-sword.co.uk
Website: www.pen-and-sword.co.uk

or

PEN AND SWORD BOOKS
1950 Lawrence Rd, Havertown, PA 19083, USA
E-mail: uspen-and-sword@casematepublishers.com
Website: www.penandswordbooks.com

Contents

Introduction

This is the story of ordinary men who did extraordinary things, the men who served in the Royal Norfolk Regiment during the Second World War. Admittedly, not every Norfolk man served in the Royal Norfolk Regiment during the conflict, but there were many who did. They were to be found in Norwich and every Norfolk town and village, and for many of us they were the dads, grandads, uncles, brothers, family friends and local men we used to know. Some would wear their medals and march again at remembrance events, smartly turned out in their blazers with regimental ties, with well-polished Britannia cap badges in their berets and medals jingling and catching the winter sunlight. Some chose to remember in their own quiet way, but every man I have ever known who served under the cap badge of the Royal Norfolk Regiment was proud to have done so.

As a young historian I was fortunate to know many of them and could count them among my family and friends. I feel honoured that they shared their stories with me. To a man they never spoke of doing anything out of the ordinary, even if they had been awarded gallantry medals for incredible acts of bravery. Some acted on orders, some acted on their own initiative, some just saw red in a combat situation. To them they just did what they did because their comrades were in a tight corner and they didn't want to let them down.

Over the years after the end of the Great War the two Regular Army battalions of the Royal Norfolk Regiment had, like so many of their county regiment counterparts, enjoyed the years of peace and had been able to take the time to promote smartness, drill, regimental sports and training. The interwar years also saw the Norfolk Regiment honoured by being made a royal regiment for their distinguished service during the First World War on the Silver Jubilee of HM King George V in 1935, which also coincided with the 250th anniversary of the regiment.

Up to 1939 there was no major recruitment drive for men to join the army nor compulsion to join, the posters at the recruiting offices simply emphasising the old peacetime legend, 'Join the army and see the world'. Joining up was simple. If you were a fit young man of reasonable intelligence, a recruiting sergeant would be pleased to see you, and you would probably be accepted. Many a young Norfolk man began his life in the army walking through the gates of Britannia Barracks in Norwich.

In those tough times of unemployment, the army offered a roof over your head, it would clothe you in uniform, issue you with boots, kit and equipment, and provide three meals a day. If you toed the line and were a team player (essential requirements in the army then as now) you would soon make friends and you would do okay. After all, the men in your intake would be in the same boat as you.

The Regular Amy battalions of the Royal Norfolk Regiment alternated between service abroad and at home. Seldom would both battalions be in Britain at the same time. For the majority of the 1930s 1 Royal Norfolk was out on the North West Frontier of India and was still there when war was declared in 1939. After a period on home service 2 Royal Norfolk went on a brief tour of duty to Gibraltar in 1937 and returned to England in July 1939.

The Territorial Force that had been stood down at the end of the First World War was reconstituted and renamed the Territorial Army in 1920 and had slowly grown in membership through the 1920s and 1930s. The training structure was similar to the pre-First World War years in that the recruit was put through his paces in drill and rifle but with the addition of new weaponry such as machine guns and up-to-date mortars. All potential recruits were advised upon joining that the TA provided a field force to supplement the Regular Army either in defence of this country or the defence of British interests abroad – no longer would a TA soldier be asked if he would volunteer for active service abroad: when a man enlisted as a TA soldier, it was part of his obligation.

Men volunteering to join the TA would need to be aged between 17 and 38 with minimum height of 5 feet 2 inches, of weight within reasonable parameters of 112 pounds and with a minimum chest of 33 inches. Minimum training consisted of attendance at annual camp for 15 days every year in addition to 20 drills a year, each drill lasting an hour (recruits did an additional 20 drills in their first year). Pay was at army rates of 2s a day on enlistment with an annual proficiency grant of £3 and a weapons training grant of 10s. Trained men also received a further payment of 1s a drill up to 30 for drills performed above twenty. Candidates for a commission should be aged 18–31 and were asked to apply directly to the commanding officer of the unit they wished to join.

The Norfolk Regiment territorial battalions were soon back in their drill halls after the new TA was created. New TA buildings were erected such as the new 5th Battalion HQ at East Dereham (1926) and drill halls at Dersingham (1930), North Walsham (1933–34), King's Lynn (1936) and Methwold (1939).

This book tells the story of the battalions of the Royal Norfolk Regiment which saw active service during the Second World War, but it should not be forgotten that the Depot and other battalions 'did their bit' primarily on home service.

The Regimental Depot at Britannia Barracks, with the former Cavalry Barracks renamed Nelson Barracks, and hutments adjoining had been used as the training centre for all recruits in the Regular Army battalions of the Royal Norfolk Regiment. On 26 May 1939, the Military Training Act 1939 (often referred to as 'the Militia Act') was passed by Parliament. It was the country's first peacetime act of conscription. It applied to all males aged 20 and 21 and required the 35,000 men in this age bracket from across the country to answer a compulsory call-up to serve six months of full-time military training after which they would be transferred to the Reserve for three and a half years when they might be recalled in an emergency for full-time duty.

During summer 1939 Britannia Barracks welcomed the intake of 'Militia' recruits. The Regular Army recruits were moved into a tented camp to allow space for the Militiamen to be accommodated in the barracks. By August there were 200 of these recruits at the barracks but facilities were limited; there had to be two sittings in the dining hall and there was a perpetual jigsaw puzzle in fitting all the squads into the limited space available. The new gymnasium was still under construction, and the number of rifle ranges really should have been doubled. It is to their credit that 'M' Company, as the militia intake was called, made excellent progress during their training though were still in training when war broke out.

After the outbreak of war Britannia Barracks was designated an infantry training centre and the long-serving and well-respected Lieutenant-Colonel N. P. Shand was appointed to command it. From September 1939 until August 1941 recruits were trained on a 16-week infantry syllabus; they were destined to be posted to one of the battalions of the regiment. During this period the Depot was known as the Royal Norfolk Regiment Training Centre.

In August 1941, the Northamptonshire Regiment sent its training staff to the Depot as its own centre was required for other purposes. The name of the unit was changed to No. 2 Infantry Training Centre or 2 ITC. The combined staffs worked well together, training their own recruits and each having their own companies.

On 2 July 1942 primary training for all recruits entering the army was instituted and 2 ITC was given an allotment of this class of training. A new addition was also made with No. 52 Primary Training Wing where a six-week elementary training syllabus was carried out. In November 1943 the Northamptonshire Regiment Depot was restored to them. In their place came the training staff of the Dorset Regiment, a regiment that was an old friend from the First World War when a battalion of Dorsets and another of Norfolks had suffered such losses during the campaign in Mesopotamia they combined and were known as 'Norsets'. In 1946 the men of the Dorset Regiment moved back to their own county and the Depot became No. 9 Primary Training Centre where all Norfolk men called to serve under the National Service Act would be trained.

8 Royal Norfolk began life in 9 (Norfolk Group) Defence Companies raised by Lieutenant-Colonel Lord Walsingham. The first party,

consisting entirely of officers, began in August 1939; recruitment began almost immediately but was only open to older soldiers, and they came forward in large numbers. Headquarters was at Tottington and companies were formed at Norwich, Yarmouth, King's Lynn and Attleborough. The battalion was primarily involved in anti-invasion activities including the 'Broads Flotilla' of armed speedboats which patrolled the waterways to counter landings of enemy troop-carrying aircraft. Early in 1940 8 Royal Norfolk was renamed 30 Royal Norfolk but their duties of home defence remained unchanged until 1943 when the battalion was deployed to Sicily and Italy on garrison duties. The battalion was disbanded in 1946.

9 Royal Norfolk began as 50 (Holding) Battalion. It was raised on 27 May 1940 under the command of Lieutenant-Colonel H. F. Watling and obtained a nucleus of NCOs from 4, 5 and 6 Royal Norfolk and the Depot. It was then brought up to strength with a company from 10 (Holding) Battalion, only to lose almost half its personnel soon afterwards in a large draft for 2 Royal Norfolk that was being rebuilt after severe losses at Dunkirk. The losses were replaced by drafts from the Depot and in two months it was back up to strength and stationed at Eaton near Norwich where they used the golf course for training exercises.

In October 1940 the battalion moved to North Walsham where it ceased to be a holding battalion, was retitled 9 Royal Norfolk and trained as a field force unit. They moved to Cromer soon afterwards and took up coastal defence duties and would remain at various locations primarily on the north Norfolk coast until 1942. In October 1941 the battalion supplied a sizeable draft for 4, 5 and 6 Royal Norfolk as they mobilised for overseas service. In 1942 the battalion was redeployed to Hampshire and quartered in barracks at Winchester. Early in 1943 the battalion moved to Bournemouth where they gave assistance to rescue work during the bombing of the town. The battalion was then transferred to the Isle of Wight to help run training camps for seaborne assault training.

In January 1944 9 Royal Norfolk was sent to Yorkshire where it took part in large-scale exercises on the moors. After a brief return to the Isle of Wight the battalion moved again to invasion training camps on the south coast in May 1944 to assist with Exercise *Fabius*. Second and third waves of invasion forces were all similarly served by the battalion, but 9 Royal Norfolk was not destined to serve overseas in its own right. The battalion was disbanded in August 1944, and its men were widely dispersed as reinforcements to units in Italy, Africa and India.

70 Royal Norfolk had its origins in May 1940 when the young men who had answered the appeal for 'young soldiers', i.e. those under enlistment age who volunteered to train and then join when old enough, were posted to 30 Royal Norfolk. Originally this battalion had both young and old soldiers. The youngsters received a lot of encouragement from the old soldiers, many of whom were veterans of the First World War, but this was far from ideal so 70th battalions were formed across the country specifically as young soldier training battalions.

Some 500 young soldiers were drawn from 30 Royal Norfolk to create five companies of the new 70 Royal Norfolk under Lieutenant-Colonel E. Thistleton-Smith. Battalion HQ was initially at The Crescent, Chapel Field Gardens, Norwich. After a six-week training course sections of young soldiers were despatched around the county on guard duty at vital points and aerodromes. By November 1940 the main invasion scares were over and 70 Royal Norfolk Battalion HQ moved to Taverham Hall. As the number of points being guarded was reduced the battalion was able to concentrate at Taverham to provide proper training.

The men of the battalion acquired quite a reputation for smartness and attained a high standard of proficiency as soldiers. Early in 1942 70 Royal Norfolk moved to Wolferton Park and finally to Peterborough where they trained as a counterattack force in the event of an aerodrome in the neighbourhood being attacked by enemy paratroops. When of age young soldiers from this battalion were sent to battalions in theatres of war all over the world. In the summer of 1943, all 70th battalions were disbanded throughout the British Army.

In August 1944 holding battalions were created to take on soldiers who had been sick or wounded after hospital treatment and to relieve congestion at infantry training centres. In November 1944 No. 2 Infantry Holding Battalion came into being at Ludham under Lieutenant-Colonel

P. H. Cadaux Hudson, MC. This was a composite battalion consisting of HQ Company (personnel from the Royal Norfolk and Dorset regiments), A Company (Royal Norfolk Regiment personnel) and B Company (Dorset Regiment personnel). In March 1945 the battalion moved to Great Yarmouth where it was accommodated in hotels and boarding houses. The battalion moved to Dorchester in August 1945 and disbanded at Aldershot in 1946.

As more men were drafted away from Britannia Barracks for active service the duties of clerks, cooks, stores workers and drivers were taken over by members of 40 (Norfolk) Company Auxiliary Territorial Service. Raised during autumn 1938 the company served at the Depot throughout the duration of the Second World War. There was also a total of 17 battalions of Norfolk Home Guard in the county who were proud to serve under the badge of the Royal Norfolk Regiment.

As far as possible this book is told in the words of the officers and men of the Royal Norfolk Regiment who were there. Drawing on hard-to-obtain volumes of regimental and battalion histories, accounts published in *The Britannia: The Regimental Journal of The Royal Norfolk Regiment* and original manuscripts, each chapter is based on original histories with additions from the relevant battalion war diaries, gallantry citations, personal diaries, memoirs, private correspondence and oral interviews conducted by the author.

Most of the veterans who served in the Royal Norfolk Regiment during the Second World War have now passed away. This book aims to preserve and share the stories of those brave men for the generations that come after them. Every old soldier would tell you there is no glory in war, but the sacrifice, bravery and enduring comradeship through adversity demonstrated by the men of the Royal Norfolk Regiment in the Second World War should never be forgotten.

Neil R. Storey
Norwich, 2025

Chapter 1

1st Battalion

When war was declared on 3 September 1939, 1 Royal Norfolk was in Delhi, India, and the battalion did not return to the UK until May 1940, after over ten years' service overseas. On 6 November after completion of foreign service leave, the battalion mobilised onto a war footing and became part of 20 Guards Independent Brigade and entered a comprehensive training programme. In August 1941 the battalion moved to 24 Guards (Independent) Brigade Group and deployed to Wimbledon to man the 'Brown Line' defences of London and remained there until September 1942. During this time many Londoners filled the ranks of the battalion.

Despite the war widening and great strides being made in the Western Desert 1 Royal Norfolk was still not deployed for active service; instead, they were subjected to yet more changes of location and training at home with 79 Armoured Division in Northern Command in the Knaresborough area. Finally, in March 1943 the battalion and the other units serving in 185 Brigade were transferred to 3 Infantry Division and the spirits of the men surged as it was known that 'Iron Division' was earmarked as a high priority for overseas service and was to be specially trained for mountain warfare. Proceeding to Belford in Northumberland the training was even more arduous than before –forty-eight-hour treks and full war-scale exercises were carried out with troops carrying 60lb loads over mountainous country, but not one fell out.

On 30 May 1943 advance parties of the battalion arrived at Inverary on the shores of Loch Fyne followed by the main body of 1 Royal Norfolk to commence assault training on 3 June. The battalion was also joined by ten officers and fifty-eight ratings from Royal Navy Commando to train the battalion from the naval side. Day and night landings, including the loading of vehicles, were carried out on landing craft accompanied by practice drills for manning Landing Craft Infantry (LCI). The course continued for seventeen days and by the end of it the battalion was well versed in combined operations and the tasks required for consolidating a beachhead in the face of enemy opposition.

Training at Inverary was followed by three weeks' rigorous hardening training at Dorlin in the remote Western Highlands and two weeks' initial brigade training at Kilbride Bay, Tignabruich. While at these locations the men of 1 Royal Norfolk were put through 'battle inoculation' exercises, which included powerful ground charges, live 3-inch mortar and small-arms fire over companies during practice landings and subsequent advances. These weeks sped by; the men would remember the training, not only for its realism but for the rain and mud – they became hardened, fit, confident and resourceful.

After the brigade training 1 Royal Norfolk moved to what would be its winter quarters in Nissen huts at Halleaths Camp, Lochaber near Lockerbie in Dumfriesshire, a camp they would share with 2 Royal Warwickshire, a battalion that would remain with 1 Royal Norfolk in 185 Brigade throughout the campaign to come. It was also while at Halleaths that Lieutenant-Colonel Hugh Bellamy took over command of the battalion on 14 September. Training continued with companies being attached in rotation to 13/18 Hussars for training with tanks in combat and attending the excellent divisional battle school at Moffat, which was commanded by Lieutenant-Colonel E. A. Carse, a former 1 Royal Norfolk second-in-command.

A four-day training break was granted from 23–26 December 1944 and the battalion was able to celebrate Christmas with some organised sports including an excellent inter-company boxing competition with the Royal Warwicks and a miniature rifle competition. On 27 December the battalion was back at full pitch with a battalion assault training week.

Early in the New Year the battalion moved further north to Forres in Morayshire and recommenced training at a divisional level. Billets at

Forres were good; most of the battalion were in and around the Hydro Hotel and A and B companies landed billets in a functioning distillery nearby.

The battalion was now organised to pretty much how it would be deployed for D-Day. The battalion formed a close liaison with 27 Independent Armoured Brigade and would take part in three full-scale divisional combined operations exercises with contingents of the Royal Navy and RAF. The first of these would be Exercise *Crown* staged in February 1944. The battalion moved to Invergordon on 6 February and embarked in LCIs. The exercise was postponed due to bad weather so the battalion had a good opportunity to become familiar with the routine on board their landing craft.

On 9 February the landing was made with the battalion in the assault brigade. Two companies were landed forward to seize and mop up the immediate beachhead, followed by the remaining companies which passed through to secure further objectives. The battalion remained ashore living off ration packs until 12 February.

When Exercise *Crown* was staged 1 Royal Norfolk was still intended to be one of the first-wave assault brigades. This was changed after the exercise and only 8 Infantry Brigade would hit the beaches at H-Hour and 1 Royal Norfolk would be the immediate follow-up about two hours later as part of 185 Brigade, and so it would remain until D-Day. The next exercise staged on 21 February was known as Exercise *Anchor* where 1 Royal Norfolk embarked at Fort George and made their landing during the night of 22/23 February. 1 Royal Norfolk played their part as they would on D-Day with nearly the identical team.

Early in March the battalion moved from Forres to the vast and gloomy Brucklay Castle near Maud in Aberdeenshire. From here companies detached at intervals to practise street fighting in Aberdeen. At the end of March, the battalion moved to Invergordon and in April took part in the last of their assault exercises in Scotland, Exercise *Leapyear*.

The battalion history records:

> The amphibious side of the invasion was fully tried out in
> this exercise, complete with live firing until H-hour. High-

ranking spectators were able to watch a full dress rehearsal of what was to be the greatest invasion ever staged. The battalion played its part again in the immediate follow up, great stress being laid on the counter-attack the enemy must launch, but which on D-Day never materialized.

A feature of all exercises was the careful precautionary briefing of all ranks on large-scale maps and models, by the commanding officer and company commanders. By this means every man was launched into battle not only knowing what he was expected to do in detail but also what everyone else was doing. The knowledge that they were rehearsing something very real saw all ranks achieve a marked degree of success on these exercises. They gained experience of landing craft, the kit they would be carrying, wading ashore and going on to fight for thirty-six hours without a break. What they did not know at the time was just how similar the coastline along the Moray Firth was to the strip of coast they would assault on D-Day. In fact they would face a few less enemies in Normandy in June 1944 for they did not have to contend with the bitter cold, snow, driving rain and mud they had experienced during the training in Scotland.

Orders were received for 1 Royal Norfolk to move again and immediately after the end of *Leapyear* the advance party left for the south of England on 12 April. The rest of the battalion that followed the next day did not know their destination and speculation was rife. After motoring the length of the country, they arrived at Camp J.9 at Borde Hill near Haywards Heath in Sussex.

This hutted camp was on the grounds of an estate that belonged to Lieutenant-Colonel Bellamy's mother. The calm country surroundings were much appreciated as was the Southern Electric service to London that provided a useful link for quick visits home or to the West End on passes. All ranks of 1 Royal Norfolk realised this was to be their last home in England before build-up to deployment. The battalion received its final equipment and reinforcements to bring it up to strength, among them Padre Jim Green and four Canadian 'CANLOAN' officers– Ken Wilson, Bob Vezina, Jack Laurie and Syd Kemsley. They all fitted in splendidly. In fact, the battalion was keyed up and ready to go. There would, however, be one last exercise, Exercise *Fabius*, staged in the Chichester area during the second week of May 1944 where 3 Division would rehearse landings for Sword Beach.

1 Royal Norfolk embarked their LCIs on 3 May and joined a convoy anchored off Newquay. At midnight the convoy sailed and reached the landing area, some men absolutely convinced this was going to be 'the real thing', but this was quashed when they landed a short distance to the east of Littlehampton at 0700 hrs on 4 May. The LCIs did not make a good run in and the landing was made in water so deep the majority of the troops were in water up to their necks as they waded ashore.

It was not the first time this had happened but at least the waters were not as cold as Scotland, so the men reached the beach together and moved forward in good order to the concentration area. The battalion reached its final objective of Bignor Hill in pouring rain and then carried out extensive patrols through the night. Exercise completed, they then returned to Camp J.9 on 6 May.

On 13 May a representative party from the battalion, together with other groups from 3 Division, were sent to Petworth where they were addressed by General Eisenhower on the coming offensive. Briefly, 1 Royal Norfolk now switched from training to ceremonial. On 19 May the brigade commander inspected the battalion, expressing his great satisfaction with the high standard of training that had been achieved and the fine fighting spirit of the troops. The battalion band came down from Norwich and the troops had the honour of being inspected along with the rest of 185 Brigade by the king and the divisional commander on 22 May. As ever, the king showed great interest in the battalion and specially asked to speak to all men who lived in the area around Sandringham.

On 1 June, 1 Royal Norfolk moved to Camp J.3 and on 3 June to Green Camp in Camp J.2, the focus now on the operation to come. The battalion history recorded:

> Briefing was a serious business. Imagine a series of large
> store tents each with special lighting and flooring and a

twenty-foot map. The master plan was unfolded to every man, but security was such that bogus place names were used throughout and even now any reference to any part of the immediate bridgehead is still referred to as 'Hillman', 'Rover' etc. During and after this period of intensive study of air photographs, maps and models, the battalion was 'sealed'. This meant no one was allowed in or out of the perimeter within which we lived; we knew the hour was at hand and that soon we should go through the marshalling camps to our embarkation yards.

The battalion history captures the last days before embarkation evocatively:

As in our practices, so in the final stage of everything 'laid on' in the finest order. The smallest detail of equipment or the replacement of a trained signaller were at instant call. Without wishing to ape the journalists, an air of grim determination had settled on the battalion. Typical of our Norfolk men, nothing much was said at the time. We all longed to get on with it, and our innermost thoughts are still secret. All eyes were on the weather, as upon this depended the sailing of the great armada, and so the destiny of empires.

The command structure of 1 Royal Norfolk on embarkation was as follows:

CO: Lt-Col Hugh Bellamy
2ic: Maj Humphrey Wilson
Adj: Maj William 'Teddy' Bagwell
IO: Capt Trevor Harrison
QM: Capt Reginald Francis 'Bandy' Howard
MO: Capt William Robert Colston Lang RAMC
Padre: Rev F. J. 'Jim' Green
RSM: WOI W. Brown

HQ Company
OC: Capt Peter Baker

A Company
OC: Capt Adrian Kelly
2ic: Capt Michael Fearon

B Company
OC: Maj Eric Cooper Key
2ic: Capt Adrian Robertson

C Company
OC: Maj Donald Smith
2ic: Capt H. J. Jones

D Company
OC: Maj Bill Brinkley
2ic: Captain R. C. 'Robin' Wilson

S Company
OC: Captain Freddie Fitch
2ic: Lt C R 'Bobby' Parfitt

At 2045 hrs on 3 June the battalion proceeded to Newhaven, had tea on the quayside and commenced embarkation at about 2225 hrs. All ranks of 1 Royal Norfolk were split between three LCIs, one led by CO Lieutenant-Colonel Hugh Bellamy, the second by 2ic Major Humphrey Wilson, with the company quartermaster sergeants of the four rifle companies and Battalion HQ, and in the third the adjutant, Major 'Teddy' Bagwell. A, B and C companies were in one LCI each, with D Company and tactical battalion headquarters divided between the three. Battalion transport was on landing craft tanks (LCTs). This was done so that in the event of any of the three LCIs being sunk the battalion could still function on landing.

Spirits were high and all were impressed by the way arrangements had been made to send mail up to the last minute. Free cigarettes and playing cards were delivered to the landing craft and bundles of Penguin paperbacks left on the craft to be distributed among the men. The first crossing was postponed twenty-four hours due to bad weather so 1 Royal Norfolk disembarked and returned by motor transport to Camp J.3 for a midday meal on 4 June then returned to their landing craft. During the evening an impromptu concert developed between landing craft by means of loud hailers to see who could make the most noise.

Their morale undiminished, keyed up and ready to go, at 2300 hrs on 4 June a signal was received that the convoy would weigh anchors and proceed the following morning. At 1000 hrs on 5 June the craft sailed out of the harbour, anchored for a few hours then set sail with the rest of the naval force for France.

Private Geoffrey Duncan was serving in 10 Platoon, B Company, and recalled:

> For most of us it was the first time in combat, our baptism of fire – as our sergeant so dryly observed, 'This is what sorts the men from the boys.' Most of the lads in our platoon including myself were still in their teens but he was a great character and hadn't been given his stripes because he could shout the loudest. … We boarded the Landing Ship Infantry at Newhaven on 5 June and were herded down below to our deck areas. I say herded as each of us was loaded down like a pack mule, we had been issued with assault jerkins, a sort of canvas waistcoat with pouches on the outside … into these you packed ammunition, grenades, Bren gun magazines, 2 inch mortar bombs plus emergency rations and many other items a front line soldier required. We estimated that each of us was carrying 80lbs on our backs not including our rifle.

Initially it was a rough crossing and many of the men were seasick but the wind dropped and the sea calmed through the night. Before they were halfway across the Channel the signal came that the landing was 'on', and then and only then the seals on the maps were broken and for the first time they saw exactly where they were going to land. Throughout training the terrain and maps had been studied in detail but all objectives had been given codenames and only Lieutenant-Colonel Bellamy and the IO, Captain Trevor Harrison, knew the truth of where 1 Royal Norfolk would be landing.

The 185 Brigade objectives were engrained in the minds of the troops. For their part, after landing 1 Royal Norfolk was to pass through the assault brigade who were intended to have taken a feature known as 'Hillman' from which the exits of Sword Beach could be observed, cross an anti-tank obstacle, push on to high ground (overlooking Caen) and if possible capture the town (Caen) itself … at least that was the plan. The intervening country was chiefly standing crops and was good going for tanks save a few woods dotted here and there.

The original battalion history published in *The Britannia* recalled:

> The preponderating feeling was of relief that the dreadful anti-climax of a month's waiting for the next suitable tides would not be necessary. As always seemed to happen in any operation, the landing point was at the junction of four map sheets, which had to be cut up and stuck together again. Both this operation and a final conference on board to tie up last details of landing drill were occasionally interrupted as someone asked permission to leave the small and stuffy cabin for a moment to return a few minutes later looking a shade less green. The night was very quiet and still, with only the sound of the engines pushing the craft steadily toward the French coast to break the silence. No ships other than the remainder of our own flotilla were to be seen and very few aircraft. Lights were out early on board, and everyone had their last unbroken night's sleep.
>
> D-Day dawned fine but cloudy. The Battalion was still well out from the coast … overhead could be heard the noise of supporting aircraft, and indeed the whole night long planes had been droning overhead, including the troop carrying planes taking in the Parachute Brigades of the 6th Airborne Division. As the coast was approached, the rumble of explosions could be heard as supporting craft and

planes covered the landing of the leading brigade, and a few columns of smoke could be seen rising from the dim and distant coastline. Soon the engines 'revved' for the run in, and everyone scanned the coast to try to pick up the landmarks they knew so well from air photographs. A water tower and a peculiar shaped white house were soon recognised, and confidence that the Royal Navy intended to land the battalion on the right beach was justified. As it approached the shore, splashes were noticed in the water, which had never been seen on exercises, but it was not until there was an explosion as a hit was scored on a returning craft that many men realised that they were under enemy mortar fire for the first time. However, the battalion continued to run for the beach, which suddenly became very close and distinct. More splashes around, but no hits so far, and then 'Stand to land' and with a bump the craft was aground, the gangways down over the bows, and men were streaming off, through a foot of water and up to the beach.

1 Royal Norfolk landed on Queen Red Sector of Sword Beach five minutes earlier than planned at 0950 hrs. As the ramps of the landing craft were dropped the men had been expecting a wade ashore but for most it was almost a dry landing. They scrambled ashore amid shell and mortar fire but many men would later confess they were only too glad to get their boots on dry land, no matter what was being hurled at them, after the severe vomiting they had suffered on the landing craft.

Private Geoffrey Duncan remembered his landing:

Struggling down the gangway I blessed the captain who kept his promise to take us in as close to the beach as humanly possible. It was ironic that during all our practice landings prior to D-Day we never had any waterproof clothing at all and got soaked wading ashore, now here I was virtually stepping straight on to dry land. Once ashore one had to discard the waterproof suit and this is where I ran into trouble, my suit got hooked upon the entrenching tool on my back. God, I thought I shall get clobbered before I even get off the beach.

I finally struggled free from my suit and must have aged ten years in as many seconds, then ran up the beach to rejoin my section who were making for the exit leading from the beach to the coast road. I turned and looked back down the beach – the landing ship from which we had just disembarked had received a direct hit on the bridge.

The original battalion history captured the first impressions of what vision met their eyes:

The beach – not the inferno all had imagined – was still not a healthy place. Many wounded were lying around, and mortar bombs still dropping regularly. A shed of white tape marked a safe lane through a coastal minefield. The first glimpse was caught of the enemy's warning notices 'Achtung Minen' with the skull and cross-bones sign, and then the coast road about a hundred yards inshore was reached. The first glimpse [was had] of the enemy dead, killed in the preliminary bombardment and by the assault brigade, a quick close up of the water tower, and the Battalion striking inland to its first assembly area. Here all companies reported present with the exception of one or two men hit on the beach, and a wireless set and a bicycle or two lost in a bog across which one company had tried a short cut. ... After a quick reorganisation, the unit was off again in the 'preordained' march, passing the first column of enemy prisoners being escorted back to the beach – always an encouraging sight. And so to the village, Hermanville. Here shelling was fairly intense, and several men were hit round an unpleasant cross-roads. There were many more dead in the street, and a few of our own men who had paid the supreme penalty so soon. A brief check while it was learnt that a strong and well defended enemy locality was still holding out, and a plan [was] made to by-pass it.

Private Geoffrey Duncan recalled what happened as 1 Royal Norfolk moved out:

As we cleared the outskirts of Hermanville we lost the cover of buildings and trees on either side of the road and emerged into open country, here we were soon spotted and it wasn't long before the 88s and mortars were giving us a pasting, we didn't hang about there too long but lost several lads on that open stretch of road. As we approached the western outskirts of Biéville we could hear there was stiff opposition on the far side of the village – in the village itself there were knocked out vehicles, German dead sprawled on the road and several lads from the Suffolk Regiment [were] lying dead in various places, one in particular had been shot down in the middle of the road and a tank had run over him. It was a gruesome sight but war is a gruesome business.

The battalion reached its concentration area near Périers-sur-le-Dan in good order and at 1200 hrs proceeded toward their first objective, wooded high ground overlooking Caen that had come to be known to the men as 'Rover' in training, but was known as Lebisey Wood. A Company under Captain Adrian Kelly and B Company under Major Eric Cooper Key were led in a detour by Major Wilson around the enemy strongpoint on a feature known on the operations map as 'Hillman' located about 1,000 yards from the village of Colleville-sur-Orne. This was the feature that should have been captured by the assault brigade but had proved a lot more troublesome than anticipated and would not be taken by 1 Suffolk until the evening. Both A and B companies were pinned down by the machine-gun fire and engaged in a firefight that lasted over two and a half hours before they could disengage. Private Geoffrey Duncan of B Company recalled:

> Crawling through the corn on one's belt with all the gear we were carrying was a punishing experience, the sweat poured down my face and I thought to myself, what the hell am I doing here, why hadn't I joined Royal Artillery like my elder brother and muttered to myself as I crawled through the corn. Lying there I was dirty, hungry and tired to the point of exhaustion, it seemed like an eternity before the supporting armour arrived, a fierce battle followed and the enemy position was finally over-run. I was mighty glad to see the last of that field but several brave lads were lying still and silent in that waving sea of corn.

Both A and B companies incurred several casualties, not only from enemy fire from Hillman but also from their own tanks which thought they were enemy getting out of Hillman and fired on them.

The rest of 1 Royal Norfolk pushed on and by evening the battalion had captured and consolidated a lone house which would come to be known as 'Norfolk House'. The battalion had suffered its first battle casualties of the war. A total of 20 men died on D-Day and Lieutenant Gerald Toft (21) died of his wounds on 7 June.

A number of men had also been wounded, among them the medical officer William Lang and several battalion stretcher-bearers who had been wounded when the regimental aid post (RAP) was hit by a mortar bomb late in the afternoon of D-Day. The MO had to be evacuated and was replaced temporarily by Lieutenant Anderson from the 223 Field Ambulance ADS. Lance-Corporal Ted Ballard (27) reorganised the RAP. He collected men to act as stretcher-bearers, and ensured the wounded received treatment and were safely evacuated under adverse conditions. For his cool-headed and swift actions Lance-Corporal Ballard was mentioned in despatches, the first award to be won by a member of 1 Royal Norfolk in the Normandy campaign. He would be killed in action at Manville Wood on 25 July 1944.

During the night enemy aircraft attacked the beaches but 1 Royal Norfolk had a quiet night. Orders to continue their advance came through at midday on 7 June and the battalion made their way through the village of Benouville that was still infested with snipers. Fortunately, the 6-pounder anti-tank gunner managed to distract them sufficiently for the battalion to pass through. Orders were then received over the radio that the men of 2 Royal Warwickshire were in difficulty in their attempt to take the high ridge at Lebisey Wood and 1 Royal Norfolk was ordered to proceed there with due haste, crossing an anti-tank ditch and through the cornfields to the edge of the wood without any artillery support.

The battalion anti-tank guns and mortars were brought up to give some support and C Company penetrated the wood only to be met by heavy fire from fixed machine guns and mortars and suffered several casualties. It soon became clear that without full artillery support it would be a very costly operation to clear the enemy from their carefully dug-in positions. 1 Royal Norfolk held the ridge until dusk while the Royal Warwicks extracted themselves. The CO of 1 Royal Norfolk now had to decide if he was going to stick it out overnight or withdraw his battalion. He wisely chose the latter.

Captain Robin Wilson had reached the edge of the wood with D Company. He soon found out the mine-clearance teams had been destroyed by enemy action, and any move forward was met by well-concealed enemy posts and heavy fire. Casualties were high; the order to withdraw had been given but Wilson was aware there were still several men from 1 Royal Norfolk and 2 Royal Warwickshire who lay wounded in the minefield in front of his position.

At 2130 hrs Captain Wilson went forward under the cover of darkness on his own initiative to locate the wounded. The minefield was covered by snipers with automatic weapons. Having located the wounded soldiers, Wilson returned and called for two volunteers to act as stretcher-bearers and a covering party to evacuate the wounded men. He led the party into the minefield but one of the volunteer stretcher-bearers was shot and killed while the other, Sergeant J. Martin, and Captain Wilson persevered under intense machine-gun fire until the three wounded men had been evacuated as well as the weaponry of the fourth man who had been killed there. Captain Wilson's example and gallantry was recognised by the award of a Military Cross.

The next day, 8 June, with 1 Royal Norfolk concentrated at Norfolk House, orders were received to hold the line from the Caen Canal to the west, between the villages of Blainville and Beauregard, covering the left flank of the brigade and about 2,000 yards in front of the battalion area. B Company, with three sections of carriers, a detachment of pioneers and two SP anti-tank guns, were sent out under the command of Major Humphrey Wilson. The position became known as 'Duffer's Drift' because of its unorthodox formation of four platoons in a straight line but it formed an excellent base for patrol activities.

As B Company advanced to take up their position in this line 12 Platoon came under fire from enemy armed with a 'Spandau' (MG 42) and light machine guns lodged in one of the nearby houses. Sergeant Cecil Parker was informed the house was believed to contain four enemy troops, so he ordered a section to cover the exits and he went in to flush them out. Two enemy soldiers immediately fled the building and were accounted for by the section outside, while Parker despatched the other two in the house. Parker was awarded the Military Medal for his leadership, initiative and personal bravery that decisively resolved this situation.

On the second day of 'Duffer's Drift' the enemy, clearly unaware of the development, drove down the road and fell into the trap set for such events by B Company. Within a week the bag was one marine officer, thirty-five other ranks, five vehicles and two motorcyclists. Patrols were carried out to varying degrees of success from this position until early July when a renewed attack was made to take Lebisey Wood.

The plan was simple and every man in the battalion was well briefed on his role. The night of 7/8 July was a full moon, and by 0230 hrs the battalion had moved to the assembly area along a route that had been carefully chosen. The assembly area itself was a spot where shell reports showed that nothing had yet fallen. From this area tape was laid to the crossing places over the stream and swampy ground through a hedge that was twenty yards thick to the forming-up place. All went well.

By 0400 hrs 1 Royal Norfolk was awaiting the barrage that came exactly on time. And it was a good one. The whole area had been 'softened' by the RAF the previous night and by 0600 hrs all was going to plan. The leading companies reached their first report line and were heading for their final objectives. Tactical HQ moved up the hill, and the supporting arms were through their bottleneck and in their allotted places despite casualties being sustained through enemy mortars and shelling. By 1000 hrs there were only dead Germans in Lebisey Wood, the mortaring and shelling continuing but with no sign of a counterattack. The men of the battalion dug in as quickly as they could to consolidate but D Company, now under Major Hubert Holden, was pushed through the two leading companies and B and C gave chase after the fleeing enemy but had to be stopped because the flanks had not yet been secured.

Casualties were heavy and occurred mainly during the severe shelling and mortar fire in the attack; taking Lebisey Wood took its toll on the battalion with seven officers wounded, twenty-five other ranks killed and eighty-four wounded. Major Donald Smith, commander of C Company, the left forward company, was wounded early in the action but continued to lead his men through heavy enemy fire to their final objective, where they contacted the supporting armour. Although weakened through loss of blood he remained at his post for another two hours until he was satisfied his company was properly consolidated and only then made his way to the RAP but insisted on stopping at Battalion Headquarters and giving the CO a full report of the situation. Smith was awarded the Military Cross. The entire operation was a great success and Caen fell to the British the following day.

The battalion spent 9 July in consolidation while heavy shelling accounted for a further twenty casualties of whom two were killed. On 11 July the battalion was pulled back to Blainville for four all-too-brief days of rest (the first since they landed). Everyone took the opportunity to have a bath and there was no stand-to in the evening.

On 15 July 1 Royal Norfolk marched across the River Orne and Caen Canal to the area that had been occupied by 51 Highland Division and 6 Airborne Division. The battalion made their HQ at Ranville for three days; one company detachment had the misfortune to be at Escoville, which was shelled and mortared day and night and which was the epicentre of patrol activity. It reeked of death. At dawn on 18 July the bombers came. It was an amazing sight to see about a thousand bombers unloading their bombs. Behind the bombing came the armour: 7, 11 and Guards divisions. It was the big breakout from the bridgehead, the country being chosen to suit the armour, with the hope of bringing the enemy armour to battle on ground of British choosing. 3 Division was to follow the armour and for once 1 Royal Norfolk was held as brigade reserve.

At 1400 hrs 1 Royal Norfolk received orders and marched toward a railway line beyond which the battle was still being fought. At about 1930 hrs the battalion was ordered to attack the left flank, assaulting Manneville Wood in echelon behind 2 Royal Warwickshire. During the advance through thick dust and tall crops the battalion incurred a few casualties. At 2100 hrs the battalion was ordered to commence the attack. A high wall was encountered around the objective and so it was rightly decided to call the attack off until the following morning. At dawn, while expecting the enemy to attack, it was found they had fled during the night and so the battalion advanced into Manneville Wood.

Here the battalion found a new home in what had been a well-appointed racing establishment complete with horses, some dead, some wounded and those who were neither understandably terrified. The enemy had suffered badly: a Tiger tank had been blown upside down by bomb blasts, and the surrounding countryside looked like the surface of the moon with enemy dead lying all over the place. The battalion had to stay here for nine days and were subjected to shelling and mortar fire every day. By the end of the stay, the enemy had pinpointed the battalion's position and so a steady stream of casualties passed through the RAP.

The weather was dreadful, rain pouring down day after day. It was at this point that the battalion had its first cases of 'nervous exhaustion'. The best answer was to keep the men's minds fully occupied, so the 'slit-trench quiz' was started. This proved most popular and, with the occasional firm word from leaders, stopped what might have become an epidemic. Everyone had had a narrow escape somewhere along the line: the CO was having an afternoon nap when a shell landed three feet from his slit; one of the intelligence section was buried by a direct hit and had to be dug out, and fortunately he was only stunned by the blast.

At last, the battalion was relieved by the Durham Light Infantry on 25 July and was to have a period of well-earned rest at Cazelle in what was thought to be a bomb- and shell-free area. Back across the river and canal they went, running the gauntlet twice on the way but no one minded as there was the prospect of no stand-to and some real sleep, no tin hats and even baths for at least four days.

3 Division was now to leave I Corps, in which it had served since D-Day and become part of VIII Corps in reserve for a while. After a planned move to relieve the Cameronians was aborted, the battalion spent a night in a bivouac area. At first light on 3 August reconnaissance parties met the staff captain at an RV and motored miles to the extreme right of the line where British forces linked up with the Americans. Eventually 1 Royal Norfolk caught up and by last light that day they were just south of Le Reculay, a village a short distance from Le Bény-Bocage. They were now attached to 11 Armoured Division and close to the enemy forward defence. The enemy was still staggering under the recent blow delivered by the surge of British armour and had not been able to concentrate his artillery to any major degree, but as ever, the mortars were always active.

On 4 August 1 Royal Norfolk attacked La Chapelle. The final objective was the hamlet of La Bistière, the outskirts of which were reached during the evening; it was a victory that was to prove hard won. Major Ian MacGillivray commanding A Company came under heavy enemy artillery and mortar fire as they approached the start line through La Chapelle and incurred a number of casualties that upset the cohesion of his company, but MacGillivray, despite being under fire, immediately went round his men restoring confidence and brought them to the line on time. During the attack his personal leadership and encouragement came to the fore again as he led and cheered the men on to their objective, as his MC commendation would state, 'by his great courage, personality and disregard for his own life'.

Major Hubert Holden was in command of D Company and personally led his men throughout the advance. He located one enemy tank which was holding up the company and his example of cool courage inspired his men, although they had suffered very heavily pressing home their attack. The spirit of his company never faltered, and due to his bravery in the face of heavy odds his company reached their objective and drove the enemy back. In the same action Sergeant Charles Christian Hansen was in command of a forward platoon of D Company, his leadership and courage bringing his depleted platoon almost to their objective when they were held up at a road swept by enemy fire. Hanson led eight of his men across, losing four while doing so, but forced the German tank that had been holding up the company to withdraw. For their outstanding bravery in this action Major MacGillivray and Major Holden were each awarded the Military Cross and Sergeant Hansen the Military Medal.

The following day La Bistière was finally attacked under a proper artillery barrage, but the enemy tank that had been the chief source of trouble had not only withdrawn, but it had also fled in the night and could not be brought to account. The renewed attack was entirely satisfactory and the position was consolidated.

11 Armoured Division had been pushing out a deep salient south toward the Vire–Vassy Road. Ahead of 3 Division was 3 Monmouth at Sourdevalle. On the afternoon on 5 August the CO of 1 Royal Norfolk received orders to relieve 3 Monmouth on the night of 6/7 August. On 6 August the order was brought forward to commence immediately. At 0900 hrs the CO met the commander of 159 Brigade at his HQ and the final plan for the relief of 3 Monmouth was completed. What ensued was undoubtedly the most significant battle the battalion ever fought, an action that Norman Scarfe, author of *Assault Division*, would describe as the 'Sourdevalle epic'.

The battalion began its advance in troop-carrying vehicles under the cover of the morning mist with B Company under Major Eric Cooper Key leading. The transport moved at a slow pace to avoid dust giving away their position. The concentration area was just outside the village of Burcy in a valley at the bottom of a long hill on the road to Sourdevalle where the enemy, the 10 SS Panzer Division, held the high ground.

Just as the leading company entered Burcy the fog lifted to reveal the bulk of the battalion still moving down the long forward slope into the village. Although well dispersed they presented quite a target to the enemy, and they took advantage of it. A Company under Major Ian MacGillivray got lost trying to avoid the death trap of Burcy and lost two officers and fifteen other ranks in so doing and did not arrive in Sourdevalle until after the counterattack. C Company under Captain H. J. Jones also got badly hit coming up, losing some key personnel.

By 1730 hrs 1 Royal Norfolk had taken over, but were still double banking on the right flank, while 3 Monmouth had not completely left the area. Shortly afterward as the relief of transport was taking place a huge artillery bombardment fell on Battalion HQ with the result that most of the fighting echelon vehicles were soon ablaze. Ammunition trucks were being sent sky high and setting off others. The scene was indescribable, blazing vehicles, dead men, cattle and to add to the commotion USAAF Thunderbolts mistook the 1 Royal Norfolk position for that of the enemy and gave it a good strafing.

Corporal Colin Thirtle was in charge of his company transport and for the next three hours he worked among blazing and exploding vehicles to salvage what stores and equipment he could. When the enemy shelled the area again he continued his work without any thought for himself and dragged wounded clear of burning vehicles. In one instance Private Edwards, an A Company carrier driver, was badly wounded and unable to move from his blazing vehicle. Corporal Thirtle made three attempts to rescue him and on the fourth attempt dragged him clear.

At 1745 hrs a heavy counterattack led by Tiger tanks supported by infantry from the Panzergrenadiers of 10 SS Panzer Division struck the hamlet of Pavée, deep in the bocage about five miles east of Vire at Perrier Ridge. Facing them were B and C companies of 1 Royal Norfolk. 11 Platoon was on the right of B Company and bore the brunt of the attack. Sergeant George Smith was acting platoon commander when his position was attacked. After 30 minutes his platoon was reduced to just seven men and the enemy had succeeded in establishing themselves in the forward section positions. Smith maintained control of all that was left and crawled forward with a Bren gun, killing and wounding several of the enemy.

On returning to the rear section he realised that more had to be done if the position was to be held till a counterattack by 10 Platoon came in. Accordingly he collected as many grenades as possible and with a 2-inch mortar moved forward once again to a good position where he continued to blast the German infantry, then followed up with a shower of 36 grenades that killed and wounded several of the enemy, but he was forced to retire owing to the heavy machine-gun fire from the tank.

Acting Corporal Cockney Sidney 'Basher' Bates (23) was commanding the right forward section of B Company, which had already suffered casualties as the counterattack came in. There were some fifty to sixty Germans in this attack, supported by mortars and machine guns. Seeing the situation was desperate Bates got up and charged, firing his Bren gun from the hip and despite being almost immediately wounded and knocked down by machine-gun fire he recovered himself quickly and continue his advance on the enemy, spraying a deadly hail of fire from his Bren. His action silenced much of the enemy machine-gun and rifle fire but mortar bombs continued to fall around him. He was then hit for the second time, this more seriously. Undaunted, 'Basher' staggered to his feet again toward the enemy. His constant firing continued until the enemy started to withdraw before him. At this moment, he was hit for the third time by mortar bomb splinters – a wound that was to prove fatal. He again fell to the ground but continued to fire his weapon until his strength left him. This was not, however, until the enemy had withdrawn and the situation in this locality had been restored. Two stretcher-bearers from B Company risked their lives to bring the mortally wounded Bates in from the battlefield. One of them was a well-loved regimental and local character from his Norfolk home of Flitcham, Lance-Corporal Ernie Seaman. In his inimitable style Ernie reminisced:

> On to Sourdevalle, what a few days there, being surrounded during the night and then being bombed by the Yanks and losing all our transport. I will never forget one incident during the night when we were being shelled and I dived into a trench and a bloody great sergeant came and jumped in too, right in the middle of my back. Of course this is

where Sid Bates won his VC, I and my partner picked him up but had no idea of what he had done.

Nothing could be done for Corporal Bates, who died two days later from his wounds, but by his supreme gallantry and self-sacrifice he had personally restored what had been a critical situation. He would be posthumously awarded the Victoria Cross. 'Basher' is buried at Bayeux War Cemetery and remains the only Normandy VC recipient to be buried in Normandy.

Major Humphrey Wilson vividly recalled the action:

> About 6 o'clock on this cloudless day the enemy came for B Coy in a big way. Cpl. Bates, one of the leading section commanders, was the first to receive the onslaught. His buddy was killed alongside him which was more than Cpl. Bates could stand. He seized the Bren gun and set about the advancing enemy. Not content with killing quite a number of enemy Cpl. Bates proceeded to charge them, getting badly wounded in so doing. … The enemy attack was in fact a feint as the real one came out of the sun about 7 o'clock and fell on C Company, or what there was left of it, and some Monmouths. Our Gunners saved the day here together with Sgt. Hopkins who personally knocked out some Tiger tanks with a PIAT until he himself got badly hit in the legs. Both Cpl. Bates and Sgt. Hopkins deserved the VC.

Major Wilson was certainly not a man prone to exaggeration. The citation for Sergeant Charlie Hopkins's courageous actions on that day states:

> On 6 August 1944, during a heavy attack on the battalion position by 10 SS Panzer Division, this NCO was acting platoon commander. Three enemy tanks and accompanying infantry penetrated his company position, which bore the weight of the attack. Sergeant Hopkins' platoon was badly cut up by machine gun fire from the tanks, but held their

ground with tanks milling around their position. This NCO was hit early on by three bullets in the leg, but he refused to be evacuated and remained to command his platoon, using a shovel as a crutch until he could cut himself a sapling in order to carry the weight of his 'useless' leg the better.

Sergeant Hopkins then found the remnants of another platoon in his area. He immediately reorganized them, and took them under his command and carried out an excellent move to alternative positions on orders of his superior commander. Here he engaged the enemy with PIAT and scored several hits, the whole time inspiring his men with his own splendid example and cheerfulness. ... His untiring efforts and devotion to duty played a very great part in the eventual defeat of the enemy. After five hours when the remnants of the enemy had withdrawn, Sergeant Hopkins, having handed over his command, reported to the regimental aid post and was immediately evacuated. ... His personal bravery and leadership were of a standard not often seen amongst the best of fighting men.

Sergeant Hopkins was awarded the Distinguished Conduct Medal, one of only two such awards recorded to 1 Royal Norfolk during the war.

One decorated hero of the day is often forgotten. Small in stature but fit, superbly trained, smart on parade, respected by the men and a man able to keep a level head no matter what, CSM Tommy Catlin of C Company was the sort of senior NCO any company commander would want under him, especially in action. To self-effacing Tommy, he just did the things that needed to be done but his story deserves to be told and it is probably told best in the words of his citation:

On 6 August 1944 during the heavy enemy attack on the battalion position by elements of the 10 SS Panzer Division, the company HQ was wiped out with the exception of this Warrant Officer. Three tanks had penetrated the company position, one of which was causing great damage and casualties to the company. CSM Catlin rightly appreciated, that this tank, a Tiger, must be destroyed or else a deep wedge would be driven into the battalion position. … Alone he remained in the company HQ area, passing the necessary orders and then saw one of our tanks moving up to engage. CSM Catlin immediately left his fire position, ran across to the friendly tank, while under small arms fire, and jumped on it to give the exact location of the Tiger. As he was talking to the tank commander, they received a direct hit and the CSM was very badly wounded. He was brought back to the regimental aid post, but not before he had passed through Battalion HQ to see the battalion CO and personally give the situation in his company area. This warrant officer did wonders throughout. His sense of responsibility, personal courage and leadership, were of the highest order. His services during this attack can hardly be equalled in this campaign.

Corporal Colin Thirtle, Sergeant George Smith and CSM Tommy Catlin were all awarded Military Medals for their acts of bravery on that day.

At about 1930 hrs around 20 Sherman tanks of the Fife and Forfar Yeomanry arrived and the troops who had been grimly hanging on took on a new lease of life. By 2130 hrs the last of the enemy had been overcome or driven out. The position was consolidated. 1 Royal Norfolk had faced the hardest day of fighting it had known to date and won against a numerically superior enemy with a fearsome reputation for its fighting abilities. But it had been a costly day for the battalion with twenty-two dead and 138 wounded.

Battalion CO Lieutenant-Colonel Robert Hugh Bellamy was also recognised for his gallantry and leadership:

On 6 August 1944 Lieutenant Colonel Bellamy's battalion was heavily and determinedly attacked by enemy Tiger tanks and infantry covered by intense shelling and mortar supporting fire. The action lasted from 1400 hours until dusk.

The enemy tanks penetrated the position. The casualties amounted to the equivalent of two companies, and included the whole of Battalion HQ and its vehicles. ... Throughout this confused and grim action Lieutenant Colonel Bellamy, by his cheerfulness, clear headedness and personal example was an inspiration to all ranks. It was the confidence which his appearance and calm control gave to his subordinates that had helped them stand their ground after having been over-run and suffered heavy losses. ... His leadership on this day must rank as an example of how a courageous and respected commanding officer can personally influence and bring about success under the most trying circumstances.

Lieutenant-Colonel Bellamy received an immediate award of the Distinguished Service Order.

Major Humphrey Wilson concluded his recollections of the battle by writing:

The battle of Sourdevalle as we always called it was perhaps the biggest and most important battle the battalion ever fought. The whole battalion was battle experienced by then and so were our supporting arms. Almost everybody had the opportunity to shoot at the enemy and there is no doubt that there were many acts of bravery which could not be written up. The Norfolk soldier is very good on these occasions, keeping his head and doing what he has been taught, he will always go on if his officer tells him to.

1 Royal Norfolk held the position for another five days; there would be no counterattack but the shelling and mortaring went on as usual and a particularly nasty heavy Nebelwerfer caused some casualties.

On 12 August 1 Royal Norfolk had the chance to sleep and rest in an orchard near Reculay. The impetus to keep the enemy at bay saw the battalion moving into action again the following day when orders came for the battalion to proceed to La Maslerie, a small village not far from the main road to Tinchebray. By 2000 hrs a dusty battalion arrived and settled in and prepared for orders. They waited all the next day until 2000 hrs when 2 Royal Warwickshire who were in front of the battalion were ordered to attack. This was met by heavy mortar fire from the outset and 1 Royal Norfolk was brought up to relieve them on the crest of a hill known as Point 214 and achieved this successfully. After nightfall no enemy patrols emerged – it would turn out later that the enemy was in retreat.

On 17 August the battalion was on the move again. Reconnaissance parties had relayed that good billets had been found just outside Tinchebray, so in a surge of traffic the battalion occupied them and for the first time since Cazelle, the battalion was complete in their A echelon, orderly room, quarter guard and even the regimental flag of Britannia was flown from a flagpole. Reinforcements also arrived and a company was reformed under Major Philip Searight. It was a time to rest and refit, and small-arms contests were arranged, as were football matches and entertainments were found in Flares.

Around this time 59 Division was being disbanded having sustained severe casualties during the Battle of Epron, so 1 Royal Norfolk lost no time in getting in touch with Lieutenant-Colonel Ian Freeland, who commanded 7 Royal Norfolk in that formation. After a few days a large reinforcement party arrived, of such a size it was the best part of a company, and also contained many specialists who were badly needed after the losses suffered in 1 Royal Norfolk. Soon the battalion was up to and even over war establishment and starting to work together as a team.

German forces were in retreat and 1 Royal Norfolk crossed from Belgium to Holland over the Escaut Canal in September. The advance was going well at that time but still shells would fall in the battalion area and pockets of enemy resistance and snipers were still encountered. On 25 September the battalion was ordered forward to occupy the town of Helmond. Units of 11 Armoured Division had skirted the town on the northern side of the canal but had not entered it. A well-protected recce party from 1 Royal Norfolk was despatched hoping not to be ambushed on the way or sniped in the town. The rest of the battalion was due to follow in troop-carrying vehicles passing through a thick belt of woodland. As the battalion reached the outskirts of the town at midday, they were met by a despatch rider who brought orders for the battalion to debus and proceed into Helmond on foot. Expecting the worst the men of the battalion advanced to contact with every weapon at the ready.

Instead of bullets the men were greeted by the most amazing welcome they ever experienced. 1 Royal Norfolk were the first British troops seen in Helmond and they were met with rapturous joy from an immense crowd of cheering civilians who gave them a flag-waving welcome. The battalion war diary recorded: 'Reception was uproarious. Crowds almost prevented our entry. People drunk with joy made it almost impossible to take up a defensive position. Curfew at 19.00 hours cleared the streets.' Had the enemy counterattacked the most fearful chaos would have ensued but fortunately they had withdrawn some distance and the battalion was left to enjoy the fruits of victory without firing a shot.

On 1 October 1 Royal Norfolk was ordered to move north over the Maas to a position no more than 3,000 yards from the German border and the great Reichwald Forest with the aim of relieving the American airborne troops southeast of Nijmegen. The battalion took up positions in a wooded area at Kiekberg near Groesbeek and regular patrols were undertaken. The men of the battalion had become adept at stalking the enemy and could get close enough to observe them undetected, hear their voices and even the rattle of their mess tins.

On 4 October 10 Platoon, B Company, was out on patrol when they were pinned down by snipers. Lance-Sergeant Ted Shepherd (22) was a tall, fit and powerfully built man; what happened next is recorded in his citation:

> Lance Sergeant Shepherd was ordered to take his section, who were in reserve and deal with the snipers. Location was very difficult, but after some time he located two in the same tree, whom he brought down by firing a PIAT with creditable accuracy. He then spotted two wounded lying in a clearing near the enemy position. Any move brought fire, but Sergeant Shepherd, leading his section with a Bren gun which he was firing from the hip, neutralised the fire and

with the aid of his section got to within ten yards of the men. Further movement proved impossible, so he decided to break off and return when the platoon operation was completed. ... In the assault on the main strongpoint, this NCO led his men forward with the utmost courage and coolness. Heavy small-arms fire was encountered and a 5in, mortar was active. As he assaulted the enemy trenches his Sten gun jammed. Confronted by 2 of the enemy, he threw it at them and then leaped after it empty handed into the trench. Sgt. Shepherd seized both by the neck and banged their heads together with such force that they temporarily lost control. He dragged them out, assisted by another member of his section, and using his fists rendered them completely docile. The Platoon, having completed its task, returned with the prisoners. ... Sergeant Shepherd was later evacuated as it was discovered he had fractured his knuckles while dealing bare-fisted with the enemy. His courage, cool-headedness and leadership were of outstanding quality and an inspiration to his section, which was 75% untried in battle. His control was remarkable throughout, and the success of the whole operation was mainly due to the two actions fought within the framework of the play by this NCO's Section.

Ted was awarded the Military Medal and was later promoted to CSM, the youngest in 1 Royal Norfolk.

The advance of the Allied forces had been halted short of Arnhem and a large pocket of enemy resistance remained to the east, up to the River Maas, so 3 Division turned south and was ordered to clear out the enemy down to Venraij (Venray). The attack began on 12 October with a barrage of 90,000 shells. 1 Royal Norfolk arrived north of Overloon on 13 October. The going was difficult after the enemy had closed sluices to raise the water level and large areas of ground became waterlogged as a result. 1 Royal Norfolk was ordered to take up a position on the right of 2 Royal Warwickshire astride the Overloon–Venraij road.

Battalion Tactical HQ was in a ditch at the side of the main road, a regular target for mortar fire with the enemy about 300 yards away. The village of Overloon was shelled and mortared continuously and 'Moaning Minnies' – Nebelwerfers – frequently wailed through the air. The only way to get to Tactical HQ was through the village, which meant those making the journey had the sickening but unavoidable experience of driving over bodies of dead German soldiers to get there.

On the morning of 14 October 1944 1 Royal Norfolk received orders to attack. At 0700 hrs, B and D companies led off. In support of each was a troop of Churchill tanks and ARVEs (Armoured Vehicles Royal Engineers), with flail tanks and SP anti-tank guns. The advance was difficult, as once through the thick woods there was very little cover and all the advantage lay with the defenders. Progress was made in three bounds: the first to the forward edge of the wood, the second to the lateral road some 800 yards ahead, and the final one it was hoped would be the line of the Molen Beek (brook), a small waterway about fifteen feet across and about another 1,000 yards farther on.

Bounds one and two were made easily, although the enemy fought hard and used all he had, which included some airburst 88 fire. Bound three failed, but the CO managed to manoeuvre all four companies into a tight formation, providing depth, about 400 yards short of the *beek*. Enemy tanks were still in the vicinity and could be heard rumbling about during the night.

Memories of the action remained boldly etched in the memory of Captain John Lincoln (a lieutenant at the time) when he wrote his personal account of the action from his perspective with D Company for his book *Thank God and the Infantry* 45 years later:

> Before dawn we had eaten breakfast brought up by the Company cooks and been given rations for the day. The sound of tanks moving up to join us was already attracting the fire of the 88s, a gun recognised by its whip-like crack and immediate shell bursts, disliked by both infantry and tanks. A last minute check of equipment and the platoon formed up near the track alongside the tanks.

0700 hours. We moved forward with the tanks attached to D Company with a flail tank, a lumbering monster of almost medieval design with massive chains fastened to a revolving shaft at the front of the tank chassis which flailed the ground ahead of it to explode anti-tank mines.

Movement through the wood by the tanks had been restricted but now, as we cleared the timber the tanks moved outwards, left and right, the platoon spread out behind them and enemy fire increased as we became visible.

Corporal Gay, commander of the right-hand leading section, seeing an enemy tank, ran across to the Churchill tank near him to use the telephone on the rear of the tank to ask the commander to engage that target – a mortar bomb burst almost beside him and knocked him momentarily unconscious to find himself flat on the ground beside the tank, its tracks within inches of his face, the tank reversing over the binoculars still hung around his neck.

Within minutes some of our tanks had become casualties and the rest had retreated to the relative shelter of the wood, leaving us on our own, without support, but we continued to push forward, crouching, trying to use whatever scraps of cover we could find, of which there were painfully few, visible to the enemy and vulnerable to his fire. I was all too aware of the din of mortar and gun fire around me, of our own mortars and artillery engaging forward targets, of enemy resisting our advance with machine guns and 88s together with Nebelwerfers, 'Moaning Minnies', producing a distinctive and frightening sound when fired. To add to our discomfort the enemy was also using air-burst shells so that we were enveloped by the noise of explosions, the rip of machine guns, the crack of bullets. The platoon had suffered some casualties, that I knew, but could only press ahead to the illusory cover of hedges and scrub in front.

Without tank support progress became increasingly difficult and finally ground to a halt in light scrub about

200 yards short of our second objective, the lateral track ahead. ... The platoon went to ground and I checked our losses. One of my platoon HQ, the PIAT man, had been killed and the three sections had suffered considerable losses. We seemed to be on our own. I could not immediately locate adjoining platoons. I was unable to contact Company HQ by radio so I sent Barney Ross my batman/runner, back to report the situation. Before he had gone far he was badly wounded in the jaw.

The company commander needed to know what was happening so I went back myself using what cover I could from hedges, skirting round a blazing tank, reported the situation and a plan was made to continue the advance to the track ahead with the support of artillery and mortar fire.

Back with the platoon I found that Lance-Corporal Stork, the NCO in platoon HQ responsible for the 2 inch mortar section, had been killed outright by a shot in the head while I was away. Lance-Corporal Stork was a married man with two small children, a kind and genuine man with whom I often had conversations during which he told me of his family. To me he seemed a much older man, although only in his late twenties, compared to the average age of the platoon which was around twenty-one. ... His death angered me so much that when the second attack started I can remember feeling only intense, savage outrage. The moment to attack again came, we got up and begam moving forward. Enemy fire increased and my immediate thought was 'I'm wounded, I'm out of this, I won't have to sleep in trenches any more.' But we were still charging toward the track ahead through the shell and mortar bursts.

We reached the track and with the surviving members of my platoon I took refuge in the shallow ditch. The ground in front was absolutely flat, the only cover a low and meagre hedge beyond the far ditch which itself was no more than two feet deep and wet, very wet. We felt very exposed.

I checked the platoon, we had suffered more casualties but had reached our objective. As soon as I could I rolled up my tunic sleeve and then my shirt sleeve – in both there were two holes showing where shrapnel of bullet had passed through but on my arm no mark at all. Then I realised that my clothing on my right buttock was wet – again my immediate thought was 'I must be wounded – I'm bleeding.' My water bottle, hanging on my right hip, had a jagged hole in it about an inch from the bottom and most of the contents had leaked onto my trousers.

It had been a close call for many and there had been a few fatalities and wounded, among them Major Ian MacGillivray who had been hit in the arm and had to be evacuated, and thus another D-Day officer and valuable company commander was out of action.

The following day 1 Royal Norfolk waited for other units to get themselves back together and a plan was made to force a crossing of the Molen Beek and the capture of Venraij. The road bridge had been blown so the plan was to cross the *beek*, silently, if possible, with two companies of infantry using a Kapok floating assault bridge while a bridging tank would lay a girder bridge for vehicles. Having formed a small bridgehead, they were then to push on with the other two companies going through, supported by tanks.

On the afternoon of 15 October Second Lieutenant Terry Rourke was detailed to recce the *beek*, which was around 400 yards from the forward positions of 1 Royal Norfolk. His task was to ascertain its width, depth and find a suitable place for the Kapok bridge. He was also to ascertain some idea of the strength of enemy opposition. The weather was driving rain and bitterly cold. Taking two men from his platoon Rourke arrived at the *beek* and soon found from the sniper and mortar fire falling around them that they were easily observed from the enemy position but he carried out the recce undaunted. Rourke returned at 0400 hrs on the morning of 16 October leading a fighting patrol to protect the bridging party, laying the tapes that would guide the attacking troops and providing the screen for the men launching the bridge. He and his party also disposed of an enemy patrol along the way. Rourke's recce and role in the establishment of the bridge were key to the success of the action and he was subsequently awarded the Military Cross for his courage, skill, leadership and determination. A brave and popular young officer Lieutenant Rourke was killed in action leading his men at the Battle of Kervenheim just two months before the end of the war.

185 Brigade was ordered to move off just before dawn on 16 October, their only light provided by artificial moonlight, searchlights angled low under the clouds. The leading companies of 1 Royal Norfolk, B Company on the right and D on the left, crossed without incident of 0500 hrs, which was a truly incredible thing after it was established later that D Company had walked through a minefield without incident and later A Company did the same thing and also did not sustain a single casualty.

A concentrated artillery barrage was due to take place, and the leading platoons were required to form up 100 yards from the barrage. Lieutenant John Lincoln of D Company recalled how he and his men crossed the Kapok foot bridge and followed the marked path to a flat, featureless field where they were supposed to wait for the barrage that was due to commence at 0600 hrs.

Lincoln and his men lay down in the field and waited and waited on that dangerously exposed position. The sky was clearly lighting with the dawn, figures could be seen moving on the nearby road and there were sounds of tanks near the blown bridge. He remembered thinking: 'It's getting lighter, we must move soon, we haven't got a scrap of cover and one Spandau would get the lot of us. For God's sake let us move.'

At 0700 hrs the barrage started … an hour late. John vividly recalled the shell fire fell so close to them he wondered if they would survive:

> For an eternity of ten endless, interminable minutes we pressed ourselves to the shaking ground, deafened, battered, helpless. When, after a lifetime, the barrage lifted I called my platoon up and out of the hell of that brutal, vicious ordeal; those men who could get up wrenched themselves off the ground. We ran forward in a ragged line. To my right

I saw the Bren gunner of that section prone beside his gun. He was a reinforcement who had joined us only the evening before with no previous experience. I thought he might be scared and intended to help him. I shook his shoulder and called his name. He was dead. I took his Bren and ran forward. Just in front was a mound of earth and on its far side an entrance covered by a camouflaged ground sheet. As I approached, a grey clad figure drew the ground sheet aside and ducked back in again. … I registered a young pale, frightened face but my only thought was that I could not leave an enemy soldier behind our backs as we moved forward. I took a 36 grenade from my belt and attempted to pull the safety pin but my hands were too cold to close the ends of the split pin before withdrawing it. I sheltered against the bank of earth while it seemed an age to press the ends of the pin closed against my belt buckle so I could pull the pin. I waited for the explosion but had no time to see the result and ran on until we gained the ditch alongside the track.

What John did not mention is how he went on to lead by example and take over command of D Company at a critical time during the action. His commendation stated:

he [Lieutenant Lincoln] again led his platoon to their objective with the minimum of casualties and the maximum effect on the enemy. At this moment when the company commander and second-in-command were both casualties and when morale was at its lowest level, he assumed command of the company. He showed himself to be the best subaltern in the battalion.

By the afternoon the enemy was feeling the strain of the sustained attack and A and C companies had pushed on to about 1,000 yards south of the *beek*. The crossing had been secured and the enemy forced to withdraw.

The men of 1 Royal Norfolk had fought hard and achieved much. A special order was issued on 16 October 1944 by Lieutenant-General Sir Richard O'Connor, KCB, DSO, MC, commander of VIII Corps, as follows:

> 3rd British Division
>
> I would like to congratulate you all on the very fine performance you have put up during recent operations against Venraij. … All of you have taken your share in this success, but I must particularly congratulate 185 Brigade on the magnificent performance of bridging the Beek north of Venraij with all the elements against them. … In this fighting you have shown grit and determination, and you have gained knowledge that you are better than the enemy. … It is probably the first action of a good many of you, and I feel that you have made a great start and have thereby gained my full confidence.
>
> [Signed] R. N. O'Connor

Their achievements had, however, come at a terrible cost. John Lincoln would recall how just two days earlier his platoon had comprised some 30 men and after the battle only a dozen were left. D Company, which had numbered 100 men, was left with just thirty-three men all told. Over the previous four days 1 Royal Norfolk had suffered 211 men killed, wounded and missing including five company commanders and three captains.

Lance-Corporal Ernie Seaman would never forget the terrible casualties and conditions under which the battle was fought. He was awarded the Military Medal for his bravery in this action, his citation stating:

> During the attack of 16 October the battalion was suffering heavy casualties and Lance Corporal Seaman was in charge of B (Assault) company stretcher-bearers, and throughout showed quite outstanding coolness and personal courage.

On one occasion, whilst attending to a casualty, he came under direct machine gun fire. His own equipment was torn by bullets in two places, but he continued working in the open and then called up the other stretcher-bearer and carried off the casualty. Throughout this time he was under heavy enemy mortar and shell fire.

Later in the day an officer [Major Hubert Holden, OC D Company] was sniped in the next-door company area. There was only one stretcher-bearer left in that company, and Lance Corporal Seaman at once answered the call. He worked on a very nasty wound while under fire and while sniping was continuous. He then placed the officer on a stretcher, and with the other man carried him off in full view of the enemy and under indirect fire to the Advanced Regimental Aid Post.

His devotion to duty, personal courage and extreme coolness were of an outstanding nature throughout the battle. The confidence in this NCO, who has worked unceasingly since D-Day, is a fine tribute to his personal conduct, and his services to his battalion and company are beyond praise.

Those who served with Ernie wondered at how he never seemed to be hit despite going out again and again under fire to help his wounded comrades. Well-liked and respected, he never lost his Norfolk sense of humour nor the twinkle in his eyes. He would remain one of only three stretcher-bearers in the entire battalion to survive uninjured until the end of the campaign, the other two being Lance-Corporal Christopher Shingfield and Sergeant 'Trunky' Allen.

1 Royal Norfolk buried their dead in the clearing of an attractive nearby plantation, observed by *Eastern Daily Press* war correspondent R. M. Gray who described it as 'a solemn little service in which bare headed men of the Royal Norfolks, tarrying in their advance to the next town, clustered around Padre F. J. Green'.

After a short rest period the battalion reequipped and then moved to take over the northern part of Venraij from 2 Suffolk where the battalion also received reinforcements to replenish its losses. 1 Royal Norfolk was soon back carrying out local patrols and by mid-November the battalion was back on its feet again and plans were being made to clear all the remaining enemy west of the Maas. For this undertaking large forces were massed in southern Holland. By 18 November the corner of Venraij occupied by the forward company of 1 Royal Norfolk was in regular contact with the enemy.

The plan for the advance was for B Company on the right to push down the main Venraij–Wanssum road to the village of Lull. C Company on the left was to move up to the line of the railway. When this move had been completed, A and D companies were to move through B and C companies to the village of Oostrum. On 25 November this advance was carried out without opposition. Mines were encountered but no casualties were caused, except Captain Allen who was blown clean out of his carrier by an 'R' mine (Riegel mine 43) but was not badly injured.

The next day, 26 November, D Company, acting as a patrol force, was sent up to Wanssum, a village about 1,000 yards from the Maas, itself divided by a *beek* now in flood. Slight opposition was met and dealt with and the company returned intact. Early the next morning Tactical HQ received a direct hit, injuring Captain Ernest Ridger the signal officer and the intelligence officer Second Lieutenant Leon Sabel who had only just got his commission after being intelligence sergeant for over a year.

At 0900 hrs the advance began with A Company on the right and B Company on the left. By midday they were firmly established in Wanssum but the enemy was still in the eastern part of the village about 200 yards across the flooded brook. B Company was withdrawn later that day when it became apparent they could not hold it alone. A major counterattack was not possible due to the flooding.

Wanssum was also a sniper's paradise. 1 Royal Norfolk had lost its trained snipers and new ones were in training at divisional sniper school, so the battalion was fortunate to be loaned the 2 Royal Warwickshire snipers for a couple of days to help clear up the sniper problem in the village.

On 3 December 1 Royal Norfolk arrived in Haps, an intact village that had not been caught up in the fighting for the Maas – even the electric lights still worked. Occupying a length of the River Maas in the area it was extensively flooded, and only local patrols were possible and it was almost impossible for either side to get across the water.

Some training was carried out over the flat fenland while the local woodland provided pheasants and woodcock for the pot. On 12 December 1 Royal Norfolk was ordered to move into reserve around Gemeert. At this point the men realised the battalion would be spending Christmas 1944 in the line. And they were not wrong: Christmas Day was spent in the line near Horst. There was always a concern there might be a shelling or a raiding party, but all was quiet. In fact, the sound of drunken German troops could be distinctly heard.

On 29 December 1 Royal Norfolk withdrew and would celebrate their late Christmas in the best style they could with a fancy-dress football match of officers vs. sergeants.

On 5 January 1945 the battalion was again deployed to new positions on the Maas. The river was now low, and the weather had turned to bitter cold and snow. On 16 January the commanding officer Lieutenant-Colonel Hugh Bellamy left to take command of 6 Air Landing Brigade and Lieutenant-Colonel Peter Barclay returned from his time away in command of 4 Lincolnshire to take command of 1 Royal Norfolk.

The battalion entered Germany for the first time in the war through the town of Goch on 25 February 1945. Billets were found in the town and a recce of the country over which the battalion was to operate revealed a thick wood, some boggy, low-lying ground and beyond that some arable fields of sticky clay that led up to the small town of Kervenheim. This town was doggedly held by enemy troops who were only too aware that the town was pivotal to the defence of the area. A ridge was to the left of the battalion and about three miles to the east flowed the Rhine. As usual, communications were going to be difficult, roads were fast becoming impassable and several bottlenecks had to be negotiated.

By midday on 27 February 1 Royal Norfolk had concentrated in the woods southeast of Goch. The woods had only just been cleared and the enemy trenches still contained detritus from their occupation. At 1300 hrs on 28 February the marching troops moved off to an assembly area about a mile along the 185 Brigade axis. A Company was on the right, B Company in the centre, C Company on the left and D Company echeloned behind B Company. It was hoped to put in the attack that evening but the flanks were not yet secure and it was a good 1,000 yards to the start line through tricky country which had not been fully cleared and was exposed from the right of the battalion. The CO decided to stay put, get everyone fed and rested then move up to a forming-up place under the cover of darkness and wait until the artillery opened up.

A forward patrol led by Lieutenant Rowe went right into the outskirts of Kervenheim, returning after dawn with valuable information. At 0415 hrs a long snake of men wound their way along the track to the assembly area. A Spandau opened up on the right but was directed against 2 Royal Warwickshire. Keeping a weather eye on that flank 1 Royal Norfolk continued to advance through the darkness and was dug in at its start line before dawn on 1 March 1945. At 0800 hrs tanks arrived and at 0900 hrs the leading companies crossed the start line and the battle commenced. The battalion history recounts the action:

> The start line was the edge of a wood beyond which lay open fields with no cover of any sort. To the right were two groups of farm buildings, and it was from these that we suffered our initial set-back. A Company on the right suffered badly. Major Donald Smith was killed, shot clean through the head, all the platoon commanders were either hit or badly wounded, only the gunner FOO remained to control what was left. B Company on the left had got on a bit better but were still being troubled by the farther farm on the right. The did not know exactly how far A Company had got and called for fire. This was answered by divisional artillery but the enemy still held on. … The left was now the only approach to the town. With three companies committed D Company was now put in to work round to the left flank, close to the KSLI [King's Shropshire Light Infantry], there being a bit more cover that way. B Company had not got very far, but C Company was now able to join up with D Company and a finger hold on the eastern extremities of the town was made.

At this point the Boche put in a counter attack, but were unable to throw out C and D Companies. Sadly, Lieutenant L Dawson was killed by the enemy getting back into a house that had already been cleared. The Boche were also firing on wounded men who were trying to crawl to safety, and on several occasions the Red Cross was disregarded. … Captain Robin Wilson MC had been wounded just as his company (D) was getting into the town. Out tank support had not been all that it might, and that intimate fire to help us on to the final objective was not forthcoming at the vital moment; it therefore became a purely infantry battle.

One of the officers who had bravely led his men 'at the sharp end' of the action was Lieutenant John Lincoln. He had already distinguished himself at the Overloon–Venraij action and would stand out again for his inspiring and leadership gallantry at Kervenheim. The author remembers John Lincoln with great respect and affection, as a good friend. His citation not only sums up his gallantry but reflects the gentlemanly qualities that were his hallmark. It is also a testimony to his modesty that he did not mention his citation in his remarkable account of 1 Royal Norfolk, *Thank God and the Infantry*. It deserves to be published in tribute to John:

he was wounded at Kervenheim when leading his platoon in the first wave of the assault into the town. It was entirely due to the successful capture of the first objective and penetration beyond effected by this officer that the subsequent capture of the town was possible. Both as platoon commander and second in command of his company his work was of the highest order at all times, especially in view of his youth and inexperience. … Lieutenant Lincoln is one of those officers who, by their quiet honesty and unostentatious efficiency, could lead their men anywhere. His influence in preparing his men for battle and his personal example and leadership have proved themselves as battle winning factors.

Sunday Times war correspondent Reginald Thompson was at 1 Royal Norfolk Battalion HQ during the battle and evocatively recorded what he saw:

It's two in the afternoon. Masses of blue smoke veil the burning mass of Kervenheim from which the black silhouette of the church steeple stands out solid against the driving mist of rain. That steeple has been the cause of a great deal of trouble. So has that house five hundred yards away to the right flank. It still is. All day the Spandaus have crackled to strew this unavoidable piece of open ground with the bodies and blood of Englishmen. The Nazis are still holding out fanatically and some of these heroes lying now on the fringe of the woodland belt will die before that house is in our hands. The colonel has come up. He speaks to each man as he walks along the positions: 'Going better now, going along much better now. D Company are well in. You've done fine. Good boys. It's been tough.' … The faces look up to him from the wet earth of the woodland fringe, red boyish faces under the netted tin hats. The whites of their eyes are very white and their eyes shine. They smile at the Colonel. They are glad of his words. They call him 'Two-gun Pete'. He may or mat not know that. Peter Barclay is the man they have faith in. Some of them answer 'Thanks, sir,' and say, half to themselves, an echo of the Colonel's words – 'Tough, yes sir.'

Every man showed outstanding bravery in the attack. Lieutenant George Dicks went above and beyond. He was in command of the right forward platoon of B Company and led a frontal attack under murderous crossfire from at least five Spandau machine guns. His citation went on:

Despite heavy casualties Lieutenant Dicks kept his men going by his drive and his own example. Within fifty yards of the objective he was wounded in the groin [and] in spite of this he was the first man to reach the heavily held building which was his objective. Then started to organise the assault on the nearest houses, when he was again wounded in the chest. Still undaunted, Lieutenant Dicks issued orders and encouragement to his men, planning their assault and directing it from the position in the ditch where he lay. His great gallantry was responsible for the company gaining its objective under the most difficult conditions and against extremely strong opposition

Lieutenants John Lincoln and George Dicks were both awarded Military Crosses for their gallantry at Kervenheim and both would make successful recoveries from their wounds. They were also great friends and remained so for the rest of their lives.

By 1500 hrs the enemy had had about enough, and C Company was able to back up D Company, and the key to the town was won. Some house-to-house fighting still took place with a few suicidal paratroops holding out – they would not give up or run away and became a menace by sniping. One tank managed to get forward to the central crossroads of the town but was bazookered from a doorway. A factory that had now fallen to D Company became a bastion from which to operate

It had undoubtedly been a severe battle. 1 Royal Norfolk had incurred thirty-six dead, 115 wounded and four missing but the enemy was beaten and pulled out from his strong position. Lance-Corporal Ernie Seaman would recall:

Kervenheim, what a place! This is where we really got cut about and the weather didn't help; drains full of water, where a lot of our people went to escape the shelling and machine gun fire. I think we started the morning with about 130 men and at night when the cooks brought the meal up we had about 26 to eat it – a terrible day for B Company. I can see us now in the woods, very depressed as we had lost so many of our friends.

After only a brief rest 1 Royal Norfolk was ordered to join in the 185 Brigade attack on the village of Kapellen. The village was surrounded by water almost on all sides and only one road led in, and from all points of view it was easy to defend. It also lay on an important road which could be of great assistance to the Allied forces and the denial of this road could hold up the advance for some time. To the left of the village was a large wood with a big country house known as Haus Winkel. To capture Kapellen this feature would have to be secured or both attacks would have to go in at the same time. The CO decided on a night infiltration to secure Haus Winkel with the whole battalion that night. It worked superbly, thanks in no small measure to the leadership and gallantry of Great Yarmouth-born officer Major Jack Dye; his citation is outstanding:

On 1 March 1945 C Company led by Major Dye preceded a Battalion night infiltration to Haus Winkel near Kapellen. The advance was wrought with difficulties, a very short time was available for briefing and the whereabouts of the enemy were not known. The advance passed through a large forest and the objective, a walled-in house and its surrounding buildings were known to be occupied. Major Dye's leadership in this difficult operation was superb. With great accuracy he marked the route as he went forward. He located enemy positions on the near edge of the wood and in between them he successfully found a way through. With such skill and silence was this carried out that the whole battalion passed between these localities without incident, save the quiet taking of a prisoner.

Passing through the woods the objective was dimly outlined. Moving forward with his leading platoon Major Dye initiated a flanking movement against some enemy in the vicinity of the house. Surprise was complete and the party of five were captured. He then moved across to the other platoon and led them in an assault against a further party of enemy in the garden. So sudden and determined was their manoeuvre that without loss this section was accounted for. Moving quickly round his company Major Dye then supervised the consolidation of his company which was then being subjected to artillery fire. So quickly and thoroughly did he complete his consolidation that the enemy counter attack directed against him two hours after his arrival was received by a fully dug in and prepared company. Consequently the counter attack was broken up and caused several casualties among the enemy.

Although suffering from extreme fatigue, Major Dye led his company forward again later that day, through the forest to an outpost on the far side. During this operation one of his platoons was attacked in the wood. Thanks to Major Dye's quick appreciation and speed with which he led his counter attack force, it was quickly driven off and he took the outpost position. Dye's leadership was so inspiring that the morale of his tired men was kept at a very high level and further efforts by the enemy to dislodge him were repelled with great determination. Throughout the period of three days and nights with scarcely any sleep this officer showed a standard of leadership, tirelessness and inspiration which impacted his entire company and a very difficult operation was successfully accomplished.

Dye was awarded a well-earned Military Cross; he carried on serving with distinction after the war and retired as a major-general.

After a period of rest the battalion marched on toward the Rhine. On 23 March the Allies made the first crossing and 1 Royal Norfolk crossed the Rhine and marched through the ruins of Rees to some farm buildings southeast of the town on 29 March. On 1 April the battalion moved back into Holland via Lichtenvoorde and Enschende, ready for an attack back across the border on Lingen, a small German town on the east bank of the Ems Canal, on 4 April. The battalion crossed a pontoon bridge into the town but the enemy had occupied several houses, and were determined to hold out.

B Company had got on well and made their objective but it soon looked like they might be cut off as the enemy began to drive a wedge between them and the rest of the battalion. C and D companies filled the gap between A and B companies but the whole battalion was fully extended. It was a soldier's street-fighting battle and the battalion would certainly have appreciated a squadron of Crocodile tanks to help. After the main square of the town was passed the forward companies encountered the stiffest of opposition. The leading platoon of the two assault companies was held up by a party of enemy in well-placed positions and C Company OC Major Jack Dye got hit and fell directly under the nose of a Spandau.

Sergeant Les Langford was in command of the only available Wasp and was ordered to move up to the enemy strongpoint with the Spandau and flame it so that an assault party could go in and Major Dye could be evacuated. Although fire was directed at and into Langford's carrier, he carried on with complete disregard for his own safety, moving it close to the enemy position, which he flamed so accurately that the Spandau team was burned alive.

The remaining occupants of the enemy machine-gun position surrendered. There were still plenty of bullets flying about and, as usual, Lance-Corporal Ernie Seaman and one of his stretcher-bearers went out under fire and brought Major Dye into the regimental aid post and the assault party consolidated the position.

While this was in progress a further enemy Spandau opened up from the flank. Using his own initiative, and with great promptness, Sergeant Langford directed his carrier at this post, knowing full well that there was no infantry covering fire sited to support him. Refusing to be cowed, the enemy kept up his fire. Once again, Langford's skilled handling of his carrier and the direction of his flaming decided the issue, and the occupants of the post were ejected screaming.

Later, Sergeant Langford was ordered to repeat these tactics against a second similar strongpoint in a cellar. The route to this was covered by snipers firing from upper storeys. Between them the enemy was temporarily frustrating all attempts of the leading elements to get forward. Manoeuvring the carrier could only be done with the greatest difficulty. Despite this and the accuracy of the enemy sniper fire Langford successfully ran the gauntlet to within point-blank flaming range of the strongpoint. Although under Spandau fire from twenty yards' range, the skill and accuracy with which this NCO completed his task was in no way impaired. In a space of seconds, the objective was a sheet of flames, the enemy bolted and eight out of ten were killed or captured.

Sergeant Langford's supreme disregard of danger, his tactics and his infectious confidence completely turned the scales in a very difficult street-fighting operation. Thanks to him and his skilful use of his Wasp the morale of the enemy was completely undermined. For his outstanding gallantry and example Sergeant Langford was awarded the second and last Distinguished Conduct Medal in 1 Royal Norfolk during the Second Word War and would be promoted to CSM.

Meanwhile, Major Humphrey Wilson had already shown his courage, enthusiasm and tirelessness on several occasions and he took temporary command of Major Dye's company after he had been wounded. This company had also suffered several casualties, their advance held up by an enemy strongpoint from which three Spandau positions commanded all the approaches. Stalking forward Major Wilson was under close fire from one of the Spandaus and when he reached a point about thirty yards' distant, he despatched the machine-gunner. Moving round all his subunits while under close-range fire most of the time, he quickly reorganised the company for a further attack and instilled in them fresh confidence. Under his leadership the flanking movement against this strongpoint met with overwhelming success.

Lingen was taken and 1 Royal Norfolk spent the next two days resting and reorganising. On 7 March the battalion moved out of Lingen to woodland southeast of the town. The following day they received orders to march to Bramsche. This was quite some distance away and it was a difficult march with no food or sleep. The battalion was given an area of responsibility along a canal at Wallenhorst where there was no direct contact with the enemy. The men were able to have a good night's rest on 10/11 April but moved on yet again on 11 April and motored to Barrien, eight miles south of Bremen.

The battalion then undertook patrols while the next operation to take Leeste and Brinkum was planned with 2 Warwickshire to take the first town and 1 Royal Norfolk to attack the latter on 15 April. Brinkum was approached across open country and the assault on the town was made in a series of bounds onto fixed objectives.

D Company led in and reached the first houses without incident, but C and A companies that passed through them were troubled by snipers and suffered some casualties. As they penetrated deeper into the town the opposition intensified. By nightfall more than half the town had been cleared of the enemy. It had been a hard slog house by house; the battalion had been in action for 14 hours when darkness fell. The decision was then made to consolidate what had been gained and clear the remainder in the morning when there would be sufficient light for the Crocodile tanks to operate.

At first light on 16 April the task was resumed, A Company with Crocodiles penetrated deep into the town. This was followed by C Company and both, after hard fighting, reached their objectives, taking many prisoners as they did so. The brigade artillery opened up on the remainder of the town before committing further troops to the assault. After 'softening up' B and D companies passed through. House by house and street by street the town was cleared and by 1200 hrs all that remained in the hands of the enemy was a small suburb of new houses to the northwest of the town. This was cleared by a company from 2 Royal Warwickshire and by nightfall the whole area was firmly held. It had been 'a model battle', which demonstrated fine cooperation between armour, artillery and infantry.

Yet again, Major Humphrey Wilson demonstrated leadership skills and gallantry. Having already mentioned his actions at Lingen, at the battle for Brinkum on 15/16 April:

> his imperturbable cheerfulness and disregard of personal danger had a most marked effect on one of the companies which was temporarily held up by a strongly defended factory. Moving down with a fresh section of Crocodile tanks he made a recce from OP to OP, each time coming

under short range Spandau and sniper fire, so that the Crocodiles could get off to the best possible start and be sure of the best routes to take in their advance. As a result, the attack took on a renewed turn of speed and opposition was shortly overcome.

Wilson had been second-in-command of the battalion since D-Day and had never failed to show a degree of courage, unselfishness and spirit that directly influenced several of the engagements of 1 Royal Norfolk; he was awarded a Military Cross in recognition of this.

At Brinkum 1 Royal Norfolk suffered three killed, among them the CANLOAN officer Lieutenant Jack Laurie who had gained an MC for his skilful leadership of a company after the OC had been killed during the Battle of Kervenheim. Twelve men had also been wounded, among them Jack's fellow CANLOAN officers, Lieutenants Ken Wilson and Bob Vezina. All three had landed with the battalion on D-Day, they had all been wounded previously and had given sterling service to the battalion. The enemy suffered 60 dead with five officers and 203 other ranks taken prisoner. 1 Royal Norfolk now headed for Bremen.

On 25 April the battalion was due to cross the flooded plain to the city, but at the last minute was diverted through Arsten to attack Habenhausen and a housing estate suburb of Bremen. Buffaloes had gone across the start line at midnight with 8 Brigade followed by 2 Royal Warwickshire. There was little opposition save a few 88 shells which were swiftly dealt with. 1 Royal Norfolk advanced with B Company under Major Denis Millar in the lead. The men were expecting another Brinkum but such was the state of the enemy at this time that hardly a round of small-arms ammunition was fired; there was no opposition and by 1300 hrs all objectives had been secured.

At 1900 hrs the pioneer officer Lieutenant A. R. Gill went out with two NCOs to prove the route the battalion was to take in the morning for the final advance into Bremen. He caused great anxiety at Battalion HQ when he had not returned by 2300 hrs. A patrol from A Company was just setting out to look for him when the sound of an approaching column was heard. This turned out to be Lieutenant Gill with three German officers and 163 troops who had surrendered to him. Apparently, they had been hiding in a brickworks and were too frightened to come out unless they could find a British soldier to surrender to.

1 Royal Norfolk would see no more serious fighting. At 0800 hrs on 5 May 1945 when the battalion was in positions near Delmenhorst, notification was received that all offensive operations had been cancelled. Most of the battalion were able to celebrate the end of hostilities that night. By some remarkable stroke of good fortune 1 Royal Norfolk had occupied Beck's Brewery when in Bremen. Of that day the late Captain John Talbot, the battalion's Royal Artillery liaison officer, simply recorded: 'Becks Brewery emptied.' On VE Day proper, 8 May 1945, 1 Royal Norfolk moved to barrack accommodation near a former poison gas factory at Espelcamp, about ten miles from Minden, and would remain in Germany as part of the Army of Occupation.

The toll paid by the battalion between D-Day and VE Day was fifteen officers and 235 other ranks killed, forty-seven officers and 785 other ranks wounded, forty-six other ranks missing and prisoners of war, plus two officers and 148 other ranks who had suffered from 'battle exhaustion'.

Chapter 2

2nd Battalion

The officers and men of 2 Royal Norfolk had been on garrison duties in Gibraltar since March 1937 when the battalion set sail to return to Britain on 18 January 1939. On arrival at Southampton, it came under Aldershot command and was stationed at Guadeloupe Barracks, Bordon Camp, as part of 4 Infantry Brigade. The spring and summer of 1939 were spent on hard and continuous training, so the battalion was at a high state of fitness and efficiency when the order to mobilise was received at 1640 hrs on 1 September 1939.

Movement orders were received on 13 September and a small advance party left for Southampton. On 16 September 1939 the battalion's motor transport left for Avonmouth where they were to embark for Saint-Nazaire. The remainder of the battalion left for Southampton on 20 September where it embarked aboard the MVs *Royal Daffodil* and *Royal Sovereign* and landed at Cherbourg in the early hours of 21 September, becoming the first complete infantry unit of the BEF to land in France. The officers listed on the embarkation were:

CO: Lt-Col Eric C. Hayes
2ic: Maj Eric Prattley
QM Lt Qmr A. E. Grant

Capts
F. R. Marshall
J. C.C. Richardson

J. H. Elwes
G. M. Allen
F. P. Barclay
R. M. Allen
A. G. Gibbons (Temp)
A. L. Gordon (Temp)
C. W. H. Long (Temp)

Lts
F. Fitch
J. N. R. Hallett
P. A. C. Everitt
E. J. Richardson

2Lts
A. G. M. Hazlerigg
J. B. Buchanan
B. E. Dillon
J. G. Woodwark
C. C. Swainson
J. T. Gain

On the same day that they landed 2 Royal Norfolk entrained for the brigade assembly area at Noyen and marched to its billets in the Commune of Pirmil (Sarthe). On 28 September the battalion moved to the brigade concentration area at Monchy-le-Preux, near Arras.

In early October the battalion moved up to the forward area on the Franco-Belgian border, near Rumegies, where it took over from the French 201st Regiment d'Infanterie. The next two and a half months were spent digging trenches and anti-tank ditches to continue the defensive system beyond the Maginot Line. On 24 December the battalion entrained for the Saar and arrived at Metz on 25 December. It took a further five days' marching in the freezing cold by night and laying up by day to reach the front and relieve 1 Black Watch on 1 January 1940.

This sector was on the extreme left of the Maginot Line and consisted of three lines: the *Ligne de Contact* was the front line, the *Ligne de Recuil* or fallback position, and the *Ligne de Résistance*, which comprised the Maginot forts proper. During the brigade's stay in this sector each battalion occupied each line in rotation for a period of five days at a time.

The duties of the battalion consisted mainly of wiring, reinforcement of defences and night patrols. Two patrols were sent out into enemy lines on the bright moonlit night of 3/4 January 1940. No. 1 Patrol consisted of Captain Peter Barclay, Second Lieutenant Charles Murray Brown, Lance-Corporal Herbert 'Mick' Davis, Lance-Corporal A. Harris and Lance-Corporal Spooner, and was sent to reconnoitre enemy positions around the railway station at Waldwisse, just over the German border below Luxembourg.

After crossing about half a mile of no-man's land Captain Barclay led the search of a house that proved to be empty. Leaving the rest of the patrol behind to give covering fire if required, Barclay took Lance-Corporal Davis with him to penetrate further to ascertain the location and strength of the enemy's defensive posts. They ran into barbed wire and were at once subjected to rifle fire, which effectively gave away the German positions. After a sharp exchange of grenades and small-arms fire Barclay and Davis managed to work their way clear and the patrol withdrew without loss. For their coolness and resource Barclay and Davis were given immediate awards of the Military Cross and the Military Medal respectively, while the remainder of the patrol were mentioned in despatches. These were the very first gallantry awards made to any members of the BEF in the Second World War.

The No. 2 Patrol led by Lieutenant Patrick Everitt consisting of Private J. Jackson, Private E. Lilley and Sergeant V. Newman also achieved a unique honour as they became the first British patrol to cross the frontier and set foot in Germany during the Second World War. Fortunately, they did not encounter any enemy while out on their patrol and returned without incident.

The battalion suffered its first loss on Sunday, 7 January 1940. Lieutenant Everitt was in charge of a party which was covering a 1 Border Regiment wiring party when he took the initiative to take part of his patrol over the crest of a hill to within sight of the enemy who opened fire on them. Everett fell and the rest of the patrol was pinned down. Eventually the patrol managed to return over the crest of the hill but Lieutenant Everitt had gone too far ahead of the patrol and had to be left behind. A search for Everitt after dark proved unsuccessful. Second Lieutenant Patrick Anthony Clement Everitt, the only son of Lady Everitt of Sheringham, Norfolk and the late Sir Clement Everitt had been mortally wounded. Several national newspapers covered the story under the headline 'First Officer killed on the Western Front'. According to the published accounts Lieutenant Everitt had gone ahead of his patrol with a French liaison agent named Jean Cognasse who recounted what happened:

> Lieutenant Everitt was so brave, it was crazy. As we approached the crest in front of the enemy lines I suggested we should crawl, so as not to be a target. We had come out to make certain observations and he wanted to see as clearly as possible. The firing began and he immediately began making a courageous charge down a hill in front of the enemy lines to attack two enemy machine gun posts. Heavy bullets cracked around him as he leapt over the snow down the hill … He had covered thirty yards when he was caught by the enemy's cross fire, which was aimed low. He fell forward, the lower part of his body badly wounded and his legs shattered.*

The rest of the patrol behind him dropped to the ground and wriggled into shallow depressions in the terrain to take cover as the area was raked by machine-gun fire. As they lay there the sergeant in the patrol believed he heard Lieutenant Everitt call out, 'I'm shot …', but he did not respond when a member of the patrol shouted back calling his name and asked if he could move.

---

* *Sunday Express*, 4 February 1940.

The patrol lay under incessant fire for about 15 minutes. Cognasse could see that trying to reach and evacuate the lieutenant would have meant certain death so he made his way back to the patrol, explained there was no other option than to withdraw and guided them back to their lines. Cognasse's action during the patrol was recognised when he was decorated with the Croix de Guerre by General Gamelin.*

German radio broadcast soon after the raid that a British officer had been captured on Sunday, 7 January. Whether he was alive but unconscious or already dead can never be known for sure. The German broadcast simply stated that he had been removed to a German military hospital and they claimed, 'The best efforts of a number of German specialists failed to save his life.'† The Germans stated his date of death as 9 January 1940. In the spirit of reciprocal honours being given to those who died on enemy territory Lieutenant Everitt was buried with full military honours by German soldiers at Weiskirchen Cemetery in the heart of the Hunsrück High Forest in the Saarland. His body was exhumed and removed under the graves concentration programme to Rheinberg British cemetery for reburial in June 1948.

The battalion returned to Rumegies on 20 January and on that day the CO departed for the UK to take up a staff appointment as commandant of a training school for company commanders which was being formed at Sheerness. Major Eric Prattley assumed command of the battalion.

The battalion moved to billets in Orchies the following day and would spend the rest of the month manning and improving defences as best they could amid vile weather of frost and thaw. On 4 February Lieutenant-Colonel G. P. St. C. de Wilton arrived to take over command of the battalion. The battalion remained in Orchies where it received reinforcements, took part in training exercises and was engaged in the improvement of defences.

March saw 2 Royal Norfolk move to billets in the Doullens training area then returned to Orchies on 19 March. At the end of the month Major Prattley left the battalion to take over command of 5 Royal

---

* *Daily News*, 14 February 1940.

† *Sunday Express*, 4 February 1940.

Norfolk in England. Leave was suspended on 10 April (it was reopened on 24 April) and the following day the battalion was placed at six hours' notice to march into Belgium should the Germans invade. There had been no direct aggression from the Germans against the battalion but on 21 April German aircraft dropped propaganda leaflets over the battalion area addressed to the French Army.

On 25 March General Georges, commander-in-chief of the French Northern Army, accompanied by Viscount Gort, commander-in-chief of the BEF, visited Orchies and a demonstration of weapons was staged on the square. Being so close to HQ, smartness in turnout, especially for guards, was the order of the day. Considering there was a lack of spare battledress and web equipment the quartermaster, Lieutenant A. E. Grant, and RSM WOI Cockaday were instrumental in keeping the standard high. A company provided a guard of honour commanded by Captain Barclay at the Marchiennes station for General Georges's departure. The smartness of the guard was much commented upon.

The battalion then returned to working on the divisional switch line at Orchies. Training during the months February to May was mainly devoted to anti-parachute exercises, digging and rehearsals of embussing and debussing battalion transport. Toward the end of April rumours abounded that a large German offensive was to be launched and all leave was stopped. During the night of 9/10 May there was considerable enemy aircraft activity, then at approximately 0600 hrs, a warning placing the battalion at six hours' notice was received and at approximately 1000 hrs the enemy made the first bombing attack on the town with bombs falling on the railway close to divisional headquarters and a couple of large fires were caused in the town. The men of 2 Royal Norfolk would soon discover Hitler had unleashed the blitzkrieg.

The battalion was ordered to a preliminary concentration area in the Forêt de Marchiennes commencing at 1030 hrs. By the evening of 10 May 2 Royal Norfolk had concentrated at Beuvry Nord, ready to cross the frontier into Belgium and at approximately 0200 hrs on 11 May the head of the battalion crossed the frontier into Belgium at Pont Caillou (Rumegies) in motor transport and motored through Leuze, Ath, Engien, Hal and Malaise. At 1100 hrs there was a delay of one and a half hours during which time enemy reconnaissance aircraft came over but were dispersed by divisional AA batteries. After the move had been resumed the column was attacked by dive-bombers near Tombeek. This was the first occasion of direct enemy air activity against the battalion. Sergeant Sellick set a magnificent example of coolness and courage, emptying magazine after magazine at the enemy from his truck.

At Tombeek 2 Royal Norfolk debussed and dispersed, occupying their new positions on the south bank of the River Dyle north of and including the town of Wavre, which appeared to be a very well-built and prosperous town. Several pillboxes were also to be occupied but there was a bit of a delay when the keys could not be found. Soon enough all was sorted and the battalion had a quiet night. Early in the morning, 1 Royal Berkshire from 6 Brigade reconnoitred the battalion's positions with a view to taking over, in order that the battalion might move back with the brigade reserve around Bois de Beaumont.

On 12 May heavy gunfire was heard soon after first light. Allied aircraft appeared active overhead for the first time and the evacuation of civilians commenced. Numbers of Belgian soldiers looking tired and unkempt filtered back through the lines. No news had been received of what was happening to the Belgian Army, but everyone was apprehensive of their appearance, as the sound of artillery grew closer. 2 Royal Norfolk closed to a two-battalion front and went into brigade reserve between Wavre and Tombeek. The battalion was busy digging in and bridges over the River Dyle in their sector were prepared for demolition. The battalion had been given a warm welcome by local people and were living very well indeed on local farm produce and shop supplies.

After a peaceful night Wavre was bombed on the morning of 13 May and several houses were hit but no casualties occurred in the battalion. In the afternoon a few long-range shells landed in the sector but the battalion suffered no loss of life. Morale remained high but the sight of streams of refugees was not encouraging and late in the day news was received that the Germans had crossed the Albert Canal. The 2 Royal Norfolk war diary recorded: 'It was our last calm day.'

Sappers arrived to prepare the bridges for demolition and over the night of 13/14 May, small parties of enemy appeared on the eastern side of the river and the bridges over the River Dyle were blown successfully. There was considerable air activity and the divisional artillery opened up on groups of enemy spotted by Lysander aircraft. It was clear the forces levelled against Wavre were armoured divisions supported by artillery and Stuka dive-bombers that bombed the passage ahead of the tanks. By the evening of 14 May 1940 Wavre was reduced to ruins.

On 15 May Allied shelling was almost ceaseless and caused extensive damage of enemy positions. During the day the enemy made determined attacks along the front supported by dive-bombers from the air. C and A companies were ordered to move to new positions at Hulpe and A Company (Captain Barclay) was to attack and recapture Bierges. Communication was difficult at the time and when A Company began their attack they found that 1 Royal Scots had already recaptured the village.

About 1900 hrs orders were received to withdraw to the River Lasne and 2 Royal Norfolk was designated to cover the withdrawal of the entire brigade. The battalion commenced its withdrawal at approximately 2230 hrs, 2 Royal Norfolk CO Lieutenant-Colonel de Wilton and the adjutant Major F. R. Marshall remaining with the battalion. Major Lisle Ryder, OC Headquarters Company, proceeded directly to Malaise to recce a position for battalion HQ, which was eventually established in a château. A Company, 2 Royal Norfolk, was the last company to withdraw.

Over 15/16 May the enemy pressed their attacks against the crossings along the River Dyle. A short distance away 2 Durham Light Infantry was fighting off sustained attacks upon the blown bridge at Gastuche, Belgium. In a notably courageous action Second Lieutenant Richard 'Dickie' Annand earned the first Victoria Cross in the British Army during the Second World War when he not only singlehandedly repulsed an enemy bridging party, inflicting over 20 casualties with hand grenades; he repeated the deed later that evening and on learning his batman Private Joseph Hunter had been wounded returned to find him and attempted to evacuate him in a wheelbarrow.

On the same night 2 Royal Norfolk received orders to retire to a new line on the River Lasne in the neighbourhood of Overijse. The first report received by 2 Royal Norfolk on 16 May was that a bridge at Tombeek had not been destroyed and B Company was hurriedly despatched in motor transport to blow it up. There was considerable air activity during the day and planes of both sides were brought down. About midday four men in khaki were seen to be swimming the river. They belonged to A Company and when questioned stated that they had been left in Wavre to load a lorry and on looking out of a window saw German cavalry in the yard below. They opened fire and were then able to escape across the river and rejoin the battalion.

The main road along the River Lasne was under intense small-arms fire all day. In the evening withdrawal orders came again and the movement was carried out in a great hurry, an officer and 10 other ranks from each battalion being left behind to move up and down the road to mislead the enemy amid intensive rifle, machine-gun and grenade fire as they did so. This ruse was apparently successful. The withdrawal was hampered by a shortage of motor transport, which had to make several trips. The battalion marched seventeen miles before the transport returned and uplifted it.

After a hurried breakfast on 17 May the entire brigade was ordered to Grammont. There was no time to make out a brigade march table. Just before moving off the brigade was subjected to a heavy dive-bombing and machine-gun attack. During this the commanding officer was seen with others engaging the aircraft with rifle fire. Units were ordered to make their way to Grammont as best they could. All roads leading west were crammed with refugees and the brigade move took all day to complete. The battalion arrived west of the River Dendre at about 1900 hrs and was billeted that night with their first good sleep for about a week.

Lieutenant-Colonel de Wilton had taken ill on 17 May and was evacuated early morning on 18 May. Command devolved upon Major Nicholas Poyntz Charlton and Major Lisle Ryder as second-in-command. In the early morning the brigade took up a position along the river between Grammont and Lessines with the battalion left and 1 Royal Scots on the right and 1/8 Lancashire Fusiliers in reserve. It was a quiet day and the battalion dug in with outposts east of the canal. That night the enemy attacked the town of Grammont and later that same night orders were received to the effect the brigade would withdraw once more.

The battalion motor transport was frequently bombed during the move and suffered several casualties. The attacks and lack of maps caused the column to become disorganised and some lost their way. One of the quartermaster's trucks found itself in Lille. During the afternoon of 18 May the battalion moved into the area of Froidmont. The battalion marched about nine miles before they were able to embus; there had been a great deal of bombing en route and most of the battalion despatch riders had been put out of action. However, by the end of the day the battalion, with only a few exceptions, had assembled at Froidmont where troops settled down for a night's rest.

On 20 May the order was issued for non-essential personnel of the British Expeditionary Force to evacuate from France. 2 Royal Norfolk assembled in a large wood near Froidmont with the officers' mess established in a house in the village. The area suffered heavy shelling during the day. Troops carried out a recce of the River Escaut between Tournai and Antoing and the battalion moved into positions after dark.

The following day, 21 May, the German attack came just after first light. A Company was the first to be attacked by heavy mortaring that caused several casualties. Battalion Headquarters had been established in a large château in Calonne and it was there the CO Lieutenant-Colonel Nicholas Charlton, Major F. R. Marshall and Second Lieutenant P. S. Buckingham were all wounded by a mortar shall which fell in the porchway of the house. All were evacuated. Captain Peter Barclay, the first officer to receive the Military Cross in the conflict, was also wounded and evacuated later in the day. Major Lisle Ryder now assumed command of the battalion. The enemy continued to put over heavy mortar, artillery and machine-gun fire and consequently the battalion had difficulty in getting through supplies of ammunition and rations.

Twice during the day's fighting an enemy breakthrough appeared imminent. The first was on the left of the battalion front, between B Company and 1/8 Lancashire Fusiliers on the left. The enemy attacking in mass and undeterred by extremely heavy casualties caused by machine-gun and small-arms fire, overran B Company's position. C Company was in reserve and was ordered up immediately and restored the position with a counterattack. A second fierce German attack was made against the centre and A Company's flank was threatened but the decisive actions of CSM George Gristock (35) turned that situation around. His citation tells the story:

> On 21 May, 1940, when his company was holding a position on the line of the River Escaut, south of Tournai, the enemy succeeded in breaking through beyond the company's right flank, which was consequently threatened. C.S.M. Gristock organised a party of eight and went forward to cover the right flank. An enemy machine gun was inflicting heavy casualties on his company, and he went on to try to put it out of action. Advancing under heavy fire, he was severely wounded in both legs. He nevertheless gained his fire position, and by well aimed rapid fire killed the crew and put the machine gun out of action. He dragged himself back, but refused to be evacuated until the line had been made good. By his gallant action the position of the company was secured and many casualties prevented. C.S.M. Gristock has since died of his wounds.

Company Sergeant-Major George Gristock was evacuated to England where he died from his wounds. For his supreme gallantry and sacrifice he was awarded the Victoria Cross, the first to be awarded to a member of the Royal Norfolk Regiment in the Second World War. A fine CSM and a tough fighting man, Gristock would always be remembered by those who served with him for his mess trick of taking a bite out of a beer glass. Gristock was buried in Brighton City Cemetery, Sussex. After the war his parents, George and Edith Emily Gristock of Sandhurst, Berkshire, presented his VC and medals to the Royal Norfolk Regiment.

Throughout the night of 21/22 May the close fighting continued and owing to casualties Major Ryder decided to put in his reserve company,

B Company, commanded by Captain G. M. Allen. Allen was wounded and evacuated almost immediately. On the evening of 22 May orders were received for 2 Royal Norfolk to withdraw to Bachy in the 'Gort' Line. By 1100 hrs on 23 May the battalion was back in its former position and ready to resist the next enemy attack, but fortunately the day was far quieter and the battalion was relieved by a French regiment at about 2030 hrs and moved back via Aubers to La Bassé in the Béthune sector where the brigade was to reorganise and refit. The weather had been beautiful up till this time but that night it was pitch dark with a thick mist and the move by motor transport was a nightmare. There was also a shortage of military police and great congestion on the route. In this new area the men of 2 Royal Norfolk were confronted by a terrible scene of destruction. Hundreds of refugees were seen lying dead on the roads, machine-gunned by dive-bombers; most of the houses were damaged or destroyed.

After no more than a few hours' rest the battalion was ordered to take up a position on the Béthune–Estaires canal near Le Paradis. The CO's recce party was heavily fired on and the recce was not completed until after dark. There was only one map per battalion. Companies of the battalion took up positions around Le Paradis and Lestrem, in the Pas-de-Calais, France.

Early on the morning of 25 May the OC Anti-Tank Company reported 100 per cent casualties at one of his guns in the Bois de Paquet; he did not think there was any friendly infantry in the area and that the wood was full of enemy. Fortunately, a counterattack by A Company drove the enemy out and regained contact with 1 Royal Scots, who were holding the sector to the right of the battalion. Although all four companies were very much reduced in strength, the length of the front held by the battalion was 5,000 yards, and the inevitable gaps between positions had to be covered by machine guns. All through the day the enemy attempted to cross the canal using sunken barges as bridges, but they were held up at all points by small-arms and machine-gun fire from the forward companies. In the fierce fighting in the confusion caused by darkness the battalion headquarters found itself in the wrong position practically in front of its forward companies. A hurried move was made and a new battalion headquarters was established about half a mile back at the Duriez F. During the night of 25/26 May B and D companies moved to their correct positions and were dug in by first light, with B Company on the right of A Company at Petit Cornet Malo and D in the gap between A and C companies.

The first attack came on at 0330 hrs against B Company on the right, with a lighter attack on C Company's position on the left flank. At the same time heavy and accurate mortar fire on the remainder not only pinned the other two companies down, but it also caused heavy casualties. The attack on the right gained a great deal of ground and although B Company and the adjacent company of Royal Scots on their right made several local counterattacks, they were unable to completely restore the situation.

Captain Straghan of the Anti-Tank Platoon received a report that Bois de Paquet was out of action so he and Second Lieutenant Hatch went over and discovered another of the guns knocked out with all the crew killed or wounded. Hatch went forward to the gun, removed important parts to take away as spare parts and returned with a wounded soldier. The soldier's condition rendered it awkward and slow for two to carry him so Lieutenant Hatch took the whole weight of the soldier himself and carried the man back about 500 yards under fire to safety.

The enemy pressure was increased during the morning and casualties mounted. Lieutenant Edgworth, the last remaining officer with B Company, was killed and by noon both A and B companies had reported to battalion HQ that they hardly had any men left after the morning attack. Captain Hastings and Captain Long were sent from HQ to reorganise the two companies and combine them into one unit. This was successfully done and the combined companies numbered about 60 men who continued the defence of their area near Petit Cornet Malo.

By the later afternoon the enemy was across the canal in strength and both B and C companies were engaged in hand-to-hand fighting. To add to the difficulties the Germans managed to get some of their tanks over the bridge at Petit Cornet Malo but many of these were knocked out by determined and skilful use of anti-tank rifles. By the end of the day all the enemy attacks had been held or driven back, though at a terrible cost, and the brigade line, except on the extreme right where a small salient had been pushed between the battalion and 1 Royal Scots, was still intact.

Shortly before 1900hrs on 26 May Winston Churchill ordered Operation *Dynamo*, the evacuation of the British Expeditionary Force from the beaches of Dunkirk, to commence. Some regiments would have to provide the rearguard to hold back the enemy as long as possible to enable as many men as possible to reach the beaches of Dunkirk for evacuation – and 2 Royal Norfolk would be one of them.

Orders were received to mount a counterattack together with a company of 8 Lancashire Fusiliers on the Bois de Paquet. This cleared the northern end of the wood of enemy. Fierce fighting continued and the battalion suffered very heavy casualties. Among these were Captain Cecil Yallop and Second Lieutenant Clem Elson who was missing presumed killed but had been taken prisoner. The enemy was still using mortars with great effect while what mortar ammunition the battalion had left was 100% smoke. No high-explosive mortar rounds could be brought up.

Casualties steadily increased among 2 Royal Norfolk but orders came that their position was to be held to the last man and the last round and the men of the battalion fought on with grim determination. They knew what their duty was, the battalion's part in stemming the German advance to save countless lives as the army fled toward the Dunkirk beaches. The men of the rearguard never showed a sign of wavering in the face of such terrific odds.

After a brief lull on the night of 26/27 May when the troops were able to eat a hot meal, at 0330 hrs the enemy let loose a barrage and at dawn on 27 May launched a full-scale attack. They had brought up barges to cross the canal, repaired the canal bridges during the night and were now pouring across with tanks in support. Several of these tanks were destroyed but without artillery or air support it was impossible to hold back the force of the enemy attack.

German casualties were tremendous, and for a short time their fire slackened. The opportunity was taken to check up on the companies of 2 Royal Norfolk. A, B and D companies were virtually non-existent and a message from Major Elwes was received that C Company was now surrounded. The situation was reported to Brigade HQ and orders were received to hold on until dusk and, if any men were still alive, to withdraw to the northeast to La Nouvelle. Major Ryder assured the brigadier that although the situation was hopeless, every effort would be made to hold on. The fighting became confused, with pockets of soldiers being lost or taken prisoner.

Arthur Brough remembered that morning only too well:

The tanks thundered closer and closer and there appeared to be hundreds of them. The only thing left to do was get rid of as much ammunition as possible, so we fired all the high explosive and smoke bombs we had. Out three inch mortars were red hot. By this time the tanks were too close for comfort and so immobilizing out three inch mortar we removed the bolts from our rifles, threw them away and scattered. We were running along side the dykes by the side of the road like rabbits, a bit degrading for professional soldiers but what could we do against tanks? It was like all hell had been let loose, tank fire and bombs bursting all around us. My best friend Johnny Cockrill was immediately behind me, we were sticking close to each other. Suddenly an explosion stopped us dead in our tracks. I could feel something in the back of my leg; I had been hit by shrapnel. I then saw Johnny had also been hit and there was a chunk out of his leg just above the knee. Almost immediately an enemy tank was on top of us and a voice rang out, 'For you the war is over Tommy.'

The tank crew left Arthur and Johnny where they were and they were taken prisoner by German infantry a short while later and were taken to a dressing station in a château to get their wounds attended to.

Massacre at Le Paradis

Approximately 100 men of 2 Royal Norfolk had bravely held on at the Battalion HQ at Duriez Farm in Le Paradis through gunfire, mortars and shelling until 1700 hrs on 27 May 1940 when it caught fire. Lieutenant-Colonel Ryder ordered the building to be evacuated, the defence to be continued from the surrounding ditches and outbuildings and the seriously wounded to be brought into the yard. The Battalion HQ radio had been smashed and it was reported that Battalion HQ was practically surrounded. They fought on until 1715 hrs when most men had retreated to the cowshed and it was there that they finally ran out of ammunition. The remaining men were then ordered to surrender by their CO Major Lisle Ryder who told a platoon sergeant-major to obtain a soldier's white towel and fasten it onto a rifle for the purpose. The sergeant-major then opened the back door of the cowshed, thrust out the improvised flag of truce, waited until the firing stopped and stepped out with five or six men behind him. Holding the white flag aloft they walked ten paces toward the German troops who promptly opened fire on them.

Those who could still move rushed back to the cowshed and shut the door. Again, the firing ceased, five minutes passed and a second attempt was made to surrender. An officer shouted, 'We are coming out now,' opened the door and there was no hail of bullets. The rest of the men of 2 Royal Norfolk then filed out with their hands up, followed by walking wounded. The Germans appeared to accept their surrender. These 99 remaining soldiers had surrendered to No. 3 Company, 1st Battalion, 2nd SS Totenkopf (Death's Head) Regiment, under the command of SS Hauptsturmführer Fritz Knöchlein.

Disarmed, stripped of their equipment then searched, the men from the farm, along with some of 1 Royal Scots who had also been taken prisoner in the village were paraded on the Rue du Paradis and were marched toward Petit Cornet Malo, hastened by kicks and blows from the rifle butts of their captors; one man suffered a blow so violent it shattered his jaw. Meanwhile, two machine guns from No. 4 Machine

Gun Company were set up on a paddock facing a barn. Private Albert Pooley recalled:

> There were a hundred of us prisoners marching in column of threes. We turned off the dusty French road, through a gateway and into a meadow beside the buildings of a farm. I saw, with one of the nastiest feelings I have ever had in my life, two heavy machine guns inside the meadow. They were manned and pointing at the head of our column. I felt as if an icy hand gripped my stomach. The guns began to spit fire and even as the front men began to fall I said fiercely, 'This can't be. They can't do this to us!' For a few seconds the cries and shrieks of our stricken men drowned the cracking of the guns. Men fell like grass before a scythe … I felt a searing pain in my left leg and wrist and pitched forward in a red world of tearing agony. My scream of pain mingled with the cries of my mates, but even as I fell forward into a heap of dying men, the thought stabbed my brain: 'If I ever get out of here, the swine that did this will pay for it.'

Some never knew what hit them, others heard a command of 'fire'. Once all the men had been mowed down Knöchlein ordered his men to go through the mound of bodies with bayonets, and pistols and rifles were used to fire more shots into the bodies to ensure all were dead. Incredibly two men, Londoner Private Bert Pooley and Dereham-born Private Bill O'Callaghan, survived this hellish experience, but both were wounded. They lay motionless among their dead mates until it was dark. Pooley had received another two bullets that shattered his leg when the Germans fired into the bodies. Bill had escaped with a wound to his arm, and he helped Pooley get out from the pile of bodies and carried him over his shoulders to a nearby woodpile and then to a nearby pigsty. It was here that they hid for the next three days, living off raw potatoes and muddy water they got from a ditch.

Fortunately, they were found by Madame Duquenne-Creton and her son Victor who owned the farm – they risked a similar fate by helping and sheltering both men. After hiding out for a few days being fed by local people Pooley's leg wound was too badly injured and was clearly becoming infected and he could not carry on. Pooley and O'Callaghan gave themselves up to the German Wehrmacht troops of 251 Infantry Division who were then in the area, and they became prisoners of war. Bill would spend the rest of the war in prisoner-of-war camps but Bert was repatriated in 1943. He was determined to alert British military authorities to what had happened but found it difficult to find anyone prepared to believe his story.

Pooley did not give up and after the war gave another statement, this time to the War Crimes Investigation unit and Colonel Alexander Scotland took the matter forward, spitting fire that army officers who had interrogated Pooley after his repatriation had not taken the appropriate action after what Pooley had told them. They were never traced so their reason for this failure to act has never been discovered.

The bodies from the mass grave at the Le Paradis farmhouse were exhumed in 1942 and reburied in graves in the farthest extension of Le Paradis churchyard. Tended by the local people, white crosses were erected and soldiers' helmets were poignantly displayed on some of the graves of those 97 brave soldiers who were cut down by the hail of bullets on that day in May 1940. Today their graves are marked by Commonwealth War Graves headstones but because many of them had been forced to remove their dog tags shortly after they were captured, they remain unknown soldiers.

Evidence was gathered about the massacre and those responsible. Fritz Knöchlein, the German officer responsible for ordering the massacre, was traced and arrested in Germany in 1947. Tried before the Curiohaus War Crimes Court in Rotherbaum, Hamburg, in October 1948, he was found guilty and hanged on 28 January 1949. No other German soldiers or officers were prosecuted for their roles in the massacre.

On the perimeter Acting Captain Peter Hugh Lyall Straghan and Second Lieutenant Dennis Hatch of Anti-Tank Platoon carried on fighting. Lieutenant Hatch suddenly became aware a shell was about to land and shouted to others to take cover but had no time to get away himself and received shrapnel in eight parts of his body. Beyond applying a field dressing to the worst part, he refused medical attention and carried on the action routine of his platoon. Always keeping a level head, and putting his men first Second Lieutenant Hatch was awarded the Military Cross for his gallantry in this and other actions during the Battle of France.

By 27 May 2 Royal Norfolk was decimated. On the morning of 28 May B echelon and stragglers were ordered to proceed via Poperinghe to the sea.

Captain Straghan of the Anti-Tank Platoon kept on firing until all ammunition was expended and accounted for two or three tanks in the process. He then spiked the guns and despite being surrounded he managed to extricate his remaining crews through enemy lines. CSM Walter Haverson got his platoon onto Aire Bridge under sniper and machine-gun fire during the night when the detachment of French troops with light machine guns withdrew. He reorganised his platoon to cover the left flank of the company, which was exposed. His platoon suffered casualties but mostly due to Haverson's fine example and leadership they never wavered. Haverson was of great assistance when various withdrawals under pressure had to be effected. For their gallantry and leadership under the most trying circumstances Captain Straghan was awarded a Military Cross and CSM Haverson a Distinguished Conduct Medal.

The road travelled by the men of 2 Royal Norfolk toward Dunkirk was jammed with traffic from III Corps, French horsed transport and refugees. Several dive-bombing attacks were carried out as the men made their way to the beaches. Most of the battalion made the Dunkirk beaches on 29 May. Movement to the waiting vessels took anything from four hours to the best part of a day from the Mole or the beaches. During the embarkations, the enemy made repeated bombing attacks when waiting ships were hit and several sunk with the loss of numerous lives.

Seventy members of the battalion were taken prisoner by other German units and were brought to a barn at Locon. Among them were Major Hastings and Captain Long who had been wounded and captured in the final action. Among them were several members of C Company whose fate up to that time was unknown because they had been defending the perimeter along with 1 Royal Scots and had suffered terrible casualties.

They had been ordered to hold out as long as they could, to the last man and the last round and so they did. Even after the last of their ammunition had been used Major John Elwes had personally led a bayonet attack against enemy armed with machine guns at short range. Elwes was fatally wounded. Turning to his senior surviving NCO, Sergeant Verdun Storey, he said nothing more could be done and ordered him and his few remaining troops to make their escape to the beachhead as best they could. Major Elwes had to give the instruction as an order because it was the only way those men would have left the ground they were holding.

Verdun Storey and one of his comrades followed a hedgerow to a field; they knew the enemy was close by so Verdun and his pal decided one was to go one way and one the other. Verdun ditched his webbing and ran across the field. As he did so there was a burst of machine-gun fire. He heard the bullets zip around his head, and recalled they sounded like bees swarming around him. Expecting to be hit at any moment but by some miracle he was not wounded so he stood still and raised his hands. The German troops who were pursuing him soon caught up and Verdun could see they were SS. Verdun's captors ordered him to kneel, take off his helmet and remove his dog tags. Verdun would recall it seemed like a lifetime that he was kneeling there as he gazed at the tags in his hand; he threw the tags in his helmet and faced his would-be executioners. Suddenly he heard a German voice shouting 'Halt! Halt!' Verdun saw the man shouting was a more senior officer who reprimanded the gunmen for what they had been preparing to do, and Verdun was taken prisoner.

Pooley and O'Callaghan had, by some miracle, survived the massacre but Private Ernie 'Strips' Farrow would also be one who got away. He had missed the massacre because he had been ordered a few hours earlier to demolish a bridge where he was wounded and taken prisoner. He escaped a few weeks later with Les Chamberlain and they spent 14 months 'on the run'; finding resistance units who could help them, they made an epic journey returning via Paris, Marseille, Spain and Gibraltar to England.

Many of the members of 2 Royal Norfolk taken prisoner during the Battle of France were initially transported to and held in POW camps in

Danzig until the latter months of 1940 when they were taken to POW camps in German-occupied Poland. Several 2 Royal Norfolk soldiers were in Stalag XXA at Thorn (Toruń), a camp of 18,000 prisoners engaged in working parties over a large area, while others were in such camps as Stalag XXB at Marienburg (Malbork), Poland, on the border of East Prussia, and Stalag VIIIB (later renamed Stalag 344), in Lamsdorf, southern Silesia. They were struck how few men of their battalion they encountered while in captivity with them. They had assumed they were probably in POW camps elsewhere. At that time, they had no idea of the terrible losses suffered by the battalion and no idea of the fate of their ninety-seven comrades who had been massacred at Le Paradis. They would only discover what happened after the war.

Not all men of 2 Royal Norfolk put up and shut up with captivity either. Among them was Lieutenant Clem Elson who made repeated escape attempts until he wound up in Colditz. Sergeant Verdun Storey also made several escape bids from Stalag XXA but did not make it home either. Punished and removed to Stalag 383, Hohenfels, Bavaria, he and others simply refused to work and played all sort of tricks on the guards during their time in captivity. Their regimental spirit was unbreakable.

After surviving the depravations of captivity until 1945 some of the Norfolk soldiers who were in the POW camps in Poland were among the thousands of British, Commonwealth and American POWs who were forced to march west across Poland, Czechoslovakia and Germany through extreme winter conditions between January and April 1945. The casualties mounted through bitter cold and exhaustion; the total number of Allied POWs who died on the 'death march' are estimated to be between 1,500 and 2,000 men. Out of a battalion that had set off to war with almost a thousand men just five officers and 134 other ranks of 2 Royal Norfolk returned to Britain during the Dunkirk evacuation.

The men of 2 Royal Norfolk who had been fortunate to make it back to England in 1940 were sent to Horton Park, Bradford, and by 7 June the battalion was reformed from this nucleus and a huge draft of 350 men from the Essex Regiment and Royal Berkshire infantry training centres went a long way to bolster the numbers. After another move to Driffield

Woods the new CO, Lieutenant-Colonel Winter, arrived. As did a draft of regular army NCOs from 1 Royal Norfolk who had recently returned from India. As it reconstituted, the battalion trained and took on a healthy shape again thanks to stalwarts such as CSM Slaughter and the RSM Gordon 'Tick-Tock' Wright.

The battalion proceeded to India aboard the SS *Orbita* with 2 Infantry Division, and after a brief stop off at Cape Town, docked at Bombay on 10 June 1942 and moved off rapidly to Chinchwad Camp. Here the battalion trained in both combined operation and jungle warfare. Lieutenant-Colonel Winter retired from command of the battalion in July 1942 and his place was taken by Lieutenant-Colonel Robert Scott, one of the most colourful characters ever to command a battalion of the Royal Norfolk Regiment.

Early in 1944 Japanese forces invaded India in the Arakan and made good ground in their offensive. At that time 2 Royal Norfolk was 1,500 miles away in western India, part of XXX Indian Corps in 2 Division, but was moved rapidly by air, rail and road to the Indo-Burmese frontier. On arrival in the theatre of operations the officers and warrant officers of 2 Royal Norfolk were:

CO: Lt-Col Robert Scott
2ic: Maj H. R. R. Conder, OBE

HQ Company
OC: Maj A. F. Boldero
Capt G. E. Bradshaw
Carriers: Captain D. Classe
IO: Capt R. G. Greene
SIGO: Lt S. S. F. Horner
Mortars: Lt O. J. F. Whitaker
RMO Capt G. Armitage RAMC
Padre: Rev C. W. Wood CF
RSM: WOI G. Wright
RQMS J. Clitheroe
CSM: WOII S. Derry
A/RQMS: WOII D. L. Atkins

A Company
OC: Maj C. C. Swainson
Capt B. Savory
Lt R. Bothway
2Lt J. T. B. Crouch
CSM: WOII Keeble

B Company
OC: Maj R. L. Twidle
Capt J. N. Randle
Lt C. A. Roberts
Lt B. T. Reeve
CSM: WOII Adams

C Company
OC: Capt C. R. Murray Brown
Capt J. N. N. Molyneux
Lt S. R. P. Solomon
Lt G. C. Barclay
CSM: WOII A. Skuce

D Company
OC: Major D. A. Hatch, MC
Capt C. E. M. Fulton
Lt G. A. Myler
Lt H. M. Davies
Lt J. E. D. Lowe
CSM: WOII W. Milne

Captain J. K. Forte (C Company) and Lieutenant M. J. Franses B (Company) brought the MT (motor transport) from India and joined the battalion later. Lieutenant D. Aikens, LO at brigade, was admitted to hospital in Bangalore just before the brigade left and so on arrival at Dimapur, Lieutenant A. D. Blount replaced him. Second Lieutenants R. A. P. Van Wren and Cole joined a few days later, before the battalion had been in action and were posted to C and D companies respectively.

By 10 April the battalion was organised and B Company was ordered forward to Ghorpani, a village thirteen miles up the road. Japanese had been reported there and in fact a small patrol was later learned to have penetrated as far as the railway. B Company reported Japanese round their wire during the night of 10/11 April but no action took place. A Company was pushed up to Priphema, Milestone 28, with the relief troops of 5 Brigade and on 11 April 2 Royal Norfolk less B Company was installed there. The battalion transport had not arrived and the journey in ramshackle MT with Indian drivers was something of an experience.

There was at that time so little information and so much of an exercise atmosphere – a very badly umpired exercise at that – that news of a successful attack by 1 Camerons of 5 Brigade on 14 April provided an excellent tonic; although the constant arduous patrolling on which the battalion was engaged from Priphema, though providing excellent toughening training, was not relieved by any contact with the enemy. On the night of 15 April, however, No. 18 Platoon of D Company commanded by Sergeant Hazell, which had been sent up the road as escort to a troop of tanks, was heavily attacked by over a platoon of enemy. Sergeant Fred Hazell held his fire until the last moment, with excellent results and his platoon got quite a good bag at the cost of Private Don Woodard who died of wounds and one other casualty.

The battalion now split up, Tactical HQ, B and D companies moving on up the road while HQ, A and C under Major Henry Conder remained at Priphema. This most unsatisfactory state of affairs persisted in spite of the loud and prologued outcry raised by the CO until 20 April when Major Conder's party rejoined and the battalion was once more a unit at Jotsoma, holding the right and rear of the division 'box' Just prior to this on 18 April, CSM Willaim Milne (36) was killed, a sad loss to D Company, the battalion and the regiment.

On 21 April troops from 6 Brigade entered Kohima, Assam, and took over from defenders. On 18 April the wounded had been evacuated under fire from mortars, MMGs (medium machine guns) and snipers with the battalion carriers taking part in the operation. This short account is concerned with the battalion but it is impossible not to refer to the gallant defence put up for fourteen days and nights by the Kohima troops. Subjected by day to constant fire from mortars, artillery and small arms, suffering heavy casualties and forced by dwindling strength to shorten its perimeter daily, the force successfully maintained its positions on long narrow ridges against repeated attacks, which eventually became a nightly occurrence; it was cut off entirely from the outside world except for wireless communication and dependent on air drops for all supplies and water.

The relief of the garrison by no means meant that the road to Imphal was open during the next four days and while 5 and 6 brigades were attempting to dislodge the enemy from Kohima the battalion was in divisional reserve, with the CO and 2ic busily engaged reconnoitring. The fog of war was thicker than ever now; so much so that in one day 2 Norfolk was under command of 6, 5, 6 and 4 brigades and no less than four 'possible' attacks were reconnoitred by the CO, none of which was practicable. Major Conder taking with him Corporal Gilbet of the battalion intelligence section and a smart escort patrolled far out to the right to obtain an observed shoot on the Japanese who were worrying the Royal Welch Fusiliers on the left of the battalion. He did not get far, however, before coming under heavy fire and thus withdrawal without casualties was a fine achievement.

From Naga village on the left the enemy overlooked the whole position. Naga village itself is only commanded by the height of Aradura Spur some three miles south and east, round the eastern face of which runs the Imphal Road.

On 23 April 5 Brigade with 1/8 Lancashire Fusiliers of 4 Brigade began a wide movement to the left flank through Merema with the object of reducing Naga village, which was occupied on the night of 3/4 May by two battalions. Later, however, after violent Japanese counterattacks, the leading battalion was forced to withdraw from its forward positions; the whole village was not in friendly hands until a month later. While these operations were in progress 4 Brigade was despatched on a wide encircling movement designed to effect surprise and capture the Aradura Spur.

On 25 April, the operation referred to by the troops who took part as 'the trek' commenced. Information on the country to be traversed was far from encouraging. There was a Naga track as far as Khonoma, but even the local Nagas had not been over a great part of the route and in fact the deputy commissioner, familiar as he was with the country, held the opinion that the operation was well-nigh impossible. The CO had spent the early part of the day reconnoitring on orders of 6 Brigade for an attack up the almost sheer face of Shrewsbury Hill, which the battalion was to have carried out to relieve pressure on 1 Royal Welch Fusiliers of 6 Brigade; on his return at about 1400 hrs he was greeted by Major Conder with the news that the operation was to start that evening and that Major Conder himself was to move ahead of the brigade column to organise the assembly at Khonoma.

Considering the last-minute nature of the plan and orders, Major Lloyd DAA and QMG 4 Brigade and his team achieved the practically impossible by satisfying most demands for stores by RQMS Clitheroe and certainly no battalion could have had a better QM and staff than did 2 Royal Norfolk in Clitheroe, Colour Sergeant Atkins and their team. Time for preparation was woefully short and there was inevitably a deal of kits and kits out, but by the time of the start the battalion was lacking nothing.

Each officer and man carried 100 rounds SAA (small-arms ammunition) or its equivalent, two days' light scale rations, half a blanket, gas cape, water sterilising tablets, a *dah* (Burmese knife) and his personal weapon and two grenades, with a pick and a shovel for every three men. Some officers preferred kukris to dahs and before many days had passed became adept in their use for wood cutting. A few carried bayonets cut down into large daggers by the armourer, Staff Sergeant Hodson.

There was no small amount of coming and going before the start. Bush hats were to be worn but at the last moment steel helmets were ordered, which entailed unpacking the dumped kit already stacked in the administrative area. The battalion finally moved off with twenty-four officers, including Captain John Mather RAMC and 549 other ranks, plus 4 (carrier) Platoon dismounted acting as an infantry platoon.

Surprise being the essence of the operation, brigade ordered the start at last light and the first stage of some three miles to Khonoma from the

Iron Bridge on the Dimapur–Kohima road, which was under Japanese observation from across the valley, began at 1930 hrs. Major Conder had gone forward with guides and porters escorted by the SS (Special Services) Company . The battalion, brigade and HQ parties of 99 Assault Field Regiment, Royal Artillery and supporting arms parties wound up the stony track in single file. The going was slow and tedious – Khonoma has many steep entrances. In the blackness guides could not be found, and time and tempers were lost on all sides. Dawn had broken before the last of B Company arrived and it was some time before the battalion and much later before the column had been sorted out. The mortar platoon and a platoon of A Company, 2 Manchester, the divisional machine gun battalion, had manfully carried their weapons and the signallers their radio sets throughout the night, but it was realised by brigade that this was taxing the men overly and from then on Naga porters carried them. The column had little or no rest, the men were heavily laden and the march had been carried out over strange country in pitch darkness; although the start of the next stage was delayed until after noon it was a weary column that moved off.

It could not be denied that the necessity of war had dictated the launching of the operation with insufficient preparation and at too short notice, and as inevitably happens, these factors reacted on the troops on the ground. However, all was straightened out. The CO held an O group (orders group), and the men were put in the picture; loads were sorted out, and Naga porters were organised into parties by Captain Molyneux who had been an Assam planter before the war. He was invaluable, and shortly after noon on 26 April 2 Royal Norfolk, preceded by 143 SS Company some distance ahead, left the base at Khonoma, leading the column. It was a case of up one steep *khud* and down the other side, then up a steeper one and down again, most of the time in pouring rain. Parties of Naga porters were interspersed in the column for their protection, and they were quite unable to understand why the troops were out of breath when they reached the top of a hill.

The brigade commander had ordered that the usual ten-minutes-to-the-clock-hour halts only were to be observed, but this somewhat understandably was found not to work in practice and short halts at frequent intervals became the rule. This did not suit the Nagas at all; they preferred to go for several hours and then have a long rest and eventually they were allowed to move at their own speed. This speed was truly amazing, their moving to the accompaniment of grunts in a minor key was reminiscent of Chinese coolies to the men who had served with 1 Royal Norfolk in Shanghai. Their loads were from 80 to 100 lb carried in one piece on the back, whereas the troops who were carrying about the same were festooned like Christmas trees.

Every day's march was of a similar pattern with the force gradually climbing. The SS Company accomplished a great job of work, a great deal of the track having to be cut through virgin jungle and paths made along the sides of steep *hiss*, and all the while it was necessary to patrol forward and to the flanks. The column was behind the Japanese lines, and the enemy could just as well have been up to the same game and have passed within half a mile or less without either column being any the wiser. Each morning the Naga porters would set off, leaving the column struggling painfully on in single file and toward midday they would return for their second loads. All movement was by day, and the night bivouacs were wet and cold. There had not been sufficient 'Tommy Cookers' for issue to all units, and it must be admitted that it rankled that 2 Royal Norfolk, leading the main column the whole way, should be without them, while troops in rear were using them.

All ranks after many 'rockets' became adept at making a smokeless fire out of wet wood, the best medium being bamboo shaved very fine. All cooking was in mess tins, and the general menu was: breakfast – porridge of crushed biscuits warmed painfully and with much blowing and blasphemy, with a little salt and powdered milk added; and of course, 'char' made with boiling water if possible and if not, stewed up to some degree of warmth. Tiffin would be a biscuit and a bit of cheese munched on the march and for dinner a bully stew with selected leaves added for flavour. The monotony was hardly noticed, as everyone was tired and hungry and so relieved when eventually a fire was got going and the mess heated.

After two days on half rations the light scale ran out and 'compo' at just below designed scale was issued. This contained tinned fruit and milk, which was a boon, but the weight and difficulty of division, each tin being normally 16 and now 20 men's rations were a problem. Now and then India-pattern rations appeared which contained ghee (clarified butter) instead of butter, which no one could eat. However, it was of great value in assisting wet shavings to light as by now each man's small bottle of American insect oil, more valued as a fire starter than for its intended purpose, was running short. Three days of up and down scrambling, the column closed up in 'Death Valley' – official codename *Hyde* – and rested the whole day. Death Valley was a deep jungle-clad cleft, with an icy stream running down it, with such steep sides and so deep that the sun scarcely penetrated it and a perpetual damp mist overhung everything. Where it had before been difficult to get a fire going, here it was well-nigh impossible and the moss-covered trees and boulders combined with the gloom and cold might well have depressed the troops had they allowed it to do so. Major Conder here took a patrol of B Company with Colour Sergeant Fitt up to the top of the mountain to the south, where it was possible that the Japanese could descend unobserved upon the column.

The column, 4 Brigade group less one battalion, was now closed up and consisted of: skeleton Brigade HQ, 1 Royal Scots, 2 Royal Norfolk, 143 SS Company, Section 5 Field Company Royal Engineers, a platoon from A Company 2 Manchester Regiment, HQ OP parties, 99 Assault Field Regiment Royal Artillery (Royal Bucks Yeomanry), two Light Sections, 4 Field Ambulance RAMC, and a detachment of 4 Brigade Company, RASC. Communication within the column was by runner only, wireless silence being broken only at stated times when the 22 set got through to division.

In Death Valley it was learned that owing to it not having been possible to capture Jail Hill, the assault on Aradura Spur was impracticable, and the brigade was accordingly directed to attack and capture GPT ridge, so named from its having been the location of the General Purposes Transport Company, Royal Indian Army Service Corps, which was one of the first positions to be captured by the Japanese when they attacked Kohima. Beyond the fact that the attack was timed for 4 May as part of a divisional operation, the CO was not in the picture and consequently the battalion knew no more than that.

By 1 May, after climbing the steepest *khud* so far encountered, where the sappers had had to cut steps and erect hand lines with loads passed up by human chain, the battalion emerged onto the second highest feature overlooking Kohima. From here, taking care not to show movement, it was possible to see the reverse slopes of the positions which 6 Brigade was fighting hard to capture, and which were unobserved from any other point. 99 Field Regiment thereupon fired their guns and the Japanese must soon have wondered how the previously unobserved shooting had suddenly become deadly accurate.

At over 7,000 feet the air was cold and clear and for once it was not raining; below the whole battlefield was spread out: Naga village, Gun Spur, Treasury, Hospital Hill, DIS Range, Garrison Hill, Jail Hill, the road running through the cutting between them, and to the south, Garage Spur and the road below Aradura. This latter was obscured by trees, but the progress of the battle could be made out clearly with glasses.

The column spent 1 May resting and sorting out loads. It was inadvisable to bring the Naga porters further and in any case, it is doubtful whether they would have consented to carry on, as an unlucky chance encounter on the way back with a Japanese patrol had resulted in two of them being killed, though there was no reason to suppose that the surprise was lost. 143 SS Company was reconnoitring the route onto the ring contour, a high pimple hill afterwards called Oaks Hill (*Oaks* being the codename for 3 Brigade) which had been selected from the map as the jumping-off position for the assault.

On 2 May the advance continued and now it was to be feared that the element of luck had deserted the brigade, for a party of three Naga porters encountered a small enemy patrol lying up on the supply route some distance to the rear. Their ration loads were taken from them, they were beaten up and left tied to trees; the patrol then backtracked them to the hilltop, where 1 Royal Scots had just concentrated prior to moving off. Unfortunately, a too-eager sentry fired on them and shot one but the remainder got away. The enemy therefore now knew of the presence of the force though probably not of its strength. That evening 1 Royal Scots was attacked by about 40 enemy in a suicide attack where they just kept on coming again and again, and they only withdrew after about 20 had been killed.

The climb up to Oaks Hill was very trying, all ranks now being much overloaded, and this despite a great amount of ammunition, battle batteries and rations that could not be carried being buried; and as from the start of this move no more fires were allowed and the physical strain began to be apparent. It was a weary 2 Royal Norfolk that led on to Oaks Hill through the SS patrol, but all could muster a grin and were buoyed by the early expectation of battle. By afternoon of 2 May the brigade group was installed on Oaks Hill and a brigade commander's recce was laid on for the following day.

From Oaks Hill nothing at all could be seen through the dense jungle and owing to the danger of discovery brigade would allow no second recce by the CO. Accordingly, at 0700 hrs, two patrols from SS Company moved out to cover the reconnaissance party led by Brigadier William Goschen, Grenadier Guards, commanding 4 Brigade. This amounted to no less than 22 bodies – brigade four, Royal Artillery eight, Manchesters two and Royal Norfolk eight. The latter party originally detailed as two only, was permitted on the representation that as the battalion was to lead the assault, at least Major Swanson and Major Hatch as commanders of the leading companies should have some chance of seeing the ground.

To obtain any idea of the trend in the country it was necessary to work south onto the lower slopes of Aradura and seldom can a reconnaissance have been carried out under like conditions. From ground level the same view of jungle five yards away, to which everyone was well accustomed, was all that could be obtained; had the chance of discovery permitted climbing a tree, an equally entrancing view of treetops could have been enjoyed. After some hours of silent crawling and scrambling, however, at last a spot was discovered whence a small but recognisable part of Jail Hill could be seen, and at precisely the right moment the divisional artillery elected to drop some 5.5 shells on it. They might almost have known of the party staring at it.

Short of Jail Hill, part of a corrugated roof could be made out, and this was taken to be on the objective (in fact it was further on and to the left but when eventually the battalion stormed the last big Japanese position it could be easily picked out. Up till then, however, it was quite invisible). The brigade party then returned, leaving Lieutenant-Colonel

Scott and Major Hatch with Lieutenant-Colonel John James, CO of 99 Assault Field Regiment, to study the ground – or rather the jungle. The bearing of the tin roof mentioned above was 85° and Lieutenant-Colonel James and the CO decided that the bearing of the axis of advance must be 110°F (43°C), which subsequently proved very nearly correct.

During the recce one platoon of SS Company had the mortification of lying up on both sides of a track unseen and unheard while thirty-five Japanese soldiers walked through them. They could probably have accounted for the whole party but could not give away their position. 2 Royal Norfolk party returned to the battalion perimeter to find that a share-out of compo rations in the brigade group had been made at 1300 hrs and each man in the battalion had:

> Tea, milk and sugar for one day
> 5 biscuits
> ½ a tin of bully beef
> 1 small tin of sardines, or one-third of a tinned salmon or one-third of a tin of pilchards
> 1 small spoonful of butter
> ½ small tin of cheese
> One-eighth of a tin of milk
> One-eighth of a tin of jam or one-eighth of a tin of fruit
> One-eighth of a tin of Machonochie

In view of the no-fires order this repast had to be consumed cold, but as there was every possibility of a hard day's fighting on the morrow, the CO determined that all should have at least a hot drink and accordingly ordered a huge hole six feet deep and about twelve feet square to be dug in the area of the RAP. This was then roofed over and an immense pile of shavings prepared. As soon as it was dusk, when the escaping smoke could not show, multitudes of mess tins were boiled up and the object of the exercise thus achieved. It is regrettable to admit that the CO aided and abetted by the best of all the RMOs, Captain John Mather, reported his action to brigade as necessitated by the large number of men whose jungle sores needed hot fomentations. In the event, the furnace was invisible at five yards' distance, at least one man had a fomentation, all had a 'brew up' and were 100 per cent the better for it with Brigadier Goschen accorded ex post facto approval.

The brigade commander issued his orders in the late afternoon and the CO got back to the battalion O group only just before dark. As the light was going fast, it was unavoidable to give the fire plan first when company commanders could still see to write and the remainder was of necessity all verbal orders. As short a time as possible was taken up, but even then the task of putting the men into the picture occupied most of the night as utter silence had to be maintained and so movement from group to group was slow, and the orders had to be whispered right into the ear of each recipient. If nothing else, this ensured that by endless repetition the officers knew every word.

Lieutenant-Colonel Robert Scott noted the outline for Operation *Key* that was given at the brigade O group. The information of the enemy was somewhat scanty. 31 Japanese Division was considered to have suffered heavy casualties. 124 Regiment was possibly taking over in Kohima. The enemy had been leaving Kohima toward the south and the east. Strengths on Congress Hill, Jail Hill and GPT Ridge were unknown. MMGs and four mortars had been located on GPT Ridge. Enemy patrols between Valley and Picket hills were probable. The battalion Jotsoma patrols reported enemy slit trenches on Congress were possibly occupied. Localities were identified at three map references. Reverse slopes of Jail Hill were held from time to time. Working parties were in the valley south of the bridge and up the Nala from the bridge. Likely counterattacks would be by artillery and mortars by movement from the Nala or from any direction. It was unknown whether the enemy was expecting an attack. 4 Brigade was to capture and hold the area of GPT Ridge, Congress Hill and Pimple Hill on 4 May.

The divisional plan envisaged four phases. Key 1 was a thrust along the road by an armoured group. Key 2 was the attack by 4 Brigade Group. Key 3 was an attack by 161 Independent Infantry Brigade to link up with the left flank of 2 Royal Norfolk after its capture of GPT, and Key 4 was the capture of Pimple and Congress hills. Key 4 was contingent upon the success of Key 2 and Key 3 but neither would take place.

A comprehensive fire plan lasting 45 minutes was laid on for Key 2 consisting of five separate concentrations, some of them of an intensity of 450 shells in five minutes, and during the whole time the two medium 5.5-inch guns that the CRA had found at Dimapur and manned with RA personnel from the divisional artillery were to fire on GPT ridge 'cap on' in the hope that this would make some shell holes, which would provide cover during consolidation. 4 Brigade orders for Key 2 were that 2 Royal Norfolk with one subsection of 5 Field Company Royal Engineers, one platoon Manchesters, two platoons SS Company and one light section 4 Field Ambulance would capture and hold the highest part of GPT ridge below the jungle and spur. 1 Royal Scots was responsible for blocking the track north of the bivouac and thereafter as reserve would move by bounds on the same axis as 2 Norfolk. 2 Platoon, SS Company, was to be responsible for protection on the right flank of the battalion. 2 Royal Norfolk was to form up for the assault at the edge of the jungle, and the CO would then give the order to division for the start of the fire plan and inform brigade, which would move with 1 Royal Scots.

With so many unknown and unknowable factors the plan had of necessity to be fluid. 4 Platoon under Captain Glasse was to be in position at the bottom of Oaks Hill by 0530 hrs to cover the battalion as it moved down at first light just before 0600 hrs. The battalion was to move by bounds, one company up in the order: A Company (Major Charles Christopher Swainson), Tactical HQ and RA OP Party, 4 Platoon to move when A Company was through them, D Company (Major Dennis Arthur Hatch), Battalion HQ, 4 Field Ambulance, HQ Company (Major A. F. Boldero) less 4 Platoon, C Company (Major Charles Russell Murray Brown), one platoon Manchesters, a subsection of Royal Engineers and B Company (Major Roger Twidle). Companies were, if the jungle allowed, to move on a two-platoon front, and Tactical HQ, which with the large RA party numbered 40, also on a wide front. The first bound was to just short of the edge of the jungle.

All were to be as light as possible, the packs containing only washing kit, gas cape, cardigan and rations. Biscuits were carried in the pocket and A Company packs were carried by C Company so that the leading company could be even lighter. In the event of enemy being found on the track below Oaks Hill by 4 Platoon, B Company was to attack them and the battalion advance would either be resumed on reduction of the opposition or start at once bypassing it.

On the morning of 4 May 1944, it being just light enough to see the sights, 2 Royal Norfolk moved down from Oaks Hill led by A Company. It was a steep scramble down and as Tactical HQ reached the bottom and was passing through 3 Platoon heavy small-arms fire broke out ahead. A runner reported that A Company had bumped into a bunker position, and that Major Swainson was reconnoitring and would report in a few minutes. The CO announced that he would wait ten minutes, he then lay down and went to sleep. Before ten minutes had elapsed Major Swainson reported. He had been slightly wounded in the left foot, and it was learned that Lieutenant Richard Bothway's leading section had come under fire from a strong bunker position about 100 yards ahead and five of his men had been killed. Lieutenant Bothway had then attempted to get round to the left flank and was pinned down and Major Swainson believed the enemy position was a pretty strong one.

Two platoons of A Company were therefore dropped off to contain the position while Company HQ and 1 Platoon continued with the battalion, and the brigade commander was informed that the battalion would continue the advance. It was now only too obvious that the enemy was not only expecting the attack but strongly disapproved of it, though if the bunkers contained by A Company could be passed without discovery, it might still be possible to get down the ridge. Major Hatch, who with D Company was now to take the lead, was accordingly ordered to go wide of A Company's right and try to regain the axis well beyond the bunkers.

Lieutenant Bothway's platoons of A Company remained in position all that day under heavy fire, and thanks to the gallantry and devotion of all ranks, and the very able dispositions of Major Swainson and his officers, the bunkers that proved of immense strength were completely contained.

A Japanese track led along the backbone of the ridge, and this proved a great thorn in the flesh, for it was of course covered by fire and so the advance had to be made below it along the steep side of the ridge while the enemy could move rapidly along it and launch flank attacks as he wished.

With D Company in the lead and Lieutenant James Lowe commanding the leading sections, 2 Royal Norfolk continued its advance. The two-platoon front envisaged in the plan became, on account of the steep slope and thick jungle, a two-section one with men crawling only two yards apart and the remainder of the battalion following in single file. It was a particularly inhospitable type of jungle, thick undergrowth that had in most places to be cut, interspersed with frequent clumps of impenetrable thorn trees and brambles with occasional bamboo. After about fifty yards heavy small-arms fire opened up and grenades were thrown from above on the left flank. Captain Charles Edward Michael Craig Fulton, 2ic of D Company was killed here, the first officer casualty for 2 Royal Norfolk in this theatre of war.

As the slow advance continued the fire increased in intensity until almost the whole column was subjected to it and casualties increased. In addition, a party of enemy got in between D Company and the SS platoons on the right and the situation began to be difficult. Major Murray Brown was brought up from his company to Tactical HQ so that in the event of casualties he would be in the picture, while Major Conder remained with Battalion HQ and shepherded the column along.

The stretcher-bearers started their difficult task and besides having to find the casualties in the undergrowth, dress them and move them back to the main axis, they were in constant danger of being sniped. Lieutenant-Colonel James RA, commanding 99 Field Regiment, was wounded and while being carried back on a stretcher was sniped again and died before reaching the Light Section. This made apparent the way the enemy might be expected to respect the Red Cross armbands. Calls for stretcher-bearers became so frequent that eventually they were able only to dress wounds and leave the casualties where they were to be picked up later.

The feeling of complete helplessness of the winding column in single file is something not experienced so forcibly in open warfare. Criticism of commanders being too far forward is not always justified. Information about the progress of leading troops is difficult enough for a leading commander to obtain, who probably cannot see more than three of his men at any one time. A general picture can only be obtained by going right up and seeing with one's own eyes. This accounts for the presence of Lieutenant-Colonel Scott and his Tactical HQ with the leading sections.

Conservation of ammunition had been stressed frequently in training and in the orders for this attack. Especially was this necessary as the reserve had been buried and all that was available was that carried by each man. The men were very reluctant to shoot at noise only; they waited, as taught, for a target. The targets never appeared and the casualties were mounting with no apparent dividends. When the CO shouted out to open fire, somebody replied, 'But we can't see a target to fire at sir.' This tribute to fire discipline provoked a long string of imprecations from Lieutenant-Colonel Scott who moved over to where the fire was coming from and hurled grenades, and very soon every shot fired by the enemy was answered by a quick burst from everything close by.

As the advance progressed grenades were thrown liberally and this had the effect of discouraging the enemy and clearing the close undergrowth. Any glimpse of an enemy almost certainly meant a hit and the great amount of weapons training that the battalion had undergone now paid a high dividend. CSM Derry was observed in the perfect Hythe standing position to get three enemy in the stomach with 'three rounds rapid' and battalion rumour had it that someone shouted out, 'Reload quickly.' In places it was so thick that flat crawling was the only method of movement, As the enemy fire diminished, so the impetus of the advance grew, encouraged greatly by the CO 'full of strange oaths, and bearded like the bard' with his sandbag of grenades.

It is not often in training that men can be persuaded to shout during an assault, but its value proved immense on this occasion, and cheering broke out when any enemy were confronted; in fact the cheering and shouting throughout the column, which rose to a crescendo when a charge was made at a bunker, most certainly had an effect on enemy morale.

D Company was magnificent; running into a clear patch in the middle of which was a large enemy bunker, they never wavered but overran the position and mowed down the enemy who tried to escape. On went the leading platoon commanded by Lieutenant Lowe and the battalion was soon heading down GPT ridge to the start line and the real objective. The speed of D Company had become so rapid that the rest of the column was somewhat strung out and in consequence the CO ordered a temporary halt to reorganise, check ammunition and casualties and make a fresh plan. Colonel Scott took the opportunity to mend his pipe, which had been broken during the crawl through the jungle.

Casualties in D Company were light once the assault had got under way, but snipers had accounted for several victims earlier on. Snipers were still active against the remainder of the column and several casualties were caused as the battalion closed up. This took about 20 minutes, and temporary defensive positions were adopted.

A short conference took place to decide the next step. The CO ordered that the battalion recce party should go forward covered by a screen provided by the remaining platoon of A Company with A Company HQ on the left and a platoon of B Company on the right, with the remainder of B Company following up.

An incident here was provided by a sharp burst of fire from one of the less frightened enemy who was inquisitive to see what was going on. This burst was intended to eclipse the O group but was inaccurate and no one was hurt. The colonel, annoyed by this impertinence, immediately ordered a 2-inch mortar into action, giving explicit orders to the firer, who promptly lost his head and fired the bomb at a bough of a tree above him. The mortar fortunately was not really needed, as by this time the Bren gunners knew how to deal with the situation.

At about 1500 hrs the reconnaissance started, covered by a creeping barrage from 99 Field Regiment controlled by the OP officers moving with OCs A and B companies. This accurate shoot was no mean feat, as the axis of the advance was practically at right angles to the line of fire of the guns. Large packs had been dumped at this spot. As it was D Company had already had to throw them off in the jungle further back to get through the undergrowth. The jungle here was thinner but visibility was seldom more than twenty yards.

The enemy had not run far and before going 100 yards he opened up again. This time it was a 70mm gun position, but it was facing the wrong direction. The halt had not been long enough for the incredible ferocity of the first assault to wear off and the same immediate response, with interest, to the enemy fire soon knocked out this opposition. Again, the CO was right forward and claimed three enemy with his pistol and again the impetus of the advance grew faster until it broke almost into a double. What had begun as a recce covered by fire and protective troops had now become another assault, and enemy resistance was overrun wherever it was encountered.

Some effective shooting at running targets was made and any enemy who stayed behind was bayonetted. There was no resisting the cheering rush, led by the CO brandishing a Japanese sword; Majors Twidle, Hatch and Murray Brown, and Major Weatherby and his gunners joined in and accounted for several enemy.

Friendly casualties were comparatively few here and many enemy corpses told the tale. The jungle cleared suddenly and looking down, a bare pimple feature was seen and below that about 500 yards away, the main road twisting upward and disappearing round Aradura Spur. The CO now decided that the impetus of the attack must not be checked and that the objective could be gained if no pause was made. And so ordered Major Conder by WT (wireless transmission) to inform brigade that he was going straight on without waiting for the fire plan. Major Conder was to bring up C and HQ companies and Battalion HQ as soon as possible and to ask brigade for at least one company of Royal Scots to secure the right flank. Unfortunately, this company could not be spared; later the battalion was to suffer many casualties from snipers in the area which it was required to occupy.

Using Brens, rifles and bayonets alone, the final objective was taken and only after repeated assurances would division believe that 2 Royal Norfolk was there; when the CO got on to division, the conversation went something as follows:

2 Royal Norfolk: 'I am on GPT and am consolidating. Casualties pretty heavy but we have killed a hell of a lot of enemy.' 2 Division: 'But you can't be there, you have not had the fire plan.' 2 Royal Norfolk: 'Possibly, but I tell you I am. You had better send someone up to see.'

The left A Company platoon and the left platoon of B Company overran the objective and were caught by heavy machine-gun fire from a bunker position about forty yards to their left front (later known as Norfolk Bunker).

A very unpleasant hour followed during which every available means was tried to get those caught in the open back over the crest. The lack of 2-inch mortar smoke was greatly felt and it was not the first time that day that a quantity of 77 grenades (smoke) would have proved a real asset. From that day forward 77 white phosphorus grenades were always carried two per man in the battalion. It undoubtedly saved many lives as well as being a first-rate incendiary weapon in offence. Those pinned down were too close to the enemy for effective artillery smoke to be laid though Major Weatherby who had taken over command of 99 Field Regiment gave all the smoke possible and Captain Brook-Fox spared nothing to get into a position to be able to observe the shooting.

Two MMGs were mounted to cover the bunkers and when these went out of action Major Conder and the CO took their places with two Brens, even standing up arguing who was doing the better shooting. Brens were also used to kick up dust in front of the bunker slits and 36 rifle grenades were thrown to keep the enemy heads down, but these measures were only partially successful. The stretcher-bearers again had a most unenviable task, which they carried out with the courage and devotion that had been so outstanding in all their work throughout the day.

After two hours most of the casualties that could be reached were back but many had been killed, especially among the A Company platoon. Major Twidle had been severely wounded, Captain Jack Randle had been hit in the knee but refused to be evacuated, Captain Barham Savory, 2ic of A Company, was hit in the neck, the bullet travelling right through him to emerge low down in his back. He crawled back under fire to effect the evacuation of his platoon and only then did he allow himself to be treated at the regimental aid post.

Sergeant 'Mick' Davis had been the first NCO in the British Army to receive a gallantry award in the Second World War back in January 1940 and now as a sergeant in A Company he would prove his gallantry, devotion to duty and qualities of leadership again at Kohima. His citation states:

> During the advance down Norfolk Spur and the attack on GPT Ridge on 4 May Sergeant Davis's platoon was part of the main body when the remainder of his company was left to contain an enemy bunker position. When the advance was checked and in danger of stopping, this NCO was sent to the right flank to make a way through the jungle. … Under heavy fire from snipers and LMG he led his platoon into position, accounted for many enemy, and by cool and efficient leadership restored the situation and enabled the advance to continue. During the final assault on the enemy position Sergeant Davis's personal example, when men of his platoon had become casualties, caused the rest to carry on with the bayonet at two bunkers which were vital to the defence.

During the action on 5 May Davis was shot through the calf but continued to direct his platoon while under fire and saw all his casualties out before making his own way to the regimental aid post. For his outstanding gallantry Sergeant Davis was awarded a Distinguished Conduct Medal to go with his Military Medal, making him the most decorated soldier of the Royal Norfolk Regiment during the war; he was promoted to company sergeant-major.

Major Conder had brought up the remainder of the battalion and the defences were laid out. Brigade HQ and two companies of 1 Royal Scots formed a 'box' on the ridge, 200 yards above the battalion. During this stage Japanese snipers, especially on the Aradura flank, were active and there were several casualties, one persistent enemy eventually getting the CO in the head, the bullet going through his steel helmet but only causing a scalp would and he was not evacuated. Earlier in the advance, Major Murray Brown was hit by LMG fire in the jaw. But it was not broken, and he refused to go down.

During his reconnaissance of his company's defences, just before dark Major Hatch was seriously wounded and died during the night.

The RAP was crowded with wounded and no praise can be too high for the work of Captain Mather RAMC and Sergeant Barrs and his staff, especially Captain Mather's untiring example and the courage shown by his repeated visits to Major Twidle over a period of nearly twenty-four hours. The latter was too badly hit to be moved and was under sniper fire. Lying in hastily dug holes and enemy slit trenches, sheltered from the rain by what little cover could be scrounged, their fortitude and cheerfulness was amazing and not a complaint was heard from those seriously hit.

During the reorganisation for consolidation of the position use was found for much captured material. Five Brens had been lost, the gunners having been sniped during the advance, but no less than seven were captured from the enemy, while 3 Platoon became the owners of two 3-inch mortars and the Manchesters' platoon received two Vickers guns. These weapons had all been captured when the Japanese had first taken Kohima and though in a bad state were still serviceable and filled a much-needed requirement. A large quantity of SAA and 3-inch mortar ammunition, two walkie talkies and an infantry gun also fell into battalion hands as well as a .50 aircraft machine gun.

It became increasingly obvious that Norfolk Bunker would have to be eliminated to clear the line of communication down to the main road, to allow casualties to be evacuated and supplies and ammunition to be brought up. It was now that the loss of surprise through contacting the small enemy patrol and the consequent dispersion of the force was painfully felt, for the brigade commander could not risk the enemy occupying the high ground behind him and so would not release 1 Royal Scots for an attack in strength on Norfolk Bunker. On the night of 4 May, a strong attack would almost certainly have cleared this position but every day that passed saw it strengthened and reinforced as well as receiving an air drop of ammunition and supplies that were supposed to be for 2 Royal Norfolk.

Captain Bradshaw now assumed command of D Company, Lieutenant Lowe took over the duties of adjutant from him, Captain Randle assumed command of B Company and Captain Molyneux of C Company. All companies reformed on a two-platoon basis. This was the situation of 2 Royal Norfolk on the evening of 4 May when the position was consolidated.

The trek had culminated in a successful action, during which 2 Royal Norfolk had been under heavy fire from 0600 hrs until its final capture of the objective at 1615 hrs. From 25 April to 4 May, all ranks had undergone considerable physical strain, and the difficulty of the country can be gauged by the fact that the actual distance that took seven days to traverse was no more than twelve miles.

The problem now was to eliminate Norfolk Bunker and the Carrier Platoon was ordered to attack on foot after dark. The attack achieved its immediate objective, which was to open the track running past Norfolk Bunker to the main road. It could not be known that the bunker that had caused the A Company platoon such trouble earlier was only the most forward of a series that ran down the narrow spur to the road a few hundred yards away. In this and the subsequent attack this position was taken but the battalion was ordered to withdraw as it was feared a counterattack would prove successful.

B Company was ordered to hold onto what they had gained, and this proved enough for opening the track. There was only one direction from which the attacks could be put in without armoured support, which was not considered possible by division. The obvious way to assault a narrow ridge is lengthways along its narrowest part, thus limiting the numbers of weapons deployed against the attackers. As well as this, operating from this direction meant having the shortest stretch of open ground to cross as well as being at right angles to small-arms supporting fire from GPT ridge.

After dark the Carrier Platoon assaulted, crossing the open at the double, storming on to the pimple and knocking out the bunker. On clearing the crest, however, they came under heavy machine-gun and grenade-discharger fire from lower down the ridge and suffered severe casualties. Captain David Glasse was killed, and the assault was held up.

The remainder of the night of 4/5 May was spent digging in and bringing in the wounded who could not be moved in daylight. Morale remained high despite the exhaustion of the troops and the heavy casualties. Volunteers as stretcher-bearers were innumerable and they did magnificent work, especially Corporal Flitton and Private Carter of A Company who went out many times and organised parties with great skill. Torrential rain started to fall soon after dark and the trenches filled with water. Although brown and heavy with mud this water was the sole means of making a cup of tea in the morning, and no one seemed to have any immediate aftereffects.

On the morning of 5 May, the men of 2 Royal Norfolk could do nothing other than watch the depressing spectacle of an Allied air drop of much-needed supplies floating down onto Japanese lines. Later in the morning Major Conder was hit in the arm and leg by an LMG sniper. He lay for some hours in a slit trench protesting that he was not badly hit and pretending to read the CO's Shakespeare, but when his wounds had stiffened up and became properly painful Captain Mather was able to stalk him while semi-conscious and inject morphia, which soon put him in a position to be evacuated without further argument.

A small plot was prepared for the burial of the dead, though most could not be brought in until many days later. Sergeant Percy Partridge, then the battalion provost sergeant, worked day and night with digging parties and the results of his labour were seen later in the impressive little cemetery inside the battalion perimeter. Those whose bodies could not be recovered were given a token grave with a cross for each man on it. A small plaque bearing the name of the regiment was nailed to a tree in the centre and it was hoped it would remain there even after the bodies had been removed to the divisional cemetery in Kohima.

Major Swainson arrived with the remnants of A Company at midday, the enemy having evacuated his position higher up the hill during the night, and the defences were enlarged a little. With so few men left the position was not more than 100 yards in diameter. A ridge ran off toward Aradura Spur and enemy snipers became increasingly active, claiming anyone who took the risk of standing up when he should have been crawling.

Lieutenant Gilbert Charles Barclay was killed during the morning by a sniper bullet from the ridge that detonated the grenade he was carrying in his pocket. A single sniper was active between the battalion position and the brigade 'box' above it. He accounted for a few from the ration- and ammunition-carrying parties. It became increasingly evident that the area would have to be cleared of these snipers and the defences extended to take in the ridge running toward Aradura Spur. The main problem of Norfolk Bunker was pressing and little more could be done about the organisation of defences for several days. Sniper activity was kept down by the general alertness and individual skill of the battalion snipers, among them Private Charles Crampion of D Company who was a recipient of the King's Medal for Champion Shots.

Dysentery was now becoming a problem and many troops were suffering from it in some form or other, though none would own up to it and morale remained high. 143 SS Company had by this time come down to join the battalion from Oaks Hill, as well as a platoon of machine guns. These greatly helped to strengthen the defences. One section of the machine guns was fortunate to have two bewildered Japanese soldiers armed only with grenades wander onto their guns that night.

A second and stronger attempt was made next morning to clear Norfolk Bunker. It must not be forgotten that the real strength and depth of the enemy positions was still unknown. What information the Carrier Platoon had been able to give was not very conclusive owing to the darkness. B Company, two platoons strong, with the remains of the Carrier Platoon under Captain H. M. 'Dickie' Davies was ordered to carry out the attack.

The plan was for close fire support to be given from battalion Bren guns, brigaded on the northern flank of the battalion position; 2-inch mortars were also lined up ready to give smoke cover if called for (bombs had been obtained from the Royal Scots). The artillery and 3-inch mortars were to concentrate on the lower end of the ridge and in the valley between GPT Ridge and Aradura Spur to stop movement of enemy reinforcements. With two platoons up, B Company would cross the start line just before dawn; the left platoon was to capture the left of the initial bunker feature and the right one to take the right side of the same feature and exploit forward down the right flank, the latter to move slightly echeloned back and behind the former. A very careful and daring reconnaissance was made on the evening of 5 May by Captain Randle, and the attack was launched at dawn on 6 May. The platoon on the left could not keep sufficiently to the left and so forced the right platoon into the open forward slopes where D Company had suffered so badly on 4 May.

It was not quite light, and the enemy was firing on fixed lines. Lieutenant Charles Ambrose Roberts was killed almost instantly but the platoon gallantly went on in the face of deadly machine-gun fire. Upon seeing Lieutenant Roberts fall, Colour Sergeant Bert Fitt went forward alone and succeeded in destroying the bunker, at the second attempt, with a well-placed grenade. In the next instant, Fitt was caught by a burst of fire which shattered his jaw. He later recounted, 'It felt like a severe punch. I spat out what was left of my teeth and sprayed the foxhole with my light machine-gun. When it jammed, I threw it in the face of a Japanese soldier who was still alive.' In the hand-to-hand struggle that followed Fitt managed to kill his enemy with his own bayonet. As he led his men across the top of the enemy position, Fitt witnessed the last, courageous charge of his company commander, Captain Jack Randle.

Randle's platoon had been pinned down by the intensity of the machine-gun fire from a camouflaged bunker that had only revealed itself as the platoon approached. Appreciating that the destruction of this enemy post was imperative if the operation was to succeed, Captain Randle charged the Japanese post single-handed armed with a rifle with fixed bayonet and hand grenades. The citation for his courageous action states:

> On 4 May, 1944, at Kohima in Assam, a Battalion of the Royal Norfolk Regiment attacked the Japanese positions on a nearby ridge. Captain Randle took over command of the Company which was leading the attack when the Company Commander was severely wounded. His handling of a difficult situation in the face of heavy fire was masterly and although wounded himself in the knee by grenade splinters, he continued to inspire his men by his initiative, courage and outstanding leadership until the Company had captured its objective and consolidated its position. He then went forward and brought in all the wounded men who were

lying outside the perimeter. In spite of his painful wound Captain Randle refused to be evacuated and insisted on carrying out a personal reconnaissance with great daring in bright moonlight prior to a further attack by his Company on the position to which the enemy had withdrawn.

At dawn on 6 May the attack opened, led by Captain Randle, and one of the platoons succeeded in reaching the crest of the hill held by the Japanese. Another platoon, however, ran into heavy medium machine gun fire from a bunker on the reverse slope of the feature. Captain Randle immediately appreciated that this particular bunker covered not only the rear of his new position but also the line of communication of the battalion and therefore the destruction of the enemy post was imperative if the operation was to succeed. With utter disregard of the obvious danger to himself Captain Randle charged the Japanese machine gun post single-handed with rifle and bayonet.

Although bleeding in the face and mortally wounded by numerous bursts of machine gun fire he reached the bunker and silenced the gun with a grenade thrown through the bunker slit. He then flung his body across the slit so that the aperture should be completely sealed. The bravery shown by this officer could not have been surpassed and by his self-sacrifice he saved the lives of many of his men and enabled not only his own Company but the whole Battalion to gain its objective and win a decisive victory over the enemy.

Captain John Niel 'Jack' Randle (26) was awarded a posthumous Victoria Cross for his outstanding gallantry and sacrifice. He is buried in the Kohima War Cemetery, India.

After bringing the survivors out after the battle Colour Sergeant Fitt was met by his CO, the redoubtable Lieutenant-Colonel Robert Scott. Fitt recalled: 'I had an old field dressing wrapped around my face, and he said, "They've got you then. Let's have a look." The MO took off the bandage and Colonel Scott laughed and said, "Well, you never were an oil painting!"' Whether or not it was due to shock, despite his painful injury, Fitt burst out laughing.

Fitt was awarded the Distinguished Conduct Medal for his gallantry and went on to be the very last Depot RSM of the Royal Norfolk Regiment. He remained a well-respected legend among the men; 2 Royal Norfolk veteran Arthur Storey, who served with Fitt, recalled: 'He was a soldier first and last. Like everybody he liked his beer and a bit of fun but he was a real fighting man. He was the sort of man you'd follow to hell and back. He never asked anyone to do anything he wouldn't do himself.' Evacuated to hospital after being wounded at Kohima, Fitt managed to wangle his way out after only three days and returned to the battalion under his own steam.

From 6 to 28 May the battalion remained in a perimeter camp and was much troubled by snipers. On 28 May they went into action again in the advance on Aradura Spur, a steep climb to a knife edge where the enemy held a very strong position. An attack was delivered but it was unsuccessful, the battalion suffering around 50 casualties. The cumulative losses in battle and sickness through malaria, dysentery and other tropical diseases left the battalion with just 14 officers and 366 other ranks but still morale remained high and they would fight again.

Returning to Dimapur the battalion reorganised and took part in the advance on Imphal. At Viswema it encountered the enemy and had a sharp fight for a roadblock. The advance continued and in two months 104 miles were covered.

At the end of 1944 Fourteenth Army began a general offensive. The battalion marched with the rest of the division across the Indo-Burmese border to Tamu, down the Kabaw Valley and over the Chindwin River. In the first month of this advance the battalion covered 300 miles. On 23 January 1945 2 Royal Norfolk provided a feint on the left flank for 1/8 Lancashire Fusiliers' successful attack on the village of Ondaw on the main road down to the Irrawaddy opposite Mandalay.

While 2 Royal Norfolk were fighting their way to Mandalay a certain Lieutenant George Arthur Knowland (22) was leading his men of No. 4 Troop, 1 Commando, at Kangaw, Burma during the Battle of

Hill 170. Knowland had joined the Royal Norfolk Regiment as a private in 1940 and had volunteered to join the commando. He would serve with them in Sicily and Italy and was commissioned in 1944. His gallantry in the action was extraordinary; his citation tells the story:

In Burma on 31 January 1945, near Kangaw, Lieutenant Knowland was commanding the forward platoon of a Troop positioned on the extreme North of a hill which was subjected to very heavy and repeated enemy attacks – throughout the whole day. Before the first attack started, Lieutenant Knowland's platoon was heavily mortared and machine gunned, yet he moved about among his men keeping them alert and encouraging them, though under fire himself at the time. When the enemy, some 300 strong in all, made their first assault they concentrated all their efforts on his platoon of 24 men, but, in spite of the ferocity of the attack, he moved about from trench to trench distributing ammunition, and firing his rifle and throwing grenades at the enemy, often from completely exposed positions.

Later, when the crew of one of his forward Bren Guns had all been wounded, he sent back to Troop Headquarters for another crew and ran forward to man the gun himself until they arrived. The enemy was then less than 10 yards from him in dead ground down the hill, so, in order to get a better field of fire, he stood on top of the trench, firing the light machine gun from his hip, and successfully keeping them at a distance until a Medical Orderly had dressed and evacuated the wounded men behind him. The new Bren team also became casualties on the way up, and Lieutenant Knowland continued to fire the gun until another team took over. Later, when a fresh attack came in, he took over a 2-inch mortar and in spite of heavy fire and the closeness of the enemy, he stood up in the open to face them, firing the mortar from his hip and killing six of them with his first bomb.

When all bombs were expended, he went back through heavy grenade, mortar and machine gun fire to get more, which he fired in the same way from the open in front of his platoon positions. When those bombs were finished, he went back to his own trench, and still standing up fired his rifle at them. Being hard pressed and with enemy closing in on him from only 10 yards away, he had no time to re-charge his magazine. Snatching up the Tommy gun of a casualty, he sprayed the enemy and was mortally wounded stemming this assault, though not before he had killed and wounded many of the enemy. Such was the inspiration of his magnificent heroism, that, though fourteen out of twenty four of his platoon became casualties at an early stage, and six of his positions were overrun by the enemy, his men held on through twelve hours of continuous and fierce fighting until reinforcements arrived. If this Northern end of the hill had fallen, the rest of the hill would have been endangered, the beach-head dominated by the enemy, and other units farther inland cut off from their source of supplies. As it was, the final successful counter-attack was later launched from the vital ground which Lieutenant Knowland had taken such a gallant part in holding

Lieutenant Knowland was posthumously awarded the Victoria Cross, the last Royal Norfolk Regiment recipient of the nation's highest gallantry award in the conflict. This brought the regiment's tally to five VCs, the greatest number awarded to any county regiment during the Second World War.

2 Division had its sights firmly set on crossing the Irrawaddy but before they could cross the river, the pocket caused by the bend in the river to the west of Sagaing would have to be cleared of the enemy. This became the task of 4 Brigade and 2 Royal Norfolk was ordered to move slowly east toward the village of Saye, dominating the area by aggressive patrolling. The ground consisted mainly of rock, sand and open undulating, scrubby terrain, completely devoid of water.

A Company went forward and occupied a small hill on the track to Saye, while B Company moved south and took over a spur from which observation of the surrounding country was possible. C Company patrolled to the east within sight of the village.

The first attack on Saye was abortive, the battalion continued to hold its ground outside but the intermittent enemy shelling and waiting was taking a toll on the morale of 2 Royal Norfolk so a request was made to try again. This was arranged for 20 February. Vigorous patrolling had provided the battalion with much valuable information about the enemy dispositions. The plan was A Company, with one squadron of tanks, would secure high ground to the right flank of the village. C Company was also to attack from the southern end of the village. B and D companies were in reserve with B Company to advance with a second squadron of tanks as soon as the village was captured and consolidated. An air strike by six squadrons of Hurribombers preceded the assault. All went according to plan. A Company reached their objective at 0900 hrs, having killed several of the enemy, and C Company, though meeting a considerable amount of small-arms fire, forced their way into the village and occupied it.

B Company advancing between A and C companies came up against a strong bunker position, but overran it with great dash, Corporal Sillett winning the MM for his gallantry in leading his section into the attack. A and C then began to work back, mopping up the area. Meanwhile D Company with Battalion HQ were held up by a detachment of enemy while they were following up. Lieutenant Deeds was wounded when he tried to get over the top with his platoon. CSM Percy Ambrose Partridge decided he was going to take that ridge. His citation relates his act of grim determination and incredible gallantry:

> On 20 February 1945 during the battalion's assault on the village of Saye, Central Burma, the reserve company while mopping up ran into a strongly entrenched enemy LMG post. The leading platoon commander was wounded attempting to knock out the post. A troop of tanks returning to harbour were passing the scene of this encounter at the

time and CSM Partridge immediately signalled them to the platoon's assistance and then reorganised the platoon.

Covered by fire from the tanks himself, he then approached the mound on which the bunker was sited three times and threw several grenades over the top, rushing over the top on his third approach. His Sten gun jammed, and showing complete disregard for his personal safety, he changed magazines. The gun again failed to fire. CSM Partridge became so infuriated at this that he rushed back down the slope, threw away his Sten gun, grabbed a rifle and bayonet and once again rushed over the top. He bayonetted two Japanese soldiers and shot one, his grenades previously silenced two others. Two LMGs were captured in the position which was wiped out largely due to the determination and speed of CSM Partridge's assault which was a great inspiration to the men of the platoon.

CSM Partridge was recommended for the MM but the divisional commander upgraded it to an immediate award of the DCM. The action cost the enemy 54 killed, while 2 Royal Norfolk casualties were in single figures. Before Fourteenth Army crossed the Irrawaddy in strength in February 1945, 2 Royal Norfolk was ten miles from Mandalay. In reaching this position in the bend of the river it had covered 500 miles, excluding patrolling, in seventy days and had existed the whole time from supplies dropped from the air.

2 Division crossed the Irrawaddy by DUKWs and pontoon ferries on 28 February 1945. 2 Royal Norfolk followed soon after then took part in bitter fighting in Central Burma, which resulted in the destruction of one Japanese army. On 13 April 1945 the battalion was withdrawn from Burma and flew to India, arriving at Calcutta on 18 April to prepare for the new offensive on Rangoon in May. The battalion trained but the offensive was not required. The battalion was committed to no further operations; in June the battalion moved to Kamareddy, about sixty miles from Secunderabad. It was here the news of Japan's final capitulation

was received when it was announced by Emperor Hirohito on 15 August and V-J Day was celebrated.

On 18 October the first eight officers and 464 other ranks all due for release left for Kaylan transit camp on the first leg of their return journey back to England.

The men of 2 Royal Norfolk had fought some of the hardest battles of the war in the Far East, probably the most difficult of all the theatres of action. It had called for extreme endurance from every man and for a high degree of personal courage in the specialised fighting necessary in the jungle. Some measure of the service of 2 Royal Norfolk in the Burma campaign may be realised by the fact 2 Royal Norfolk was awarded more individual gallantry awards than any other in 2 Division.

Most poignant of all, however, was the memorial erected by 2 Royal Norfolk to their fallen comrades on one of the lonely hills near the town of Kohima. It takes the form of a large teak crosscut from one of the huge jungle trees, erected upon a base of native rock, with a pathway of the same stone leading to it. On the cross piece is carved 'The Royal Norfolk Regiment'; upon the base is a plaque bearing the three battle honours 'GPT Ridge,' 'Aradura Spur' and 'Viswema' and the dates April–June 1944. Not far away, on the slopes of Garrison Hill, is the divisional cemetery, now in the care of the Commonwealth War Graves Commission. Here lie the 108 men of the battalion who were killed in those actions. In the cemetery is the memorial to 2 Division; upon it is inscribed the epitaph:

When you go home, tell of us and say,
For your tomorrow we gave our today.

Chapter 3

4th Battalion

This chapter is based on the account compiled by
Lieutenant-Colonel. E. C. Knights, MC MM TD

The year 1938 had ended dramatically on the world stage as Britain teetered on the brink of war with Germany to the degree that 'key men' of Territorial Army battalions had reported to their drill halls to prepare for mobilisation. Every household was also sent a copy of *The Protection of Your Home Against Air Raids*, which provided homeowners with practical advice on how to protect their homes from bomb blast and gas attack; the first pilot for the government's evacuation scheme was carried out and everyone was issued with a gas mask.

Fortunately, an agreement had been reached between British Prime Minister Neville Chamberlain and Hitler and conflict was averted, at least for the time being. Norwich went ahead with the grand opening of its brand-new city hall by King George VI and Queen Elizabeth on 29 October. 4 Royal Norfolk paraded a guard of honour under the command of Captain R. F. Humphrey on St Peter's Street in front of city hall that was inspected personally by the king. It was a wonderful occasion said to have been witnessed by an unsurpassed crowd in the Norwich Market Place.

Much to the chagrin of many army officers, even after the Munich Crisis, the British government still had no immediate scheme for the expansion of any of Britain's armed forces save the usual recruitment advertisements. In fact, many experienced TA officers found the situation deplorable and firmly believed it really should have been addressed in the mid-1930s when the Nazis began to militarise Germany and rebuild their armed forces on an ever-growing scale. Speaking at the Annual Dinner and Smoking Concert of HQ and A companies of 4 Royal Norfolk (TA) held at Samson & Hercules House in December 1938, the Lord Mayor of Norwich, Mr Percy Curl, stated: 'If the voluntary system is to be maintained every facility must be given to any man who shows any inclination to join the Territorial Army.'

Speaking of the apathy by some people in the county to join up he thought it fair to say:

> most people considered we should not require anything but a very small army. There was a tremendous revulsion against the whole idea of war and they placed a great faith in the league of nations. … The position had changed today and we were faced with a problem greater than any we had met in the history of our country.

He concluded that he was glad employers and the corporation were treating their employees with every consideration and was proud to announce there were just 130 men now required to bring the Norwich companies of 4 Royal Norfolk up to strength.

It was only after Germany breached the terms of the Munich agreement by invading and occupying the remnants of the Czech state on 15 March 1939 that it was announced on 29 March that the Territorial Army was to be doubled in size. Norfolk Territorial Army units rapidly organised recruiting events across the county. The *Diss Express* was particularly generous in the space it gave to the recruiting advertisements for 4 Royal Norfolk; a feature published on 5 May 1939 detailed the reasons and terms of service offered to men joining the battalion:

> Diss should do its full share. We know that men would come forward at once if the country was attacked, but we have to point out that until they have been trained, they would be no more use against practised troops than say,

a scratch team against Portsmouth or Wolverhampton. Certain nations count on getting their way by threatening to deal a knockout blow to those whom we are pledged to support, or to ourselves. If we are ready, we can face with confidence the consequences of such a blow, not without hope that those nations who now rely on force will prefer peaceful negotiations to the probability of ultimate defeat.

Recruits for the Territorial Army must be between the ages of 18 and 20, and 21 and 38 but men in certain callings can serve up to the age of 50. While with the consent of their parents or guardians, youths of 17 to 18 can enlist, and a few boys of 14 to 17 can be accepted as buglers. Under the new Bill all men between 20 and 21 will be called up for six months' training. Men who join the Territorial Army while under 20 will be called up in their turn, but they will have the advantages of already belonging to His Majesty's Forces, and of having made a good start with their training.

Territorial Army training consists of 15 days' camp and 20 drills a year, with 20 additional drills in the first year. Those who can only find time for eight days' camp, can do 10 additional drills instead. Each hour's training counts as one drill. While in camp, men receive pay at 2s or more a day, and, if married and over 21 family allowance at 17s or more a week. In addition, trained men can draw proficiency pay of up to £5 in a year. The normal liability [is] for service both inside and outside the United Kingdom; and after mobilization the pay and conditions are the same as for the Regular Army.

The 163 (Norfolk and Suffolk) Brigade held their 1939 summer camp at Falmer, near Brighton, East Sussex. The experiences of an unnamed recruit in 4 Royal Norfolk written, I suspect with some help from the recruiting officer, but nonetheless an evocative account of the experiences and feelings of new recruits at that time, regardless of regiment, was published in the *Diss Express*, 28 July 1939:

> After parading at the Drill Hall and receiving our equipment we marched to the station, some of us new and very raw recruits, feeling very self-conscious as we met the gaze of some 'old sweats' to whom we were known. By the time the station was reached this had worn off and we realised that for some of us we were on the first stage for a great adventure – camp and what it meant. Some of us had never been away from home on our own before. Now we were all members of a happy party and the trained men of the company did their utmost to make us feel at ease. Punctually at 9.30pm our train drew up and we were all comfortably seated, some in corridor coaches and others, of which I was one, secured places in the saloons. The whistle sounded and we were off. To what? We wondered.
>
> After a time, we were issued with a box containing a meat pie, two cakes, a sausage roll and sandwiches. This was to last us through the night. Soon it was dark outside and those who could settled down to get a little sleep, but not me. Everything was so new and so strange. Despite that, the journey became somewhat boring and we were not sorry when Falmer, our destination, was reached. Here we formed up and marched to the camp, a distance of about one and a half miles. On arrival we were served out with ground sheets and blankets and detailed to our respective tents, seven to eight in a tent and then we turned in and 'kipped down'.
>
> Sunday was an easy day for us, naturally. We just got up, washed and cleaned up and went to Brighton in the afternoon. I must say that the meals on the first day were not so good, but they have improved since. After turning in on Sunday night we were all soon asleep and reveille at 6am was too early for some of us but there it was and up we

had to get out to wash, and here I must say shower baths are provided. First parade is 6.25, when we do a little rifle drill and inspection. Breakfast is at 7.30 and the weekly menu shows a good variety, such as eggs and bacon, bacon and tomatoes and bacon and beans, all washed down with an ample supply of tea.

Our next job is to get ready for parade at 8.40 when the real business of the day starts. We get ready for company manoeuvres, some men being stationed as enemies and others having to rout them out (we are carried in lorries for these). We get back in time for dinner and after a rest we tackle the meal with a gusto. There are always two courses and tea to follow.

Then comes rifle inspection, after which we are free for the rest of the day to do a little cleaning of kit etc. For tea there is as much bread and jam as one likes after which we loll about or go for a walk, some walking into Brighton. The NAAFI supplies us with our needs for supper.

Games are played and we have an inter-battalion football match coming off soon. ... For our second week the really serious work will commence for us with Brigade exercises and we are looking forward to it with great anticipation. A word as to the weather. It has been 'lousy', absolutely 'lousy' but we are making the best of it and having a darned good time.

The poor weather was unfortunate to say the least: the two weeks the Norfolk and Suffolk lads had for their summer camp were some of the worst of the whole summer of 1939; they were not alone and many units suffered training and camping on ground that soon became cold, wet, muddy mires. Old hands, however, recalled the Territorial Army summer camp of 1939 was filled with training that seemed more purposeful than before and those who had recently joined up were observed for any who showed potential for promotion. Many a good young soldier came away with his first stripe and by the time of the outbreak of war some of them had even made sergeant or had been selected for officer training.

The telegram ordering mobilisation was received on 1 September 1939, the battalion under the overall command of Lieutenant-Colonel J. H. Jewson, MC TD, and his second-in-command, Major A. E. Knights, MC MM. Knights recalled:

> It was probably with mixed feelings that the order for embodiment of 4 Royal Norfolk, in common with all other units of the Territorial Army, was received. Memories of the 1914–18 war were still in the minds of many, the war to end all wars had failed to achieve its object, and the prospect of further drawn-out struggle lay before us, but it was what we had been training for years.

In general, the companies remained at their home stations, the structure of the battalion being as follows:

Battalion HQ
CO: Lt-Col J H Jewson, MC TD
2ic: Maj A. E. Knights, MC MM
Adj: Maj F. W. Chapman
SIGO: Lt L. A. Barrett
MTO: Maj J. S. Clarke
IO: Lt J. M. Drane

HQ Company: Capt R. F. Humphrey (Drill Hall, Chapel Field Norwich)

A Company: Capt A. E. Tunbridge (Drill Hall, Chapel Field Norwich)

B Company: Capt W. L. Faux (Queen's Road, Attleborough with detachments at Wymondham, Thetford and Watton)

C Company: Capt L. H. Tibbenham (Harleston with detachments at Diss and Long Stratton)

D Company: Major F. P. Molyneux (Drill Hall, York Road, Great Yarmouth)

Lts

T. Eaton

J. Barratt

T. F. Phillips

M. Gowing

F. Nicholls

P. Hall

E. Cary-Elwes

T. Burne

D. Steward

P. Farrelly

M. Gaymer

WOs and senior sgts

5765544 A/RSM: WOI H. Clark

733993 CSM: WOII H. Gilmore

5764812 Sgt L. Long

5767434 Sgt G. Hunn

5766688 Sgt C. Yallop

5767244 Sgt C. Chamberlain

The full strength on mobilisation was twenty-nine officers, thirty-nine warrant officers and sergeants and 607 other ranks. On 2 September 1939 four sergeants and ninety-one other ranks were transferred to 6 Royal Norfolk, leaving a total of 551 other ranks. The battalion was brigaded with 4 and 5 Royal Norfolk and the Suffolk Regiment to form 54 Infantry Brigade, under Brigadier E. H. W. Backhouse, as part of 18 Division.

The early weeks of the war were spent largely in providing guards at vulnerable points and aerodromes, although as much individual training was carried out as possible under the rather difficult and scattered conditions. A move in October to Gorleston brought the battalion together as a unit, with Battalion HQ, HQ Company and two other companies in the Gorleston Holiday Camp, one at the Great

Yarmouth racecourse (which prompted the nickname of the battalion – the 'Galloping Fourth') and D Company at its home station at the York Road Drill Hall, Yarmouth. This move greatly simplified training, which now began in earnest.

A draft of NCOs and other ranks from 2 Royal Norfolk proved a great help in assisting the training. Among them was CSM Arthur Lunn, who later became RSM but was killed in action in Singapore. Also in the party were Corporals F. E. Brown, later to become RSM, W. Nelson a CSM and A. Sell a CQMS. In addition, parties of officers and men attended the 18 Division School at Cromer; there was a steady stream of officers and other ranks to specialist courses of instruction.

The disaster in France during May 1940, and the end of the French participation in the war brought in its train the threat of invasion of British soil. At once the battalion was called upon for a new role, that of coastal defence, and vigorous steps were taken to put it into effect. Beaches were wired, minefields and strongpoints constructed and manned day and night. Roadblocks consisting of herring barrels filled with sand and lashed with timber were constructed all around the perimeter of Yarmouth and Gorleston. Even a tank ditch traversed the Great Yarmouth golf course and a gap was blown in Britannia Pier to prevent its use as an enemy landing stage. However, the Flag-Officer-in-Charge (FOIC) ordered torpedo warheads to be installed in the seaward end of the pier with an electrical firing connection so if the enemy landed, they would truly be blown sky high.

The idea was undoubtedly good, but the switch for making the necessary connection was installed beside the side of the switch that operated the beach floodlights. It was always a tense moment when orders were received to test the floodlights in case the NCO in charge of the post closed the wrong switch! Great ingenuity was also shown by young officers, NCOs and men installing cunningly prepared tripwires, claxon horns and bell alarms in the vicinity of their section posts; these, however, caused inconvenience to senior officers unaware of their existence when visiting the posts at night. It must not be forgotten, however, that the first casualties of the battalion were incurred during this period when two men from A Company were killed while laying mines in front of the racecourse.

54 Infantry Brigade had a stretch of twenty-five miles of coast to defend, from Cromer to Lowestoft, the battalion being responsible for Great Yarmouth and Gorleston. This was no easy task, for the perimeter of the battalion's sector measured twenty-two miles, but with the assistance from a pioneer battalion, the 8 (Home Defence) Battalion, the Royal Norfolk Regiment, the 11 Royal Norfolk Regiment Home Guard and a party of ratings from HMS *Watchful*, HQ of the FOIC, Naval Base Great Yarmouth, it was successfully done.

During June 1940, the strength of the battalion was brought up to twenty-nine officers and 950 other ranks by drafts from the ITC Royal Norfolk Regiment, No. 10 Holding Battalion at Billericay and ITC Wiltshire Regiment. They were quickly absorbed into the battalion and soon found their feet under the guidance of Captain W. L. Faux and CSM Rice. Also, in June, came the first air raid warnings, the precursors of some hundreds of others during the battalion's stay at Yarmouth and Gorleston. Occasionally the battalion area was subject to bombing by enemy aircraft. Although some posts had near misses, no casualties were suffered by the troops, although several civilians lost their lives because of direct hits on their houses.

During the battalion's occupation of Great Yarmouth and Gorleston defences, visits were received from several VIPs and the Racecourse Company's post on the east side of Caister Road became known as 'General's Corner'. Among the visitors were Prince Henry, General Sir Edmund Ironside, then Chief of the Imperial General Staff, the Rt. Hon. Neville Chamberlain, Mr Anthony Eden, General Sir Alan Brooke and most notably in August, George VI visited Battalion HQ and inspected a detachment of nineteen officers and 323 other ranks at Gorleston Holiday Camp. After the inspection the king visited the officers' mess.

A move to Langley Park near Loddon took place on 18 September. Four days later the battalion went to 'action stations' on receipt of the *Cromwell* codeword for imminent invasion. For about fifteen hours the tension remained high, men wore gas masks for much of the time, but eventually the alarm was cancelled and the battalion settled down again to its rigorous training programme. In October 1940, the battalion moved into company area billets at Acle, Belton and Haddiscoe with Battalion HQ at Brooke Hall. By the end of 1940, with the invasion scare diminishing, and the Home Defence Units sufficiently trained and equipped to take over the duties of coastal defence, 18 Infantry Division was withdrawn for more active operations. In November 1940 54 Infantry Brigade was concentrated in the Cambridge area for more specialised training, and for the next two and a half months all ranks were hard at work, with frequent specialist courses to bring variety to the training. Gradually 4 Royal Norfolk was taking real shape and settling down into an efficient and well-trained unit.

Shortly before Christmas 18 Division received orders to proceed overseas to Egypt, to complete training. After spending an enjoyable festive season in Cambridge, the battalion, as a preliminary, was ordered to Scotland and on 8 January 1941, 54 Brigade was concentrated near Hawick. The battalion was quartered in Stobs Camp, about five miles from Hawick, together with 4 Suffolk and soon settled down to the Scottish scene.

The first few weeks were intensely cold, 38° of frost being recorded on 18 January and deep snow lying on the hillsides and roads rendered them almost impassable. The barrack huts were warmed by means of tortoise stoves; from a heating point of view they were excellent, but they had a nasty habit of backfiring and smothering everything in soot. The snow lasted well into February and interfered considerably with training, although it served an excellent purpose in toughening up the battalion and in bringing opportunities for skiing, introduced by the CO, a lover of winter sports. The sight of the men skiing was a vision of amazement to more than one visiting general.

During March, brigade and divisional schemes were carried out to exercise the movement of troops, to test marching powers, and to practice the seizing and holding of bridgehead positions with a brigade group. It was all very strenuous – on one occasion the battalion marched twenty-two miles in one day from Hawick to Melrose – but it was excellent training and by the time the next move came along, the whole brigade was working together as a team. Despite the rigorous conditions many men left the camp with happy memories and feeling exhilarated.

The decision to move 18 Division to Egypt was cancelled in the early part of 1941, a change of plan that was to have far-reaching effects on the battalion when its turn came for action. Instead of Egypt, 54 Brigade moved to Blackburn in mid-April, the division here being under the command of Major-General M. B. Beckwith-Smith. Divisional exercises were continued in the neighbourhood throughout May and in June the battalion underwent a two-day endurance test, consisting of a route march, night operations, a scheme that included field firing, and a final route march back to Blackburn. All ranks came through it well, earning the congratulations of the divisional commander and the brigadier.

On 13 August the battalion moved from Blackburn to Ross-on-Wye for the next stage of its training. This consisted at first of route marches, with a return cross-country in the fastest possible time, and night operations. Later it included river crossings in assault boats, by day and night. Lieutenant-Colonel Jewson was promoted on 9 September and was succeeded in command of the battalion by Lieutenant-Colonel Knights. Both had contributed greatly to the mounting efficiency, having been with the battalion since mobilisation. Major J. N. Packard became second-in-command.

The battalion, with other units in the division stationed in the vicinity of Ross-on-Wye, was inspected again by the king shortly before leaving the area. On this occasion Lieutenant-Colonel Knights was decorated by the king, receiving from him his Territorial Decoration, rather a unique honour as His Majesty did not usually make a personal presentation of this award.

During September, instructions were received by the battalion to hold itself in readiness for operations overseas. Tropical kit was issued, vehicles prepared for shipment, and reinforcements received to replace men unfit for service abroad. On 28 October most of 18 Division proceeded to Liverpool, where it embarked in a fleet of transports, the battalion sailing in RMS *Andes*. The destination was unknown, but there was a tremendous feeling of excitement, and of relief, that at last the long months of training were past and that the future held hopes of more stirring days.

The convoy, heavily escorted by destroyers, sailed out into the Atlantic on 29 October. On 2 November, midway between Great Britain and Canada, an American squadron, including a battleship and the aircraft carrier USS *Lexington*, took over the escort duties and it became known the first destination was Halifax, Nova Scotia. There the *Andes* went alongside and the battalion transhipped into the American transport USS *Wakefield*, a ship of 27,000 tons. The voyage continued on 10 November, the convoy now consisting of six American troopships escorted by the aircraft carrier *Ranger*, two cruisers and eight destroyers. Still the destination of the division remained unknown.

A month later the convoy steamed into Cape Town. By now the Japanese attack on Pearl Harbor had taken place and the United States was in the war. The Japanese landing in Malaya was still in its initial stages, and in fact the war in the Far East gave to some a suspicion of the destination of the division, although the most popular guess was Suez and the Middle East.

Three days were spent in Cape Town, giving all ranks a chance to stretch their legs and enjoy the lavish hospitality of the inhabitants. On 13 November the convoy left again, steaming up the East African coast past Madagascar and then out into the Indian Ocean. It was announced that the destination of the 18 Division was Bombay, which was reached on 27 December after a total sea journey of 17,011 miles. The battalion disembarked on 28 December and moved by train with the remainder of the brigade to Ahmednagar. Here further training was carried out, though the heat during the day made conditions arduous. Added difficulties arose from the fact that the battalion's transport was in another ship and had not yet arrived, and that the battalion was held in constant readiness for a further move.

It came on 11 January 1942, with orders to proceed to Bombay. Even though the destination was still a secret, few could now doubt that this was the first step toward Malaya, where the Japanese had been advancing with alarming rapidity down the peninsula and where the situation was already critical. At Bombay, reached on 15 January, 54 Brigade once again embarked the USS *Wakefield* with the remainder of the division in other ships.

The convoy sailed at 1300 hrs on 19 January, its destination given as the South-West Pacific area. Pamphlets on jungle warfare were issued, and all ranks attempted to learn something of the new type of warfare that lay ahead. As the convoy passed through the Banka Straits on 28 January it sighted a Japanese plane which dropped six bombs without result. That night, to avoid any bunching of the ships in narrow water, the three fastest vessels were ordered ahead at full speed. The USS *Wakefield* won the race to Singapore and the 54th Brigade disembarked in Keppel Harbour, Singapore, on 29 January. Although the news from Malaya was not encouraging, spirits were high in the battalion. It could not be known that, within a period of seventeen days, all the months of hard training since 1939 were to be wasted. The curtain was only just beginning to rise on the last act of this great tragedy.

The battle for Singapore fell into two distinct phases and during the first, from 29 January to 9 February 1942, there was little activity for 4 Royal Norfolk. 18 Infantry Division was responsible for the defence of the northeastern sector of Singapore Island, their area stretching from Fairy Point, near Changi, on the right, to Seletar Aerodrome on the left, and extending as far south as the Tampines Road and Thompson Village, near MacRitchie Reservoir. On disembarkation the battalion was taken by lorries to a tented camp on the Tampines Road and, during their second night under canvas, the last British troops to escape from the mainland of Malaya made their way to the island over the causeway across Johore Straits. The causeway was blown behind them and Singapore Island, separated from the mainland, was hurriedly prepared for a last stand against the enemy.

Already the difficulties of defence were being appreciated. Perhaps the most obvious was the complete lack of fighter cover overhead, leaving the air for the Japanese bombers, who made the most of their opportunity. There was, too, a shortage of full equipment, some not landed from the transports until 8 February, some lost in the daily air attacks on the docks of Singapore. A third reason was the thinness of Allied troops on the ground, for Singapore Island is roughly twenty miles long by ten miles wide; the defenders consisted of 18 Division, less one brigade, 11 Indian Division, with 53 Infantry Brigade under command, and the remains of an Australian division. None, except for a few Indians and Australians, had been trained in jungle warfare.

For the first few days the battalion remained in brigade reserve to form a force for counterattack should the Japanese attempt a landing in the brigade area. Battalion HQ, HQ Company (Major R. F. Humphrey) and A Company (Captain M. Gowing) were stationed in the Teck Hock area, B Company (Major W. L. Faux) about two miles from Teck Hock, C Company (Captain T. C. Eaton) in the Serangoon Jetty area and D Company (Captain T. F. Phillips) in the Sergangoon Church area. Frequent reconnaissance was carried out by officers and NCOs with the object of becoming familiar with the terrain over which the battalion would have to operate, and especially with the best lines of approach on the forward area.

The only brush with the enemy during these days occurred during the night of 7/8 February, when the Japanese attacked the island of Ubin, which lay in the straits on the right of the brigade sector and was occupied as an outpost by alternate platoons of C and D companies. The enemy attack coincided with the normal relief of the occupying platoon, and the relieving platoon had just reached the landing beach as the others retired onto it. The enemy was estimated at about 1,000. Four men were cut off during the withdrawal to the beach. On the following night a patrol under Lieutenant P. C. Barr returned to the island but found it deserted and with no trace of the four men who had failed to return. The night marked the end of the first phase in the defence of Singapore Island.

The second began with the forcing by the enemy of the Straits of Johore, where they narrowed to a width of about half a mile in the west. That night they penetrated the forward defences manned by the Australians, and by the morning of 9 February had advanced to a depth of about two miles. Here they began fanning out into a three-pronged attack, the northern aimed at Pierce Reservoir and Seletar Aerodrome, the centre at the MacRitchie Reservoir, and the southern one at the village of Bukit Timah.

On the morning of 10 February the battalion received orders to form part of a composite force under the command of Lieutenant-Colonel

Britannia Barracks, depot of the Royal Norfolk Regiment, Mousehold Heath, Norwich. Built by Norwich City Council, the barracks was presented to the Norfolk Regiment as its first permanent depot in 1887.

The Chapel Field Drill Hall, Norwich. Opened in October 1866, 4 Royal Norfolk Regiment (TA) mobilised here for two world wars.

Guard of honour provided by 4 Royal Norfolk for the opening of Norwich City Hall being inspected by King George VI on 29 October 1938.

The Dersingham Drill Hall, opened in 1930, was one of the first of the new purpose-built drill halls in the county after the First World War. C and D companies, 7 Royal Norfolk, were billeted here on mobilisation in 1939.

1 Royal Norfolk on the march at Arora on the North West Frontier, India, 1939.

Sergeants' mess, 1 Royal Norfolk, Halleaths, Dumfriesshire, Scotland, Christmas 1943.

Troops storm ashore from Landing Craft Assault (LCAs) during Exercise *Fabius*, May 1944.

Captain Oakley and Lieutenant Paul Buckerfield examining a map at Asten, Holland, shortly before the liberation of Helmond by 1 Royal Norfolk on 26 September 1944.

C Company, 1 Royal Norfolk during a break on the march to Wanssum, Holland, November 1944.

1 Royal Norfolk enters Wanssum, Holland, 26 November 1944. The dangerous clearance of enemy troops in houses in the town was to follow.

Lance-Corporal R. Hearn with an MP40 Schmeisser and Private F. Slater, of 1 Royal Norfolk, the first men to enter Kervenheim, Germany, March 1945.

Men of 1 Royal Norfolk demonstrate how they dodged snipers' bullets dashing across a roadway at Kervenheim, Germany, March 1945.

General Bernard Montgomery decorating CSM Tom Catlin with the Military Medal for his gallantry at the Battle of Sourdeval on 6 August 1944.

Captain Peter Barclay and Lance-Corporal Mick Davis being congratulated by their comrades in 2 Royal Norfolk following the announcement of their awards of the Military Cross and Military Medal in January 1940, the first gallantry medals to the British Army in the Second World War.

Guard of honour provided by A Company, 1 Royal Norfolk, being inspected by General Georges, commander-in-chief of the French Northern Army, 25 March 1940.

Carriers of 2 Royal Norfolk advancing up the Dimapur–Kohima road, Nagaland, Assam, 1945.

2 Royal Norfolk Regiment come ashore from a DUKW having just crossed the Irrawaddy River at Ngazun, Burma, on 28 February 1945.

Lieutenant-Colonel Wilkins (seated centre) with officers, NCOs and men of 2 Royal Norfolk, India, 1945.

Officers of 4 Royal Norfolk Regiment at Falmer Camp, near Brighton, Sussex, 1939.

George VI accompanied by Lieutenant-Colonel J. H. Jewson MC, TD inspecting members of 4 Royal Norfolk at Gorleston, Norfolk, 23 August 1940.

4 Royal Norfolk during a practice assault on a pillbox at Great Yarmouth, August 1940.

Medical Section, 5 Royal Norfolk Regiment, 1941. Many of these men were captured at the fall of Singapore in 1942 and did so much good work to help others during their years of captivity in Japanese hands.

British prisoners of war queue up for a pittance of rice for their meal at Kanchanaburi Camp, Thailand, 1945.

Some of the men of 4, 5 and 6 Royal Norfolk on Bangkok airfield, Thailand, September 1945, ready to board the plane home after years in Japanese captivity.

Officers of 7 Royal Norfolk photographed in 1939, shortly before their departure for France.

Carrier Platoon, 7 Royal Norfolk, shortly before their departure for Normandy, June 1944.

Officers and men representing all battalions of the Royal Norfolk Regiment on parade in front of Norwich City Hall when the regiment was being granted the Freedom of the City, 3 October 1945.

Contingent representing all battalions of the Royal Norfolk Regiment for the Victory Parade through London, June 1946.

The five Royal Norfolk Regiment recipients of the Victoria Cross: CSM George Gristock, Corporal Sidney 'Basher' Bates, Captain David Aldjo Jamieson, Captain John Niel Randle and Lieutenant George Arthur Knowland.

L. C. Thomas of the Royal Northumberland Fusiliers. It was called 'Tomforce' and its object was to back up 12 (Indian) Brigade and to stem the tide of the advance toward Bukit Timah. At 1230 hrs the force proceeded in buses to the Bukit Timah Road, advancing on the northern side of it toward the village. On the southern side of the road a similar advance was made by the 5 Sherwood Foresters.

That night the Japanese captured the village. On the morning of 11 February the battalion continued the advance through the thickly wooded country on a two-company front – A followed by D Company on the left, B followed by C Company on the right. There was considerable enemy activity in the air and as B Company reached its first objective it was subjected to a low-level bombing attack. Its position, too, was marked by smoke signals dropped by the attacking aircraft, followed by heavy machine-gun and mortar fire from concealed Japanese positions.

B and C companies both suffered heavy casualties but continued the advance after the Carrier Platoon had given support with 2-inch. mortars. Once again it ran into heavy opposition, with a withering fire from the enemy on high ground to the north. It was obvious from this attack that the Japanese were infiltrating straight to the north of the 'Tomforce' position, and that their objective was the reservoir near Thompson Village. After consultation with the force commander, it was decided to withdraw the battalion to the area of Singapore Racecourse to beat back this advance. As good a position as possible was selected and occupied on the racecourse, and contact was made with 4 Suffolk on the right to form a perimeter defence covering the MacRitchie Reservoir.

A blunder on the night of 11 February made the situation worse. 4 Suffolk was ordered to advance toward the Swiss Rifle Club Hill, near the junction of the Bukit Timah Road, an objective impossible to reach because of the Japanese strength on the high ground to the north. All it did was to uncover the right flank of the battalion, a situation of which the enemy took full advantage. By first light on 12 February the battalion was almost surrounded, with only one small gap left to the east.

At 0900 hrs on 12 February the Japanese put in a heavy attack on the forward company (A Company) which was astride the Bukit Timah Road. The enemy used tanks in the attack, which caused several casualties, and forced the company to withdraw. The CO at once planned a counterattack to restore the position, but before it could be mounted, orders were received to withdraw the whole battalion to Adam Road, running south of the MacRitchie Reservoir. The withdrawal was carried out successfully through the open gap to the east of the battalion positions, except for the carriers, which had to run the gauntlet of the Bukit Timah Road. Here they came up against enemy tanks, but successfully fought their way past without loss, a wonderful achievement of the crews who, at one time, were facing almost certain annihilation.

Back again at Adam Road the battalion once again came under the command of 54 Infantry Brigade, 'Tomforce' being dissolved. The positions were put into as strong a state of defence as possible, barbed wire being used as an added deterrent against attacks. A reasonably quiet night on 12/13 February, although it gave some opportunity to the tired troops of catching up on their sleep, proved only the prelude of a heavy attack on 13 February, enemy shelling and mortaring causing further casualties in the battalion. The attack itself was largely broken up by fire from supporting artillery, although in the afternoon, further heavy shelling added to the casualties.

During the evening of 13 February the battalion was relieved on the western side of Adam Road by 5 Sherwood Foresters, withdrawing into brigade reserve on the eastern side of the road. Shelling continued through the night of 13/14 February, allowing only a little sleep, and proving that the enemy was well informed of the battalion position.

At about 2300 on 13 February orders were received to despatch a party of officers and ORs to Brigade HQ for a special mission. The party consisting of Major W. Leslie Faux, TD, Captain Michael Gowing, Lieutenant Hubert Hockley, CSM Charles Chamberlain, Sergeant Arthur Smith, Corporal Ted Clarke and Lance-Corporal Arthur Watson was given orders to embark HMS *Laburnham* at Clifford Pier and escape to India.

Major Faux takes up the story of the official escape party in his report:

On arrival at the docks we discovered that the naval transport due to take us off had been unable to get near the docks owing to the heavy shelling and had dispersed. ... It was decided to still endeavour to get away. At this time the shelling was still fairly heavy and it was approaching dawn on 14 February, therefore the whole party moved back to the YMCA in Singapore. During the day we were all organised into groups of about 18 people each and my party consisted of ourselves, some gunners from 148 Field Regiment and one or two men from the Bed & Herts. In the afternoon of 14 February the recce party who had been looking for boats returned and reported there were very few available and we were told that we should have to try to find our own means of getting away. As there were a fairly large number of officers and men there at this time, we were informed that we must move down to the docks with our complete parties at half hourly intervals and the time for our party to move was 2130 hours. At about 2100 hours shelling began again and eventually the YMCA received three direct hits with shells of 105 or 150mm calibre. One of these shells penetrated the building and burst on the concrete floor of the hall, where my party was waiting. Lt. Hockley was mortally wounded, Sgt Smith and L/Cpl Watson were wounded. Captain Gowing could not be found, and as it was pitch dark, it was very difficult to identify anyone. There was a badly mutilated body near where Captain Gowing had been lying, but only the trunk and legs were there. For this reason, I was unable to say definitely that this was Captain Gowing although I am, certain in my own mind it was he.

As the shelling was now getting worse, we decided to make for the docks, and this we did, picking up the remainder of our party. On arriving there we found an Indian Engineer Officer trying to get a small boat into the water and we helped him and eventually left Singapore on 15 February. After four days and five nights in a rowing boat we arrived at Tembilahan in Sumatra and from there moved bit by bit through Rengat, Aire, Moloch, Savalento to Padang. Here a form of movement control was organised by Lt Col Sydenham as there were so many service personnel and all kinds of civilians trying to get away, that something had to be done, I was among the officers asked to stay and for this reason I went no further with my party. Lieutenant MacDonald turned up two days after we arrived and he together with CSM Chamberlain, Sergeant Smith and Corporal Clarke were put on a small Dutch coastal vessel bound for Java … Later we were informed that this ship was torpedoed off the coast of Java and the only two survivors were two Malay seamen. L/Cpl Watson was sent to India on a destroyer and was later killed in 1944 at Kohima whilst serving with 2 Royal Norfolk. I eventually left Padang on a Dutch coastal ship SS *Palima* and arrived at Columbo on 14 March 1942.

Back to Singapore and the rest of 4 Royal Norfolk. The fire became heavier during the morning of 14 February, added to by repeated bombing attacks, and again there were many casualties. The enemy put in several determined attacks, one breaking through to the north of the battalion positions and a second, made in the early hours of the 15th, forcing back the Sherwood Foresters. B and C companies were ordered to counterattack and, by 1100 hrs, had restored the position, although at a very heavy cost in casualties.

In the meantime, the situation in the rest of the island had become critical. The speed of the enemy advance had been so rapid that 11 (Indian) Division had been overrun, and the commander-in-chief had been forced to abandon the defence of the northern beaches. Singapore itself was in a sorry state, its street choked with rubble from repeated bombing attacks, and the harbour area in a state of chaos as attempts were made to evacuate civilian and non-combatant personnel. As rumour succeeded rumour, it became obvious to all that the end could not be far off.

It came with a dramatic suddenness. At about noon on the 15th a car was seen proceeding along the Bukit Timah Road flying a white flag above a Union Jack. Even though at first it was thought to be a Japanese fifth-column trick, it had a depressing effect on morale. An hour or so later news was received from Brigade HQ that firing would cease at 1600 hrs. Although this was later altered to 2000 hrs, it made little difference to the feeling of bitter disappointment among all ranks. The end had indeed come, and the future held only dim and doubtful visions of the unknown horrors of prison camp.

Chapter 4

5th Battalion

This chapter is based on the account by Major H. T. Crane

In early 1939 the strength of 5 Royal Norfolk stood at 620 other ranks. The TA had been ordered to double in size, the result being that practically up to the time of going to camp in August 1939, recruits were joining the battalion. It was therefore planned not to split the two battalions until 1 October, thus allowing the new unit (7 Royal Norfolk) to grow up alongside the trained one. The battalion area would also be separated geographically so that each battalion would be approximately the same strength. The training went well but the weather at the summer training camp at Falmer was not what was hoped for. The report from A Company, 5 Royal Norfolk in *The Britannia* recounted:

> The training before camp proceeded smoothly and everyone worked well and hard. The attendance at drills was excellent, both the trained personnel and recruits. The CO's drill took place on the last two Sundays in April and comprised of schemes set out by the company commander. These were very instructive and many lessons were learnt by all that attended. The trained personnel fired their Annual course during May, and a very good standard was attained who fired the LMG. The recruits will fire their Course on 9/10 September, and we hope they will maintain the good average set up by the trained men.

And

> Now for the annual camp. We moved off and after an uneventful journey, everyone was soon between the blankets and asleep. Sunday was devoted to sorting the Company into original and duplicate Companies, ready for training on Monday. Monday greeted us with a downpour of rain which, with intervals, lasted for about the first ten days but everyone made the best of it and the spirit of the Company was excellent throughout, and the only occasion it flagged somewhat was when the promised issue of rum was cancelled. … The original Company carried on with the normal training which consisted of Platoon and Company schemes, etc whilst others carried out a programme set by HQs which covered some valuable subjects, ie, in addition to the usual, wiring, digging and so on. The weather caused the programme to be curtailed somewhat, but by the time camp was finished the recruits were proving their prowess in various subjects.

Most of the men were glad to get back from the foul weather of camp. The only saving grace had been the enjoyable get-togethers in the evenings that made up for the dull days, not to mention the payment of the bounties and cycle allowance shortly after their return, which put smiles back on their faces. It was also harvest time and many of the men earned good money out on the golden fields of the county.

When the Territorial Army was embodied on the outbreak of war, 5 Royal Norfolk had been the subject of a reorganisation that saw the Headquarter Wing become Headquarter Company (Support Company) at King's Lynn with a detachment of Headquarter Company at East Dereham. The companies embodied at East Dereham, Aylsham, North Walsham and Holt and the troops were billeted with subsistence in the towns: A Company (HQ Swaffham with detachments at Methwold, Stoke Ferry and Downham), B Company (Fakenham), C Company (HQ at Aylsham with detachments at North Walsham and Sheringham) and

D Company (Dersingham with a detachment at Hunstanton). Senior warrant officers and sergeants serving in 5th Battalion in 1939 were:

>5764584 A/RSM WOI C. Sutton,
>5765682 CSM WOII F. Unwin
>2556118 Sgt A. Howard
>5767914 Sgt W. Melton
>5767596 Sgt F. Jolly
>5768298 Sgt J. Hubbard

A large detachment was sent to form part of the ITC at Norwich, and officers and NCOs attended a brigade cadre course at Norwich. These latter formed the staff of the battalion cadres held in Dereham. At the same time guards were placed at various aerodromes and vulnerable points in the area.

During early October, the invasion scare started, and the battalion was concentrated at Holt on very short notice (about twenty-four hours). Again, the troops were billeted and dining halls requisitioned. Shortly afterward the battalion moved to Weybourne anti-aircraft camp and accommodated in huts. Weybourne had only been designed as a summer camp and offered very little protection against the bitterly cold winter of 1939/40. Indeed, as one of the coldest winters on record it was so cold even the sea froze and only one toilet did not require defrosting before use in the entire camp.

During this time cadres, individual and section training were carried out, with troops still manning vulnerable points. Positions were sited for the defence of a large area of the coast. Another group of 'Army Class', otherwise known as 'Militiamen', joined and were trained here. At the same time a large number of soldiers who were under 19 were transferred to the AA Command. In November 1939 the colours of the battalion were laid up in Sandringham Church, Lieutenant-Colonel George Scott-Chad carrying the king's colour and Captain Barham Savory the regimental colour for the ceremony. In December Captain J. Alley took over as adjutant from Major H. T. Crane who had held that position since 1936.

At Christmas the battalion had the honour of providing a guard for George VI during his stay of six weeks at Sandringham. The guard were about a company strong under Major E. Thistleton-Smith, Captain E. P. Hansell, Captain T. D. Savory and Lieutenant J. M. Woodhouse (Essex Regiment attached). Quartered in York Cottage the duties of the special company consisted of manning LMG anti-aircraft posts and patrolling the grounds.

In March 1940 Lieutenant-Colonel Eric Prattley came from 2 Royal Norfolk in France to take over from Lieutenant-Colonel G. N. Scott-Chad. In the same month section training began. After Dunkirk and the threat of invasion hanging over the country, the battalion occupied their beach defence positions at Weybourne almost continually. Additional defence posts were constructed, barbed-wire entanglements erected, anti-tank ditches dug and fields of fire cleared. At the same time, when possible, company training was carried out.

Later in the summer as vehicles and carriers arrived, more advanced training was undertaken and gradually the battalion achieved an excellent degree of skill and cohesion. As the Battle of Britain turned in Britain's favour and the imminent danger of invasion waned, training was stepped up to brigade level as vehicles, carriers and other equipment arrived. Soon the battalion was taking part in more advanced exercises and special toughening schemes to fit the battalion for an active service role.

In September the battalion went into brigade reserve and was billeted in Holt. The bulk of the battalion were in Gresham's School. The battalion was now brigaded with 6 Royal Norfolk and 2 Cambridgeshire to form 53 Brigade, 18 Division. Brigade and battalion training was carried out with a complete establishment of vehicles. Major E. Thistleton-Smith went to command the Young Soldiers Battalion and Major Crane returned from working on the GHQ Defence Line and was appointed second-in-command.

In November the battalion was moved to King's Lynn, relieving 4 King's Own Scottish Borderers and were billeted in cold, dark and uncomfortable warehouses on the docks. While here several air raids were carried out on Lynn. On 5 November a lone German plane machine-gunned people in South Lynn causing one casualty when a railwayman was injured while diving for cover. More severe damage was caused during the bombing on 9, 19 and 20 November; due to several bombs failing to explode the casualties were far fewer than they might have been.

On 21 December another bomber dropped incendiaries near the chemical works but caused little damage. In December Captain M. T. Keith took over as adjutant on account of Captain Alley being invalided out of the service. The battalion was again chosen to provide a guard during the king's stay at Sandringham, but owing to the impending move and mobilisation, the guard had to be relieved, and one provided by another unit.

After a peaceful but somewhat uncomfortable Christmas and New Year at Lynn, in January 1941, 18 Division was ordered to mobilise in southern Scotland. Arriving on 7 January Battalion HQ and three companies went to Castle Douglas and two companies went to Dalbeattie. To the relief of all, everyone was accommodated in billets. The local people were most hospitable. Intense training was carried out including divisional schemes. The battalion was getting very fit and well-trained, which brought a new confidence to the battalion as a whole and most of the mobilisation equipment had arrived.

Except for a raid on Glasgow, after which the battalion was employed in assisting the civilian services, this area was 'siren free', which was a great relief after the East Coast. This also enabled the battalion to get down to almost unbroken training. Divisional exercises and brigade schemes were combined with strenuous practice over assault courses. By the end of this training period 5 Royal Norfolk was 'very fit and hard', so much so that to everyone's surprise when the division was ordered to move in April, it was not off to active service abroad but to the west of England. 53 Brigade was to occupy an area in Cheshire. The bulk of the brigade went by road, staying in Preston at the depot of the East Lancashire Regiment of the Loyal Regiment.

The move was on 7 April, the journey of 186 miles being long and tiring owing to the number of towns en route. The battalion was accommodated at Marbury Hall, Northwich, mostly in huts which were quite comfortable. Considerable training in the form of attack and defence exercises was carried out here with a good deal of participation in Home Guard exercises and training. The battalion also sent large detachments into Liverpool for fire-watching duties during a period of heavy raids on the city. Specialist courses drew their quota of officers and other ranks from the battalion and by the end of September when orders were received to prepare to go overseas, the battalion was working together as a fit, efficient and formidable unit.

Shortly before departure, on 22 October a detachment of one officer and fifty-five other ranks was sent to Crewe Hall on the inspection by the king of a representative body from 53 Brigade before its departure overseas. On 25 October, the battalion sent an advance party to the ship. This included OC ship, ship's adjutant, RSM and OR clerk. On 28 October the brigade concentrated at Gourock, Scotland, and the battalion embarked on the SS *Duchess of Atholl*, in peacetime a Canadian Pacific Liner of about 21,000 tons, which had been converted into a troopship. The following officers and NCOs embarked with the battalion:

Battalion HQ
CO: Lt-Co. E. C. Prattley
2ic: Maj H. T. Crane
Adj: Capt M. T. Keith
QM: Lt G. Clarke
Carriers: Capt B. Savory
SIGO: Capt D. R. Gray
IO: Lt K. A. S. Potter
Defence Pl: Lt C. J. Brereton
Anti-Aircraft: Lt T. W. Higgs
MTO: Lt L. A. Collins
Mortars: Lt W. B. Battersby
Pioneers: Lt P. G. Bambridge
Interpreters: Capt F. Wallace and Lt R. Carey FMSVF joined on arrival at Singapore.
MO: Capt R. W. W. Brown RAMC
RSM: WOI L. G. Burrows
Chaplain: Rev J. O. Dean CF

A Company
OC: Capt R. Hamond
Capt H. E. Schulman
Lt Lee-Smith
Lt P. J. Ramm
Lt Turner
CSM: WOII W. A. Stephenson

B Company
OC: Capt A. J. Self
Capt R. A. Ferrier
Lt G. H. Pallister
Lt McKean
Lt P J Sayer
CSM: WOII T. Brandwood

C Company
OC: Maj C. P. Wood
Lt T. R. Cubitt
Lt J. Taylor
Lt F. W. W. Kettley
Lt W. J. Warrington
CSM: WOII W. Melton

D Company
OC: Capt S. C. H. Boardman
Lt R. A. Bowman
Lt H. R. Cook
Lt R. A. Burne
CSM: WOII A. E Patrick

HQ Company
OC: Capt E. P. Hansell

First reinforcements
Maj R. C. Briegel
Lt J. V. Willins

Lt E. F. Adie
Lt L. W. Curtis
Lt E. A. Parker
CSM H. Ward

Posted to 53 Brigade: Capt C. S. M. Brereton
Posted to 198 Field Ambulance: Capt J. Hendry RAMC

The ship left the Clyde the next day and met other ships from the West Coast ports carrying the division. There was a small escort of two destroyers. About halfway across the Atlantic, a large convoy was sighted which seemed to stretch right across the horizon. Presently the air was alive with planes flying around the ships which, much to everyone's surprise, turned out to be American aircraft. The escort was now relieved by US Navy ships consisting of a battleship, a large aircraft carrier, two 10,000-ton cruisers and about six destroyers. Everyone felt rather more secure.

The weather was very kind for the time of year and later became quite calm. There were about 2,500 troops on board the ship, which was more comfortable than the peacetime troopers and good food was served. After an uneventful voyage of about eight days the convoy entered Halifax. Here the division transhipped into American ships. The battalion embarked on the USS *Mount Vernon*, formally the American liner *Washington* of about 26,000 tons. The troops were rather crowded but quite comfortable having iron and canvas berths to sleep in. After a stay of about twenty-four hours, the division left Halifax with a large escort.

A few days later the weather became much warmer, and battle dress was discarded for khaki drill. The first stop was Trinidad. No one was allowed ashore but it looked a very beautiful island. After taking on water and fuel the voyage continued in calm, warm weather. The 'crossing the line' ceremony was held on 23 November just off the South American coast. Training and games were held on deck during the day and concerts in the evenings. The one drawback was that in accordance with US Navy orders the ship was 'dry'. Before making Cape Town, the convoy went far south down into the 'roaring forties' or 'westerlies' but a ship of that size was steady in the following wind, although the escorting cruisers and destroyers had rather a rough time.

The convoy arrived at Cape Town on 9 December and were addressed by General Smuts in the evening of the day of arrival. Everyone was given a very good time by the residents, who set themselves out to give all ranks as much entertainment as possible; the South African ports had a high reputation for the way they entertained convoys passing through. After four days of leave everyone was sorry to leave.

The convoy carrying the 18 Division left Cape Town on 13 December, bound for Bombay and proceeded up the African coast between the mainland and Madagascar. On 23 December the *Mount Vernon* was ordered to turn back and proceed at once to Mombasa. The ship arrived on Christmas Day. All ranks were given shore leave and bathing parties were organised. On the morning of 28 December *Mount Vernon* and 18 Division sailed again for an unknown destination, announced later in the day as Singapore and joined a convoy bound for the Far East.

This announcement had a sobering effect on all ranks, for already the Japanese landing at Kota Bharu had made remarkable progress and the outlook in Malaya was hardly promising. But none the less, lectures on Malaya, typical Japanese tactics and TEWTs (tactical exercises without troops) now became the universal form of training in an effort to prepare the battalion for the difficult fighting that lay ahead, already recognised as likely to be very different from the training carried out at home.

The next call was a fuelling station in the Indian Ocean and after a short stay of about six hours, the convoy put to sea again, passing through the Sunda Strait to Singapore. During this latter part of the voyage heavy tropical rainstorms probably prevented the convoy from being sighted by enemy aircraft. The ship went into the large graving dock in the naval base and the troops disembarked in pouring rain on Friday, 13 January 1942.

The battalion was quartered in the Woodland Camp near the naval base; this was a comfortable hutted camp. The next two days were spent in getting ready for battle. The battalion transport had not arrived, so new transport had to be drawn and organised on a different scale. In the evening all the officers were given a lecture by Lieutenant-General Percival on the campaign, and lectures on Japanese tactics were given to all ranks by officers and other ranks who had battle experience in Malaya but little more than the merest rudiments could be given in the short time available.

On 16 January the CO with a reconnaissance party reported to 2/M Battalion AIF at Jemalung on the east coast of Johore. The next day the battalion moved by MT to Ayer Hitam in the centre of Johore. The first reinforcements were left in Singapore.

As the battalion was about to take up a defensive position that evening in the village of Yongpeng, orders were countermanded. On 18 January, the battalion moved to Jemalung by MT and took up the prepared defensive position from the AIF, which had previously been reconnoitred. The next day patrols were sent out and at noon orders were received to move back to Ayer Hitam. Owing to the shortage of transport this had to be done in two relays. The 20th was spent in a harbouring area, the battalion being in 11 Indian Division reserve.

On 21 January, patrols were sent out during the morning and clashed with a Japanese patrol, with two men wounded and one missing. The enemy was attacking the coastal town of Batu Pahat in a two-pronged drive down the coast while, at the same time was attempting to put forces ashore further south in the vicinity of the villages of Senggarang and Rengit, some ten and twenty miles respectively down the coastal road. During the evening the road to Batu Pahat on the west coast was reported blocked. At dawn on 22 January, patrols made contact with the troops from Batu Pahat at the milestone 73 and reported the road open.

The battalion was ordered to keep the road open throughout the day. At about 1600 hrs, D Company made contact with the enemy near milestone 73. One platoon was ambushed and several casualties sustained. Captain Stuart Boardman, the company commander, was killed, with Captain Harry Schulman taking over. Orders for the battalion to move into Batu Pahat were received at about 1730 hrs. In the meantime, it was reported that the road was again blocked. The battalion was then ordered to concentrate for the night near milestone 72 and move on to Batu Pahat next morning. At dawn on the morning of 23 January, the advance guard encountered a strongly defended roadblock.

B Company under Captain Self attacked the roadblock but was unsuccessful and were driven back, suffering several casualties including Second Lieutenant Peter McKean who was killed and Lieutenant Guy Pallister who was seriously wounded (he died of his wounds two days later). C Company under Major Wood attacked round the southern flank and succeeded in getting two platoons around the roadblock but did not reach the road again, when at 1130 hrs the division commander ordered the battalion to withdraw to Ayer Hitam.

At 1300 hrs, orders were received to move to Batu Pahat by MT, taking the road south and then up the west coast via Skudai and Pontain Kechil. The battalion moved at 1600 hrs and harboured for the night near Skudai. On 24 January, the battalion left the harbouring area at 0400 hrs and arrived two miles south of Batu Pahat at 0700 hrs where contact was made with HQ 15 Brigade. 2 Cambridgeshire had been ordered to withdraw from the town the previous evening but had been stopped when just clear of the town. The battalion was ordered to retake positions in the centre and east of the town and hold them for 48 hours to enable other British units in the area to be extricated.

The attack commenced at 1045 hours assisted by one troop of Royal Artillery which could only shoot by the map. The attack was successful on the left, but the right sector became heavily engaged. No further forward movement was possible owing to the difficulty of getting 3-inch mortar and artillery support. In addition, there were indications of an enemy flank attack from two high points east of the main road. At 1500 hrs, B Company was ordered to occupy these high points, which it did but was counterattacked by superior numbers and had to withdraw below the crest. It was then decided to regain these positions at night.

At 0400 hrs on 25 January C Company, with the remainder of one company and 2 Cambridgeshire attacked the heights again. This was unsuccessful after heavy mortar and machine-gun fire held them back just short of the crest. At about 1300 hrs it was clear any further advance on Batu Pahat would be impossible and the battalion was ordered to hold its present position and cover the withdrawal of 2 Cambridgeshire.

The positions were finally abandoned at 2100 hrs. The battalion marched back about four miles and were ferried by MT to a position near the aerodrome, arriving at midnight. On the morning of 26 January, information was received that the coastal road in rear of the battalion position had been blocked by the enemy in several places south of the battalion position.

At 1000 hrs, the battalion was ordered to move south, sending all transport ahead. At this time some 250 vehicles were on the road in Senggarang, head to tail, waiting to get back when the roadblocks were cleared. At 1745 hrs, the brigade commander ordered all transport to be destroyed and all troops to make their way south through the jungle and assemble about eighteen miles back, A bridge across the river was to be blown at 1830 hrs. At this time all ranks were extremely fatigued having been in battle almost continuously for five days with little or no rest.

On 27 January, most of the battalion, about 500 men under Major Wood and guided by Captain F. Wallace reached Benut and were taken back by MT to B echelon, near Skudai. Captain Hamond was following up this group; having started with twenty men, by the time he reached Benut he had collected many stragglers including a whole company of 2 Cambridgeshire who, not knowing where they were going, asked Captain Hamond to take them across, along with some Australian troops who had been moving south for a week after their battle at Muar. Another party under Captain Schulman made for the coast and were evacuated by small craft of the Royal Navy. The commanding officer, who had remained behind to supervise the blowing of the Senggarang bridge, got separated from the battalion but eventually with about eight men, made their way down the coast in a small canoe.

On 28 January the main party was taken back to Serangoon Road Camp on Singapore Island by MT. From 29 January to 2 February, the battalion reorganised, reequipped and rested. The first reinforcements also joined the battalion.

On 3 February, the battalion proceeded to the naval base on the north of the island and began to put it into a state of defence. During this time all forces, upon C-in-C's orders, were leaving the mainland and coming back to defend the island. On 4 February, the battalion worked on the defences, digging, wiring and sandbagging. Shelling commenced and battalion headquarters had to move twice. This shelling continued on 5, 6 and 7 February, the battalion suffering some casualties including Major Wood who was wounded. Major Crane left to take command of 6 Royal Norfolk.

On 7 February, Lieutenant Potter and Lieutenant R. Carey and three other ranks went across the strait of Johore and spent twenty-four hours in enemy territory. Work continued on the defences and on 9, 10 and 11 February Royal Engineer demolition parties began blowing up the dockyard.

On 12 February, the battalion was ordered to withdraw from forward positions in the brigade sector, finally taking over an area on the perimeter of Singapore City. D Company, who always seemed to be the rearguard, was the last official company out of the naval base; everything was being looted and under heavy fire. This was necessary owing to a successful enemy landing on the west coast of the island. During the withdrawal the battalion suffered several casualties from air attacks.

On 13 February, the battalion took up a defensive position in the Braddell Road area. During the early part of the night the right forward platoon of A Company was attacked. This attack was beaten off with few casualties. Captain Bob Hamond recalled:

As soon as we had stood down after dusk on 13 February (after visiting Battalion HQ), I went back to 'A' Company and decided to visit 8 Platoon which was under the command of Lieut. Peter Ramm as he was rather out on a limb. The ground I had to cross was about 300–400yds from HQ to 8 platoon and was a small valley which ran east and west with a small track at the bottom which we had to cross. I took my runner and started down the slope (the area was part of a large Chinese cemetery), all gravestones hidden in long grass, lalang, so one had to go slowly in the dark. I had just crossed the track and started to climb the slope of the ridge up to 8 platoon when shooting, shouting and screams broke out just ahead of me as Japs attacked.

This went on for several minutes then there was silence except for the screams from a man who had had his ear cut off with a sword and was wandering about the ridge. I did not know the strength of the attack or if 8 Platoon had been overrun and eliminated or if the attack had been beaten off so I could go forward; in fact, if I had started my journey a few minutes earlier, I would have walked right onto the Japs who were crawling up the slope in the long grass to attack. I decided to get back to my HQ.

This was not easy as I had to pass through one of my rear platoon positions and by now everyone was very trigger-happy and liable to shoot anything that moved. However, by calling out names in that platoon as I approached them, I got back without being shot and regained my HQ where I reported to the CO by telephone. During the next hour or so we recovered the screaming man who had wandered along the ridge to a 'C' Company platoon area.

L/Sgt Oswald Griffin of 8 Platoon reported to me personally. The attack had come from a Jap patrol, commanded by a Warrant Officer with a sword, who had crept up close to 8 platoon before rushing in with shouts in a hand to hand fight. Sgt Griffin had taken on the WO personally and won but not without being stabbed through the right arm. Some other Japs were killed and we had more casualties before the rest of them were beaten off and withdrew.

Captain Hamond took Sergeant Griffin to the regimental aid post and stayed with him until an ambulance took him away to hospital. Heavy firing and shelling continued all night. It was from the fighting, much of which was hand to hand in this area, that the battalion sustained heavy casualties.

In the early hours of Saturday, 14 February, many men from the battalion were evacuated to Alexandra Military Hospital. The water supply to the hospital had been cut off in the early hours, and shelling from the air, mortar and artillery became intense. Having penetrated from the Ayer Rajah area the first Japanese attacks were seen toward the Sisters' Quarters; Japanese troops were about to enter the hospital from the rear. Lieutenant Weston went from the recreation room to the rear entrance with a white flag to indicate surrender of the hospital. The Japanese took no notice and bayonetted him to death. Then they entered the ground floor of the hospital and ran amok; incumbents pointing to the Red Cross brassards or shouting the word 'hospital!' had no effect.

Next a Japanese party entered the theatre block where operations were being prepared. In the corridors male and female personnel held up their hands but the Japs, for no reason, set among them, bayonets flailing. Even a soldier on the operating table was bayonetted to death. Lance-Sergeant Oswald Griffin (26) was a prewar NCO and keen boxer in C Company who had been transferred on promotion to A Company after mobilisation. Realising the situation, although already wounded in combat on Bradell Road and ordered to hospital, he mustered those he could to hold back the attackers and assisted those able to get out and run for the British lines. By their selfless act several lives were saved but Sergeant Griffin and his small group of brave men fighting off the enemy with their fists could only hold on for so long; they did not make their own escape and were never seen again. Captain Hamond recorded of Sergeant Griffin: 'He was a stalwart NCO but above all a tough, courageous soldier for whom I had great admiration.'

Early on the 14th a second attack on the 2 Cambridgeshire area resulted in the battalion left flank being exposed. The line was readjusted by a counterattack by 2 Cambridgeshire. During the night, the enemy infiltrated the left flank and established several posts in the C Company reserve platoon area. RA support was excellent when SOS fire was called for by C Company. In the evening two enemy grenades were thrown into a weapons pit occupied by men from A Company. Withe great coolness and bravery Private Charles Frost picked up both grenades and hurled them back at the enemy. They exploded in mid-air. Frost's actions undoubtedly saved the lives of his section and he would later be awarded the Military Medal for his gallantry.

It is traditional that the British Army never lets a complete unit be taken prisoner; consequently, on the 13th, the official escape party consisting of three officers and about eight other ranks were ordered away. They were lucky and all, except one who was recaptured, eventually reached India via Java.

On 15 February, the enemy attacked on the battalion front from dawn but were kept at bay by determined resistance and accurate fire. At 1600 hrs orders came through to cease fire as the garrison had been ordered to capitulate. The regimental history records: 'It was a bitter disappointment to all, especially as the Japanese had been well held on the battalion front and had been unable to make any progress.' But further south the enemy columns had broken through the defensive lines and threatened the reservoirs upon which Singapore relied for its water supplies.

Many men of 5 Royal Norfolk swore to their dying day that they could have fought on; indeed, at the time of the capitulation one senior officer was seen sitting by the side of the road crying in despair with his head in his hands; but on the wider front, in the face of the threat to the water supplies, the lack of military supplies, air defence and troops against mounting numbers of enemy the fate of the battalion, 18 Division and Singapore Island was sealed. The only small consolation on that night, the first in captivity, was the men who were still standing had come away with their lives and although deeply fatigued and battle weary, they could at least sleep. The strength of the battalion on the capitulation was thirty officers and 660 other ranks, though several others turned up later in captivity.

Chapter 5

6th Battalion

This chapter is based on the account compiled by
Lieutenant-Colonel H. S. Ling MC

In April 1939 when the TA expanded, battalions of the Royal Norfolk Regiment duplicated and 4 Royal Norfolk provided the nucleus for 6 Royal Norfolk. The first parade of the new battalion took place at the Chapel Field Drill Hall, Norwich, and was attended by 250 recruits, all in civilian clothes. Their first serious training commenced at Falmer Camp, near Brighton, in July and on 1 September 1939, the unit, then known as The City of Norwich Battalion, was mobilised under the command of Lieutenant-Colonel D. C. Buxton at the Aylsham Road Drill Hall, Norwich. The battalion was then at a weak strength, specifically twenty-four officers, twenty-seven warrant officers and sergeants and 483 other ranks. The officers holding executive positions were:

CO: Lt-Col D C Buxton
2ic: Maj H. S. Ling, MC
Adj: Capt P. M. Westgate
QM: Lt H. G. Clark
HQ Company: Lt R. D. T. McClintock
A Company: Capt H. A. Cooper
B Company: Lt B. O. L. Prior
C Company: 2Lt J. Francis
D Company was not formed until 30 November 1939

Immediately after mobilisation A and B companies were despatched to Hemsby, where they were billeted in the holiday camp adjoining the village. C Company took over guard duties at Watton aerodrome, and the remainder of the unit remained in billets in Norwich with HQ at the Aylsham Road Drill Hall.

The battalion being so weak in strength, the transfer of sixteen of its best NCOs to the depot at Britannia Barracks as instructors, created some difficulties in the training of the young soldiers. These troubles were, however, soon overcome by the promotion of keen and promising men, so that when the first draft of 'Army Class' or Militiamen arrived on 19 October 1939, it was possible to 'squad' the whole 100 recruits and commence their training without delay, and with further drafts the total strength of 6 Royal Norfolk was soon up to 785 all ranks.

Toward the middle of November, the battalion was ordered to Aylsham and were quartered in billets in the town; A and B companies rejoined the unit from Hemsby. Here training was carried out on Blickling Park, which proved a most useful area. During the month, Major R. H. T. Reynolds, MC joined the battalion and was appointed OC HQ Company.

After a fortnight in Aylsham a quick move was made to Sheringham; the 287 Field Company Royal Engineers arrived in the town at the same time. All ranks were quartered in various hotels and private houses in the town, and really serious training commenced. Shortly after arrival, the first Army Class, having completed their six weeks' recruit training in Norwich, rejoined the unit.

The battalion took up defensive positions along the coast from Cromer to Weybourne with specific orders to prevent seaborne landings between Beach Road and the Old Hythe with company alarm posts in Augusta Street, Waterbank Road, Montague Road and Holway Road. Three vital points to be held were the sea wall from Beach Road to the Burlington Hotel, the stretch of beach from the lifeboat house to the Old Hythe and the area around Dead Man's Hill and the northern side of Oak Wood. Reserves were held in readiness south of Golf Course Hill (Skelding Hill) with Battalion HQ at the golf clubhouse. Each soldier was issued with 120 rounds of ammunition and 2,000 rounds were allocated to every Bren gun.

The battalion's first sight or war came at 0300 hrs on Wednesday, 5 December 1939 when a Heinkel 111 crashed on the beach in front of Sheringham lifeboat house, and the pilot and crew were all killed or drowned. The RAF arrived quickly and parts of the aeroplane were taken away for closer inspection – but not before some unauthorised trophies were secured by a few locals (the compass and pilot's seat were squirrelled away and used by a couple of local fishermen for years after the war) and those of the battalion near at hand. The articles removed by the battalion were handed over to the RAF authorities later.

The first Christmas of the war was celebrated here and the whole battalion sat down to a fine dinner of turkey and plum pudding in the basement of the Grand Hotel. The CO, Lieutenant-Colonel Buxton, visited each company in turn, and 'took wine' with each mess room. He was afterwards entertained in the sergeants' mess. On the evening of Christmas Day, when 25 per cent of the unit was on leave, a stand-to was ordered, and positions on the coast were manned for several hours.

January 1940 was a cold and bitter month with heavy snowfalls in early February that saw working parties sent out from the battalion to clear the roads of snowdrifts, some of them twelve feet deep, to assist the county council and make way for battalion transport (which consisted of impressed civilian vehicles) to get through to Dereham to collect the rations. The bad weather caused an outbreak of sore throats and mild influenza among the troops.

A temporary hospital stocked and staffed mainly by the Sheringham branch of the British Red Cross was opened in two rooms of the Grand Hotel. After the snow had partially disappeared the roads were so icy that it was found impractical to carry out the normal route marches which were usually held at least once a week. Musketry training in the form of elementary exercises in rifle, Bren gun and anti-tank rifle were carried out inside the commandeered dining room of the Sheringham Hotel. With the return of the Army Class, it was now found possible to form D Company under the command of Major R. Graham IARO, who had recently joined the battalion.

As the weather improved, considerable use was made of the golf course for training, and the hills and rough ground to the south of the town toward Cromer for both day and night exercises; in spite of the location of two rifle companies at various aerodromes in northern Norfolk, considerable progress was made in the efficiency of the battalion as a fighting unit as route marches were carried out and all companies could cover up to fifteen miles without distress.

By late spring companies were carrying out night operations with transport, whose drivers were learning night convoy work and discipline. A short range was dug by the battalion at Upper Sheringham but it must be said the weapons training was somewhat hampered by the equipment shortages, the battalion only being issued a total of six Bren guns, a 2-inch mortar and one Bren carrier. Drill was not forgotten either and battalion parades were regular features on Sunday mornings. During the spring Captain J. M. Smyth joined the battalion from the Jersey Militia where he had been serving as adjutant and Major Ling and Major Reynolds changed appointments at their mutual request.

On 10 May 1940 the battalion was directed to send a platoon to guard Cromer Pier with all companies ordered to battle stations the following day on a front from Sheringham to Overstrand. Serious works were carried out installing roadblocks, digging weapons pits, sandbagging and reinforcing defensive emplacements at vulnerable points across the area and on the main roads. Special watch was to be maintained for enemy parachutists. Battle headquarters was moved from St Bernards in North Street to Ledbury in Abbey Road. A Lewis gun post located at East Runton claimed a German aeroplane which was brought down to the east of Cromer.

Shades of the invasion scares of 1914 were relived on 14 May when a baker's roundsman put the battalion on alert after he reported seeing German parachutists landing at Felbrigg. A platoon from A Company made an exhaustive search of the woods in the vicinity but drew a blank. A further search at dusk was equally unproductive. A cross-examination of the roundsman proved he was suffering from nothing more than 'hallucinations'.

At the end of May Lieutenant-Colonel F. L. Cubitt relieved Lieutenant-Colonel Buxton in command. The international military position being even worse, the whole battalion remained in the defensive positions they had dug, sleeping and eating in their battle positions and working during all the hours of daylight on improvements to their trenches with extra sandbags and razor wire laid across all possible invasion landing places. Everyone stood-to for an hour before dusk and until well after dark, and again an hour before dawn. In June large drafts from the Northamptonshire Regiment and Essex Regiment joined the battalion, the 140 reinforcements then arriving, bringing the battalion to somewhere near its war strength.

During July orders arrived stating there would be no withdrawal from any position and full preparations were to be made to repel the anticipated German invasion. Mines were laid in the gaps in the cliffs and at all exits from beaches that were potentially passable by enemy infantry. An armoured train was brought up from Melton Constable to support local defences and beach lights (in fact adapted car headlamps) were issued to D Company. Installed at Lifeboat House Gap and Dead Man's Gap the strict instructions for their deployment were that

> they were only to be used as fighting lights and to be sited not less than 10 nor more than 50 yards from any emplacement. They were not to be exposed until any leading invasion craft had struck the beach and were to be used in close cooperation with Bren gun positions, with great care to be taken when fixing the lights to ensure they did not blind or impair the vision of other weapons or defensive position crews.

At the end of August the battalion was relieved by 2 Cambridgeshire and moved into brigade reserve at Holt and were quartered, principally, in the grounds of Gresham's School. Here there were no obstacles to training and with the assistance of a platoon of Irish Guards, who were attached to the battalion for a while, great strides were made in drill and soldierly bearing, which had been neglected during the more pressing activities on the coast. Over the previous few months there had been several postings, promotions and changes to the command structure of the battalion viz:

CO: Lt-Col J. F. Ross
2ic: Maj F. M. E. D. Drake-Briscoe
Adj: Capt P. M. Westgate
QM: Lt H. G. Clark
HQ Company: Maj S. Ling MC
A Company: Capt P. S. Campbell-Orde
B Company: Capt J. M. Smyth
C Company: Capt H. P. Pilkington
D Company: Capt J. Francis

On 21 September the battalion moved to Weybourne and took over the coastal defences from 5 Royal Norfolk who, in turn, moved into reserve. The ensuing month was spent in defensive positions, and much work was carried out in making improvements to the trenches and courses and demonstrations continued until the end of October.

In November the whole brigade moved back into reserve and the battalion was stationed in Swaffham where they spent the second Christmas of the war. The rifle companies were billeted in the town with Battalion HQ and HQ Company at Petyards, a large farm about three miles from the town. The generosity of local people saw to it that the battalion enjoyed another fine Christmas dinner. The CO visited all the companies in turn and later entertained the officers at Petyards. During this time some good boxing contests were held at the Drill Hall, the enthusiasm of the boxers themselves atoning fully for in some cases their lack of skill.

In early January 1941, Major Drake-Briscoe left to take command of 1 Royal Norfolk and so did not accompany 6 Royal Norfolk when it moved to Scotland on 7 January, preparatory, it was thought, to it proceeding overseas. During the loading of the battalion stores onto the train at Swaffham on 6 January a German aeroplane suddenly appeared out of low cloud and dropped several bombs on the station yard. Owing to the low visibility the teams of Bren gunners positioned around the station yard did not see the plane until it was over them and it was out of sight before effective fire could be brought to bear. Unfortunately, five men from the fatigue party, Privates Gordon Stevens, Leonard Batch, Frederick Smith, Albert Sewell and Christian Cobbold were killed, and Private James Furness died the following day from the wounds he sustained because of this incident.

After a long journey by train, the battalion arrived in Dumfries in the early hours of 8 January and were quartered in a large disused jute mill on the outskirts of the town. 2 Cambridgeshire and the Norwegian Army who were then in training in the district, comprised the remainder of the garrison of the town. Dumfries proved to be a happy station and although the weather was often bitterly cold and snow lay on the ground training was rigorous and there were long marches into the hills over an entirely different country from that of Norfolk, which proved extremely beneficial for field training. There was no sign of strain or over-training; indeed, the battalion reached an extremely high state of efficiency. Much practice was gained in motorised movement over long distances, and the unit took part in several exercises with the remainder of the division and other divisions over the whole area from Dumfries to Berwick and Edinburgh.

Toward the end of March Major Alan B. Cubitt was posted to the battalion and took over the duties of second-in-command. The long-expected move overseas was still postponed although the battalion was now fully mobilised and in possession of tropical kit. When orders were received for a move south again, it was thought for a time that the only service that the battalion would see would be inactive in England. On arrival in Western Command the battalion was stationed in Hartford, Cheshire, the rifle companies being billeted in large houses and scattered over an area of about five miles with Battalion HQ and HQ Company situated centrally at Sandiway.

Captain Francis was posted to another unit and Captain Westgate, who was succeeded as adjutant by Captain P. R. Hill, took over command of D Company. Many large-scale exercises were again carried out over areas such as Shrewsbury and Birmingham with assault crossings of the rivers Weaver, Teme and Severn. Each rifle company carried out a three-day march, covering not less than sixty miles and concluded with a night attack. It was noted the companies demonstrated they had achieved an advanced level of fitness, efficiency and endurance and it was noted 'casualties caused by sore feet were comparatively few in number'. While the battalion was stationed here they also had the opportunity to take part in properly organised games and cricket matches were played against teams in the district. Efforts were also made under the 'Dig for Victory' scheme to produce more vegetables to relieve some of the increasing food shortages. Each company dug large gardens around their billets, being supplied with seeds and the proper tools by the military authorities.

In May, enemy bombers could be heard passing overhead in their attack on Liverpool and the battalion was sent, two companies at a time, to take over fire-watching duties from the exhausted civil ARP personnel. Despite several heavy raids during this time the battalion escaped without any casualties. In the early part of June, the depot band under Bandmaster Burgess paid a welcome visit. This was the first and only occasion during the war that the men of 6th Battalion had the privilege of hearing a military band. On 15 July Lieutenant-Colonel Ian Lywood, the man who would eventually take the battalion abroad, relieved Lieutenant-Colonel Ross in command.

In August a move was made to Knowsley Park, the seat of Lord Derby, near Liverpool where the battalion relieved 5 Suffolk. There were many large-scale exercises during the time the battalion was stationed in the district, notably a weeklong exercise across Westmorland and the Yorkshire moors to test the defences of Carlisle plus another exercise in Otley, Yorkshire, with a battalion of the new Churchill tanks. The weather then became much colder, and there was a great deal of heavy rain. The normal pasture of the park was churned into heavy mud, while the battalion's tents streamed with water. Conditions were so uncomfortable a section of the 278 Field Company RE, who arrived to erect hutments, was given a very warm welcome and parties of the men from the battalion worked with a will under the sappers' direction to complete the new camp buildings.

It was in October that representatives from each company were, with parties from the other two battalions of the brigade, reviewed by the king in Crewe Park. The troops lined each side of the drive to Crewe Hall, and the king passed down the whole lane on foot, stopping frequently and saying a few words to individual officers and men. He was greeted with hearty cheers as he approached each unit.

It was now realised the battalion would soon see active service. Everyone was fighting fit when orders came for the move abroad. Some, of course, had to be left behind with the home details, but it was not known until the last moment who these unfortunates were to be. When the time came it was found that Captain Clark who had only recently joined the battalion from other duties, had been selected to stay behind. Another sad loss for the battalion at this time was Captain McClintock who was posted for duty with the Royal Engineers.

The battalion moved out from the railway station on 27 October 1941. After a long night journey the battalion detrained at Gourock, and at once embarked RMS *Duchess of Atholl*, which remained moored in mid-stream for two days before it sailed on 29 October. It was a pleasant voyage across the Atlantic to America and was marked by an event that must have impressed itself very forcibly on the memories of all who witnessed it. Before arrival in Canada, what appeared to be a mighty fleet approached over the horizon on 2 November. It quite overshadowed the small British naval escort, which had overseen the convoy during the early part of the voyage. This flotilla was part of the US Navy, which upon meeting our ships divided and turned inward, taking the place of the original escort, which turned outward and away, disappearing into the mists to the west.

Norwich soldier Private Ralph Gant of Wellesley Lodge, Water Lane, New Costessey described this sight in a letter home describing his voyage to Singapore and sums up well the sense of wonder many of these young men felt at the sights they saw; after all many of them had often not travelled far outside of their home county, let alone travelled anywhere abroad before the war:

> out to sea one day we sighted a very large number of naval vessels of all kinds and we were encircled by aeroplanes bearing the American star sign, these planes were from an aircraft carrier and the ships were our new escort taking over from the British and my what a sight, battleships, cruisers, aircraft carriers and destroyers, never had I seen such a sight before, the sea was alive with ships, and the sky alive with planes, this we were told was the first time it had ever happened, Americans escorting British troops and so we created a new page in history. America certainly does things in a big way.

As the convoy steamed up the estuary toward Halifax, Nova Scotia, the early morning sun was rising and a good view of the harbour and town was obtained. Immediately on arrival at the docks all personnel of 53 Brigade were transferred to USS *Mount Vernon*. Within 36 hours the division was again on its way. Passing through the West Indies the convoy reached Trinidad to refuel and take on water and set off again. No land was seen again until Cape Town three weeks later where all troops were granted shore leave. The welcome could not be bettered and the four and a half days of holiday were enjoyed by all and would be recalled many times over the harsher years to come.

The brigade sailed from Cape Town on 13 December, and steamed north and was approaching Bombay when the ship carrying the 53 Infantry Brigade turned about and proceeded without escort toward Mombasa, arriving at midday on Christmas Day.

Escorted by the cruiser HMS *Emerald* across the Indian Ocean, the year closed with the arrival of the convoy at one of the Maldive Islands for refuelling and to take on water. Escorted by the cruiser *Exeter* the convoy sailed to Singapore and on 13 January 1942 the battalion disembarked from USS *Mount Vernon* at the naval base on Singapore Island during an air raid.

The battalion structure at the time was as follows:

Battalion HQ
CO: Lt-Col I. C. G. Lywood
Maj A. B. Cubitt
Capt P. J. Hill
Capt R. F. Griffiths
Capt W. R. Jackson RAMC
QM: Lt Qmr H. G. Clark
RSM: WOI C. Leveridge
RQMS: WOII H. Hendrey

HQ Company
Capt A. R. Stacy
Capt R. R. Evans
Lt E. J. Goddard
2Lt R. O. C. Goddard
2Lt D. G. Horner

A Company
Capt P. S. Campbell-Orde
Lt C. J. Calder
Lt A. W. Nock
Lt H. R. C. C. Cook
2Lt G. A. Kidner
CSM: WOII M. Rudling
CQMS: WOII C. Reeve

B Company
Maj J. M. Smyth
Capt J. C. Stratford
Lt R. R. W. Garrett
2Lt H. C. C.. Ross
2Lt A. E. Cox
CSM: WOII N. Twiddy
CQMS: WOII L. Smith

C Company
Capt H. P. Pilkington
Lt J. C. Race
2Lt J. C. Race
2Lt J. B. Kelf
2Lt N. E. Parker
2Lt R. H. Nutt
CSM: WOII E. Kelf

D Company
Capt P. M. Westgate
Lt R. T. F. Daykin
2Lt G. J. Smith
2Lt A. E. Jones
CSM: WOII C. Lord
CQMS: WOII S. Hardwick

First reinforcements
Maj H. S. Ling, MC
Capt D. P. Apthorp
Lt J. L. Mackwood
2Lt M. C. Mitchell
2Lt J. A. Salter
2Lt E. L Weymont

Total officers: 38
Total other ranks: 877
Battalion strength: 915

A tropical rainstorm providentially prevented the convoy from being bombed at anchor after arrival but the Japanese planes were heard passing overhead. However, the rain successfully soaked all personnel and their baggage during transit to Tyersall Park Camp, where the battalion spent its first two days.

On 16 January the battalion embussed for the journey to the mainland of Malaya, leaving the first reinforcements at No. 7 MRC, the command of which had been taken over by Lieutenant-Colonel H. S. Ling, MC. Four Federated Malaya States Volunteer Force (FMSVF) officers were attached for the interrogation of natives and to act as interpreters; their services proved very useful during operations. It was thought at first that the battalion was proceeding to the mainland for training in jungle warfare, and to get its 'land legs' after three months at sea. There was further indication that this was the idea when four Indian Army officers were appointed for this class of training. But this was not to be the case and upon arrival at Ayer Hitam, the battalion was ordered to take up a defensive position astride the Jalan Muar–Yong Peng road, on a ridge ten miles south of Muar. The task was to cover the lines of communication of 45 Infantry Brigade at Muar, who were being heavily attacked by the enemy, and to cover the possible withdrawal.

On 17 January the battalion was in position supported by one troop of 4.5-inch howitzers, and on the next day had its baptism of fire in a dive-bombing attack by enemy planes on the forward companies, D and C, and on the Battalion HQ. The position was in thick jungle save for the forward slopes of the ridge, with deep irrigation ditches and swamps at the sides of the road which made it extremely difficult to get vehicles under good cover off the road. On 18 January patrols had contacted some Japanese patrols to the west. Later some Australians from two battalions that had passed through the 6 Royal Norfolk lines to reinforce the 45 Infantry Brigade, reported that the Japanese had cut off the 43 Infantry Brigade and attacked the Australian B echelon transport some six miles to the north of the battalion positions.

During the morning of 20 January, a patrol from B Company was ambushed near the river and suffered some casualties. In the afternoon the enemy attacked C Company on the left from the jungle on the west flank of the battalion. They overran C Company and managed to get astride the road on top of the ridge behind D Company. D Company, though now cut off from the forward companies, held out but C Company was almost completely disintegrated, partly because two platoons of the company were out on patrol in the surrounding jungle at the time of the attack, and because of the sheer numbers of the enemy involved in the attack a counterattack by one company of the Loyals and B Company was unsuccessful. Captain H. P. Pilkington, OC C Company, was wounded and Second Lieutenant Norman Parker was killed.

Private Ralph Gant of B Company wrote of these events while they were still fresh in his mind over two letters home to his wife:

My section was chosen again for a fighting patrol and with other chaps we numbered twenty, we were put into a lorry and went out into enemy territory, with the sole intention of meeting a Japanese patrol which was operating somewhere in front of our positions. … All of a sudden the lorry stopped, and we all jumped out quickly, in front of us in the ditches were dozens of bicycles, which meant only one thing, Japs, and these devils were all around up in the tree tops, which is their favourite way of fighting, and to our disadvantage they were used to this kind of country and warfare. …The lorry driver started to turn his lorry, but was killed while doing so then away dashed Bill Lambert to drive it, but he was shot in the back as he ran toward it, and the chaps in the lorry who had not got out in time were subjected to a hail of fire from all directions, the results of which I did not have time to watch.

I and the chaps who had got out just laid down on the ground completely in the open, although surrounded by jungle which was being held by the Japanese who were sitting in the trees, in a complete ring all around us and firing down at us like madmen, but they were rotten shots. … I got my Bren gun alongside a pole (about 6 inches in diameter) and the bullets were chipping lumps off it very close to my head without the ones which were spurting dirt all around me and the rest of the fellows. … It was sheer murder to say, as we could see nothing to fire at although the Japs could have been not further than five yards from us, but concealed in the top of these dense rubber trees, so the officer told us to get up and make a dash for the jungle and take our chance which we did with the loss of my section commander, and several other chaps on the ground killed and wounded.

As I trotted into this open patch I braced my body to counteract the thud of a bullet which I thought might come between my shoulder blades, but my luck held and God was with me, and although it might seem fantastic, I was very cool and not in the least nervous throughout the whole show, but after we had got some distance into the jungle I got a reaction, and had to rest, but of course we could not do this for long, so the chaps helped me along through swamps, streams and very dense jungle to our own lines, which took us eight hours to cover two and a half miles, bathed in sweat, dirt and very thirsty. ...Charlie and Geoff had heard all about it after we had been back a few minutes and they came running to me with a smile of relief and joy on their faces because they had heard some of the chaps had been killed, but I laid on my back on the ground panting for breath while old Charlie and Geoff taxed me with questions.

After this little 'do' we were ordered to make a bayonet charge attack on the top of a hill, and consolidate the position, so off we went with me panting like a dog and pains in the chest, which was entirely my fault because I could have gone back to the ADS but I would not trouble them, as it was some way to the rear, so on to the attack. ... Charlie's platoon made the crest of the hill and killed a Japanese mortar crew with hand grenades, but we all had to withdraw because of the opposing fire was heavy and terrific and remember we were going up a very steep hill. ... As we withdrew to positions further back, I dropped out of the single file, and Charlie passed by me. Enquiring where I was going as he passed, I said I was going to the M.O.s and he just waved and told me to take care of myself like he always did do ... and that was the last I saw of him or Geoff and now I am alone it breaks my heart to think we parted in such an offhand manner after all those years of close friendship but I thought I would be back with him the same day, instead I was put into an ambulance and taken to

> a hospital in Singapore. … This trip was not very healthy because the Japanese even dive bombed and machine gunned the road as we travelled along, although the Red Cross was plainly marked.

Private Gant was diagnosed as suffering from pleurisy and was sent to a convalescent home to recuperate.

Sporadic fighting continued through the day and night of 20 January until in the early hours of 21 January; the 3/16 Punjabis, having moved up by night, delivered a dawn counterattack on the ridge to relieve D Company, but suffered severe casualties and were unsuccessful. A further attack by 2 Loyals was to have been launched the next day but owing to the inaccuracy of the supporting artillery fire, it had to be called off. The line was finally consolidated at the road junction east of the defile but with D Company still cut off. On 22 January the Loyals advanced to launch a full-scale attack on the defile but, again, there was no covering artillery fire, so the attack was aborted.

6 Royal Norfolk was now reduced to little more than two companies and was in support of two other battalions in a hastily assembled composite brigade under Brigadier Duke covering a swamp over which the road passed. At midday on 22 January the brigade was ordered to withdraw down the road to Yong Peng, eight miles to the south, with 6 Royal Norfolk as rearguard. The enemy, having obtained a commanding position, quickly followed the withdrawal. Headquarters, HQ Company and B Company fought a bloody but successful rearguard action until 1930 hrs as the other two battalions of the brigade withdrew to Yong Peng and later moved to Skudai, south of Ayer Hitam. Lieutenant-Colonel Lywood fell sick and was evacuated to Singapore and Major Alan Cubitt took over command of the battalion, which now consisted of A and B companies with the remains of C Company.

On the night of 24/25 January the battalion moved to Senggarang with Battalion HQ and B Company, leaving A Company at Rengit, nine miles south of Senggarang. The battalion was to hold the river crossings at both places in support of 15 Infantry Brigade at Batu Pahat, nine miles to the north on the west coast of Malaya. 15 Infantry Brigade comprised

5 Royal Norfolk, 2 Cambridgeshire and the 'British Battalion' that was made up of the remnants of the regular battalions of the Leicestershire Regiment and East Surreys.

This was the first occasion during the battle when other units of 53 Brigade were near at hand. Information was received that there was no enemy south of Batu Pahat, but soon after dawn on arrival at Senggarang, the enemy attacked with heavy machine-gun fire from the south and established roadblocks between Senggarang and Rengit. A force composed of 6 Royal Norfolk reinforcements from Singapore, armoured cars and a section of 4.5 howitzers endeavoured unsuccessfully to clear the roadblocks from Rengit on 26 January but suffered severe casualties. Rengit was attacked soon afterwards and A Company, having held off all the attacks, was ordered by Brigade HQ to withdraw to Benut by the jungle, which they accomplished successfully.

On 27 January, 15 Infantry Brigade, on becoming acquainted with the situation in the south, withdrew to Senggarang, and attempted to clear the enemy from the roadblocks. Eventually the bridge at Senggarang was blown and by 1800 hrs, the brigade with 6 Royal Norfolk were ordered to withdraw independently by units through the jungle to get back to Benut. In the meantime, A Company had been surrounded at Rengit. The Japanese launched several fierce attacks but A Company held them off. Eventually they managed to make their way through enemy lines and into the jungle, where after a forced march they reached Singapore with just two officers and eighty-five other ranks.

The fighting at Senggarang had cost the battalion dearly: among the officers killed were Captain Richard Evans and Second Lieutenants Ronald King, Richard Harwood Nutt, Arthur Jones, Michael Mitchell, James Salter and Eric Weymont. The regimental history records that before becoming a casualty the 30-year-old Second Lieutenant Richard Harwood Nutt 'had shown conspicuous gallantry during the engagement, displaying the greatest initiative, drive and personal bravery'. He received a posthumous mention in despatches.

The battalion, now reduced to about 200 men, moved west of the road and next day, in conjunction with the 'British Battalion', after a very tiring march contacted naval gunboats at the fishing village of Ponggor on the west coast. Here, reliable information was received that the enemy had captured Benut and the troops were therefore evacuated by sea on the gunboats to Singapore. This took three nights and did not prove at all easy, as the river was narrow with mangrove swamps on either side with the enemy only a mile away on the main road.

At Singapore, 53 Infantry Brigade was reorganised and re-equipped in preparation for the defence of the island. Though the remainder of 18 Division had now arrived, it remained under the command of 11 Indian Division. The British forces now having been evacuated from the Malayan mainland, on 3 February 53 Brigade took up a position on the north coast of Singapore Island from the naval base to the River Seletar. 6 Royal Norfolk was on the right flank north of the river and on the other side were 5 Royal Norfolk and 5 Beds and Herts of 55 Brigade, 18 Division.

The battalion now consisted of A, B and C companies. D Company, most of whom had managed to extricate themselves from Yong Peng, had returned to the battalion via the jungle, being posted to the other companies to bring their strength nearer establishment. From this time until 12 February all ranks worked feverishly in the construction of defences, which were non-existent when the battalion arrived in the area. Most of this work was carried out under the cover of darkness because the enemy had good observation posts on the Johore side of the straits opposite and made easy pickings for the Japanese shelling from the northern side of the Johore Straits. Despite the 'mauling' the battalion had suffered, its morale remained high, as at last the measure of jungle warfare had been taken, and the role of coastal defence was more familiar. With the defences prepared, the impending Japanese attack was anticipated with confidence.

However, the Japanese attacked on the west coast of the causeway, and on 12 February, after a succession of rumours of victories by the enemy the brigade was ordered to withdraw as quickly as possible, as the enemy had all but gained possession of the bridge at Nee Soon. The men of 6 Royal Norfolk now covered the withdrawal of the brigade over the Seletar, and took up positions at the seventh milestone on the

Naval Base–Singapore road with 2 Cambridgeshire and 2/19 Australian Battalion. Next day, the enemy made a particularly aggressive attack in the dense jungle, and managed to penetrate defensive positions, causing several casualties including Captain John Stratford who was killed during the confused fighting and Lieutenant Ronald Garrett who was severely wounded and later died of his wounds. At dawn on 14 February the battalion withdrew to a position on Braddell Road in reserve behind 5 Royal Norfolk.

On 15 February, orders were received at 1400 hrs that hostilities would cease at 1600 hrs that day. Later, information was received that the British forces had capitulated and that the battalion was to concentrate in its present position and await orders. Casualties had been severe in the fighting and there were still more to come. Captain Peter Campbell-Orde was killed when a stray bomb landed on the hospital and the CO, Lieutenant-Colonel Ian Lywood, along with about another 200 others were brutally murdered when Alexandra Hospital was overrun by Japanese soldiers.

Thus ended the short campaign, and it is fair to say that the battalion fought with considerable merit, especially as it had received no training in jungle warfare, and did not act as a motorised battalion, for which role in 18 Division the battalion had been training so long in England. Captain W. R. Jackson RAMC carried out the evacuation of casualties under extremely difficult conditions and Sergeant Albert Branson was awarded the Military Medal for his conspicuous gallantry in the evacuation of the wounded, often under heavy enemy fire.

On 17 February 1942, the majority of 6 Royal Norfolk marched to Changi Barracks on the east coast of the island and there started the three and a half years of life as prisoners of war. At the end of the fighting the battalion had suffered 179 officers and men killed and seventy-five wounded.

There was, however, at least one member of the battalion who successfully escaped from Singapore. After a short spell of convalescence from his attack of pleurisy, Private Ralph Gant had been given a duty that may just have saved his life and described what happened in a remarkable letter home:

From the convalescent camp I was posted to an island just off Singapore separated by water about the wide of the River Wensum to guard an ammunition dump (1 Sergeant and 4 men).

The island itself was not very large, one could walk all around the water's edge in half an hour quite easily, so you can imagine the size of it, and this small island was manned by 2 x 6-inch shore guns, let into the ground and covered with concrete and camouflage, the entrance and exit to it was by a tunnel, and from this position I made my escape.

The battle of Singapore was on, the noise was terrific, and the was no lull in the noise from the time it started to the time it finished, and I was between Singapore and another island behind us which was getting shelled and bombed day and night, so I actually did not share so much danger as the chaps in Singapore, but it was not very cosy standing over tons of ammunition of all kinds with bombs and shells dropping all around, and on the last two days shells dropped within twenty or thirty yards of the dump, so we rallied around the 6-inch guns on top of the hill, under the orders of the captain in charge to fight to the last round which we did until the surrender.

On the day of the surrender [Sunday, 15 February 1942] when things were at a critical point the captain blew up the guns and us with them because we caught the blast through the tunnel, but nobody was hurt and the guns had to go in preference to the Japs getting them.

By this time the docks opposite us were one mass of flame, and from a ring of this flame and heat a solitary AA gun was still firing, it was hopeless against the Jap bombers, but it did something for us lads in the fort to see such magnificent fortitude and courage against very superior odds. From our position on the top of the hill we could see the battle of Singapore and it seemed just one mass of flame, bursting shells and debris flying through the air from bomb explosions.

About four or five that same afternoon everything went dead silent, then one long blast on an air-raid siren was sounded for about five minutes, we all looked at each other in wonderment, and thought we had all gone mad, but no, at two o'clock [in the early hours on Monday morning] the captain informed us of the surrender, and if we wished we were at liberty to make our escape, but he warned us of the dangers we would probably encounter, but we still intended to escape, then after shaking hands with the captain (he stopped behind with his Indian gun crew) we left the island in a small motor boat (it held six) towing a large lifeboat behind which held the rest of the chaps, about thirty of them.

Everything was silent. The noise of the motor boat sounded like thunder as we travelled down the narrow strip of water between Singapore and our island, very close to the flaming docks which lit up the whole place like daylight so we all got below the gunwale except the chap steering the lifeboat and the officer and myself steering the motor boat. The Japs must have been asleep because we were not fired upon although they had been sniping from the docks at us all day while we were loading shells into small boats to feed the AA guns in Singapore.

Our first stop was the boom which we crashed into and was tangled in for half an hour, then on across the minefield outside the boom, the officer steering the motor boat with his feet and his head through the top of the cabin, my writing this tells you we did not strike any mines, so on we travel.

About two miles from Singapore we could still see it burning and it was showing us up, the motor boat began to sink so we all clambered aboard the lifeboat and then ran aground on a sandbank quite some way from a small island we could see and which were plentiful around this particular part of the world. ... A volunteer was asked to swim to shore with a rope, or test the depth of the water which was shark infested, but one chap did it without the slightest hesitation, and then all of us had to get out and form a chain holding the rope to the shore, by this means we got the rifles and stores ashore which lightened the boat, thus getting it nearer to land. Half of us could not swim but we stood there up to the chin in water, regardless of what was swimming beneath the surface.

The next day we had to wade out to the boat again very hurriedly as we had been informed the Japs were taking the island over at 12 o'clock and it was then ten minutes to twelve, so imagine the energy we pit behind those oars which did not seem to go fast enough for us but we did our best without oars, even this worry was topped by Japs planes above but they must have taken pity on us as it was hopeless for us to get far because they did not harass us or our tiny craft with its human freight low in the bottom of her except for the oarsmen.

The same night we ran into a rock and this time we were miles from shore so we were all ordered out regardless of our ability to swim, to push the boat off the rock. We all got out and I managed to land on the rock as the sea was just above my ankles, but it was a rotten feeling all the same not being able to swim, with big black waves coming at you, and miles from land, not only this, as we heaved, I stepped off into deep water and was hauled aboard by the rest of the chaps, because by this time she was afloat again. … The officer said, 'We must now row around in a circle till daylight because the tide is low and the water is studded with rocks.' This we did for eight hours in a circle of about twenty yards diameter till daylight having twenty minute breaks at the oars, and by morning we were practically all in but we saw a Malayan fishing boat whose owner guided us some of the way to Sumatra.

We kept landing at native villages where we took on stores of coconuts and different fruits which was our main diet for eight days on the sea in an open boat, through treacherous seas, storms that almost capsized our boat, and intense heat. We also traded our tropical kit for Malayan kit which consisted of sandals, sarongs and a little black hat, all this being disguise against Jap planes who were out spotting after us. At last we reached Sumatra, not to rest but to carry on down a very wide river. This time a tug boat, thank goodness, organised by the Dutch people who were the main factor in our escape.

The river was about ninety miles long to where we landed and on its banks could be seen crocodiles, while floating on its surface were logs of wood and great clumps of earth like small islands, so it is very lucky we were not in our rowing boat else we should not have made it against the current, which certainly was travelling. ... From the boat we travelled across the rest of Sumatra by bus, over very rough roads, and round tops of mountains with drops of several thousand feet at the edge of the road, this trip was a nightmare itself with a Malayan driving like a madman. ... From here everything was organised secretly, and we met other groups of chaps who had got away, and who all made one large party, when we got the word to move suddenly but silently to a destroyer waiting for us at the docks.

We boarded this at 7 o'clock that night, fourteen days after leaving Singapore, and we were glad to see the British Navy. From this boat after two hours travel out to sea we clambered up the side of an Australian cruiser which was steaming outside the harbour waiting for us. ... After this everything was like a holiday and certainly a rare one because not many people have had the pleasure to be aboard a man o'war at sea travelling at speed, it certainly was grand. ... The cruiser landed us at Columbo where we slept in a convent, then once more we went aboard a British naval vessel which brought us to Bombay where we now wait for fresh developments.

Private Gant would be transferred to the Suffolk Regiment and spent the rest of the war fighting in the Burma campaign.

Prisoners of War

When it seemed the situation on Singapore Island made capitulation just a matter of time, the tradition of no British Army division ever surrendering in entirety saw an official escape party consisting of Carrier Officer Captain Barham Savory, Signal Officer Captain Douglas R. Gray, Intelligence Officer Lieutenant Kenneth Potter and thirty-four men, mostly from 5 Royal Norfolk, leave the island. A few weeks later the following account was published in a local paper, 'They Rowed out of Singapore – Dereham Man's Luck in Escape':

> Capt. Douglas R. Gray, Royal Norfolk Regiment whose home is at Dereham has sent his wife news of his and other Norfolk men's exciting escape from Singapore. Captain Gray has now reached India via Columbo. After the retreat to Singapore Capt Gray and 34 officers and men, believed all of the Royal Norfolk Regiment, except an Australian Major, put out to sea in a boat found on a burnt out ship. Capt Gray left his battalion on a special mission on the night of February 13th–14th, after which fighting continued for two days.
>
> From another source it is known that among the men who escaped with Capt Gray were Sgt. Catling, Cpls Disdale and Cocks (Signal Platoon), Cpl Carter and Pte Catling (Carrier Platoon) [two other members of the Norfolks' party were Sgt Wilson the Provost Sgt. and Pte Chadwick of C Company]. Describing their 'amazing luck' in getting away Capt Gray says 'Nearly all the boats leaving on the previous nights had been fired on but we rowed out of the harbour in full daylight and never a shell or shot was fired at us. Twice Jap plane flew over, but luckily they were too much intent on

having a last crack at Singapore to worry about us. We just kept on rowing as hard as we could, four oars on each side. About half our crowd were sea sick in the first half hour, but seasick or not they took their turn at the oars. We prayed for it to get dark. By sundown the buildings of Singapore were getting low behind the horizon, and we reckoned we had rowed six miles out. The whole town seemed canopied by a pall of thick black smoke.'

During that night the boat was caught in a rip tide off an island, but the crew survived the ordeal and at dawn, after some attention from Japanese planes, they landed on a small island, and made a bargain with two natives to tow them with a motor launch. Gray picks up the story: 'By various stages we made our way to a town in Java. … Here we had to wait for several days. The Dutch were very good to us. I was surprised how many of them could speak a bit of English.'

On the voyage from Java to Columbo as Captain Gray was reading on deck an enemy submarine periscope popped out of the water 100 yards away: 'The submarine fired three torpedoes at us, which all missed. The first went across our bows, and the others went right underneath us midships. We all thought she would surface and sink us by shell fire, but after a good look at us she dived. We saw her surface again about three miles away.'

The rest of the 18 Division were now in the hands of their Japanese captors.

The two days immediately after capitulation saw the battle-weary men of 4, 5 and 6 Royal Norfolk develop intense speculation over their future. They would find out soon enough but most of the families back home would have no idea of the fate of their loved one until Christmas 1942. Even then many would receive a notification that their loved one was 'missing in action' and would be left with the agony of just not knowing what had happened to them. On Singapore efforts were being made to clear up loose ends, contacting those who had been separated from the battalion during the confused fighting on the island and many men collected what personal effects they could muster for the inevitable captivity that lay ahead.

On 17 February all three battalions marched about seventeen miles to Changi Barracks on the east coast of Singapore Island. Some men, however, found transport hidden in rubber plantations and were relayed to Changi without interference from the Japanese and joined the rest of the 18 Division in captivity. The barracks had escaped serious bombing and remained in good condition but there was no water or light, a situation soon rectified by the Royal Engineers. There was, however, serious overcrowding and huts had to be erected as overspill. Many of the Norfolks were crammed into the NAAFI of Robertson Barracks. The officers were in the Chinese coolies' quarters, two and three officers in the space usually occupied by one coolie.

Food was scarce, there was practically no meat and rice appeared to be the main diet – the shape of things to come. And this change of diet did not help the constitution of many soldiers and resulted in many of them not going to the toilet for over three weeks. Attempts were made to organise concerts to relieve the boredom of captivity and vegetable gardens were started whenever possible to supplement the meagre rations. There were also various forms of study and education for all ranks in the form of a 'university'. It was also during the incarceration at Changi that a renegade Sikh battalion mutinied and was put in charge; they put up roadblocks, demanded stringent respect and made the situation even more difficult.

Soon dysentery was prevalent and one of the early deaths was the popular 35-year-old padre, Captain the Reverend John Oswald Dean. He was sadly missed by all ranks. At the end of April men were marched to Singapore and accommodated in tents in Farrar Park Camp. Here food improved considerably. Also, some pay was issued to those who worked, about 25 cents a day, the equivalent of about 4d, so that a little extra food, especially bananas and pineapples, could be bought. It was often possible to steal food from the Japanese, and other items that were sold to the Chinese. An equally comic and tragic incident occurred at this time when a party of men acquired some flour they'd bought from the docks. The treasure was then made into some fine-looking Norfolk dumplings but the smiles of anticipation dropped when they turned out hard as bricks – the supposed flour was in fact plaster of Paris.

During this period there were practically no medical supplies, but the health of the battalion remained good. The Japanese treatment of their prisoners was always harsh. A Japanese store was raided one night by a party of Malays and some were killed in the ensuing fight. Their heads were put up in about eight prominent places such as the railway station as a warning to others.

During the summer the Japanese issued paper declarations to every man upon which he was expected to sign his name and agree not to escape. At first the men refused so the prisoners were ordered to Selerang Barracks where the Australians were held. Prisoners held in the southern area of Singapore had to travel the farthest, approximately two miles, over steep hills to Selerang. The two roads to Selerang were soon covered with troops from 18 and 11 Divisions, many of them in teams pushing trailers, handcarts and even wheelbarrows, piled dangerously high with rations, cooking stoves, fuel, utensils and bedding.

Lads who were suffering from beri-beri or who were recovering amputees struggled along on crutches and for so many reasons men, who could only just manage to walk, remained determined to get there – somehow. Some men took over four hours to cover just one mile. Spirits were kept high; after struggling to the top of a hill, men would simply laugh and joke and cries like 'Off to Brighton for the weekend!' were heard. All these men were crammed into a barracks built for just one battalion of British infantry. After a couple of days all supplies, including those for medical needs, were cut. Diphtheria and dysentery rapidly became epidemic and nobody was allowed to be removed to hospital. One poor man had to be operated on for appendicitis. In these dire conditions the British commander ordered all ranks to sign the declaration saying of course, that as it was done under duress, it had no meaning. The men having pacified their captors were then allowed to trek back to their original camps.

The senior British and Australian commanders were made to witness the shooting of two British and two Australian soldiers who had previously attempted to escape. Subsequently the Japanese general responsible was himself sentenced to be shot, and the sentence was carried out in the same place. Many Eurasians and Chinese gave great help to the battalion with gifts of food, medical supplies, musical instruments and later wireless parts. The Japanese camp commander in Farrar Park at this time was a Sergeant Asouki, who also did a great deal to help.

A railway was ordered by Japanese high command to support their troops deep into Burma and Siam (Thailand). It was to be built in 18 months; however, this order was countermanded and construction was to be completed in a year – which it was, but at a horrific cost in life. At this point, to recount the experiences of all three battalions as bodies of the Royal Norfolk Regiment becomes difficult because men from all battalions in captivity made up the railway work parties which were constantly demanded. Latterly even very sick men were sent from Singapore up country to work during 'Speedo' (the building of the railway). Notably F and H forces, which consisted of large numbers of Norfolk men, experienced tremendous hardships and casualties. Toward the end of June, the camp at Changi began to split up. The first party to go was from 6 Royal Norfolk, under the command of Captain Goddard, its destination Siam, where it was to assist in building a railway. At the time of its departure, it was rather envied by those they left behind. None yet knew what the railway was to cost in human life and suffering.

In September 1942, 5 Royal Norfolk was removed a mile distant to Serangoon Road where a camp was being rebuilt. The accommodation consisted of palm leaf huts. The men had to sleep in very crowded conditions on wooden platforms in two tiers, which very soon became full of bedbugs. This camp was 2,000 strong and commanded by a Japanese officer. The guards were changed from fighting soldiers to POW guards who were Koreans with Japanese NCOs – all of whom were 'a very bad lot'. Lieutenant-Colonel Eric Prattley was British camp commander. One evening he was beaten over the back with a rifle by a drunken Japanese lance-corporal.

In September the officers, at last, got a little pay, about $10 a month. The British commander laid down certain contributions toward messing and hospital upkeep. A good concert party and band were now forming. Also a few selected canteen suppliers were allowed into camp once a week. Eventually electric light and shower baths were erected.

In October a Red Cross ship was allowed in, with a very welcome issue of clothes, medical stores, food and cigarettes. It was also in October that the move to Thailand was accelerated. Further parties were ordered there, including a large one from 4 Royal Norfolk under Lieutenant-Colonel Knights, while others were sent off to Burma, Indo-China, Formosa (now Taiwan), the Philippines and the Japanese mainland. It was impossible to keep a check on all men in the three battalions as they became split up, a factor that caused many regrets among both officers and men.

After Christmas, 5 Royal Norfolk moved back to Changi and were accommodated in a barrack room block in Roberts Barracks. There was now much more room after the working groups had been despatched. Some really good concerts and plays were performed in Changi. During this period of captivity the battalion medical officer was Captain Chopping RAMC, who apart from being a very good doctor, was also a wireless expert, and had made a very fine compact wireless set so there was no lack of news from the outside world. As 1943 progressed more men were shunted up to Siam for work on the railway; only the sick, the wounded and those attending to them remained in Singapore.

On 18 March 1943, a party of 550 other ranks (400 5 Royal Norfolk and 150 6 Royal Norfolk) and five officers, namely Major Crane, Captain Hamond, Captain Self and Lieutenants Curtis and Batterby, were ordered to Siam to work on the railway between Bangkok and Rangoon. The party was taken by MT to Singapore and then put into steel goods wagons, twenty-five men plus kit to a wagon. The railway was a metre gauge, so the overcrowding and heat turned the wagon into ovens. The journey took five days; the men ate two meals a day, chiefly rice. By the time the men arrived at Non Pradok (the southern starting point of the Burma Railway) they were completely exhausted.

The Japanese issued five unripe bananas per man and a nearby POW camp was able to provide tea. The party was moved into another train of open trucks, fifty men were put in each truck and were wedged in like sardines. The track was very uneven and the train proceeded very slowly at 5–10 miles per hour, a speed that was not enough to provide any cooling draught. It was blazing hot, which was not made any better when the train stopped for about an hour and a half at noon while the guards went and had a meal. No prisoners were allowed to leave the trucks. The party arrived at Kanchanaburi and were marched one mile and ordered into the jungle. This had to be cleared, and everyone bivouacked in the open. Just before dark rations were delivered which were much better than had ever been issued before: rice, vegetables, pork and eggs.

The great difficulty was cooking, as the Japanese would not allow any cooking pots to be taken from Singapore, and only a few were issued. The next day working parties had to be found to work on the railway. Troops were allowed to bathe in the river about a mile away. In the evenings it rained and everyone got soaking wet. It was not until after eight days that some tents and tarpaulins were issued. In the meantime, further parties from Singapore arrived daily until there were about 5,000 troops in the area.

About 3 April 1943, the party was ordered to move on again. It was transported by the trolleys that carried the rails for laying and were drawn by diesel rail cars that could also be converted for road use. About fifty men were left behind suffering from malaria and dysentery, and these were moved to the base hospital nearby, run by a British medical officer and staff.

This journey was not too bad as the trucks went faster and the day was cooler. In the evening the party was detrained at Wompo, which was then the railhead, further progress being stopped by a viaduct that had to be quarried out of a cliff face. Five tents, each about fourteen feet by eighteen feet, were issued and a camp was made on the riverbank. The following day work started from daylight and carried on until dark. One party had to work for twenty-four hours on end. The guards here were Koreans. Beatings by guards and Japanese railway engineers were frequent. No pay had been issued since leaving Singapore until the last evening in this camp. The pay issued in Singapore was no use in Siam as it took three months to exchange.

On about 14 April the party had to march about ten miles to Tarso. About fifty men were left behind for evacuation to base hospital. No transport of any sort was provided, and everything had to be carried; this was a very hard march. The stay in Tarso was only for a few days; again, men were simply put into a jungle clearing without cover. On around 17 April the party started to be moved by MT in three lifts, one each day, to Takanun. In this, the party was very lucky because every subsequent party had to march about ninety miles. On arrival at Takanun, tents were issued on a scale of one per twenty-five men. All ranks were made to work on the railway and on a Japanese camp. No one was allowed to build a cookhouse or dig latrines. The food was very bad, practically rice only. The camp was situated on the riverbank with the trace of the railway on the other side. The surrounding jungle was of very dense, prickly bamboo and practically impenetrable. More parties started to arrive and pass through the camp daily. Meanwhile the hard work, exposure, lack of proper food and medical supplies began to take its toll.

The two medical officers with the party, Captains Donaldson and Petrovski RAMC, did wonderful work with what little medicine they had. When the monsoon broke at the end of May, conditions became terrible as the tents were made of poor-quality material and not only did they fail to keep the wet out but became completely rotten after about a month. Cholera hit the camp causing a great many deaths. Not for some time did the Japanese allow the camp to build any hospital huts to cope with the growing number of sick men with other ailments such as bronchitis, beri-beri, malaria, amœbic dysentery and diphtheria.

All the fit men of the camp were moved out to another camp about fifteen miles above Takanun and a mile above Tameroh Parh. Captain Robert Hamond was in command of the fit men of the Norfolk party, which consisted of two other officers, Lieutenants Bill Battersby and Ned Holiday, and 100 men. Captains Hamond and Self both had cholera (Hamond had also suffered tropical typhus) but managed successful recoveries, but after the move Hamond went down with scrotal beri-beri and could not walk for a time so Bill Battersby took over the running of the camp. In ten weeks 98 per cent of the men suffered from malaria. It was several days before the Japanese would allow any sick to be evacuated to base hospitals. This was a long journey by barge. Altogether during this period, the entire Norfolk party in captivity in the two camps suffered about 170 deaths.

We must also remember that the constant abuse and torture of prisoners took a horrific toll. The work was murderously hard. In places the railway ran through rocky hills, and here the track had to be levelled by hand with crowbars and sledgehammers. The tools provided for the work were primitive in the extreme, adding to the labours of the construction. So, the work went on and the 'Railway of Death' forged its way through the jungle – for every sleeper laid a British, Australian or Dutch life was taken (about 13,000). Add to this toll inestimable thousands of coolies from Malaya.

In effect, most of the Norfolks' role in completion of the railway was done by October 1943. Conditions improved and huts were built of bamboo and palm leaves. Parties were organised to work in the cemeteries, a stage was built for entertainment and the food improved considerably. During that winter it used to be very heartening to hear Allied bombers flying overhead at night on their way to and from objectives such as Bangkok and Saigon. Quite a good amount of food was available for Christmas, and all ranks had a riceless day; a pantomime was put on by fellow prisoners in the evening.

In February, all fit men were organised to go to Japan; no officers of 5 Royal Norfolk were allowed to so RSM Spencer was put in command of the men in this party. Early in March 1944, Takanun camp was evacuated and everyone was moved by rail down toward Bangkok to a base camp at Chunki. This was a large camp accommodating about 11,000 POWs. The place was very well organised although everything was improvised because the Japanese supplied nothing. There were tailors, bootmakers, a laundry, a theatre, a band, and good cookhouses and canteens. The hospital, although it had very little equipment and practically no medical supplies, did wonderful work. The cemetery at that time was looked after by senior officers and was well laid out in grass and tropical flowering shrubs.

Men evacuated sick from up-country working parties were, when discharged from hospital, taken into a combined Norfolk battalion commanded by Lieutenant-Colonel Alan Cubitt. In May working parties were sent up country again for railway maintenance and firewood cutting for the locomotives. During the monsoon, owing to washouts and bombing, the railway did not operate at all efficiently. In the summer, some American Red Cross parcels arrived and were distributed: about six men shared each parcel. Some other camps did not receive any because the Japanese guards took the contents of the Red Cross boxes for themselves. At the same time quite a good amount of medical supplies also came. These were very much needed and made the critical difference between life and death for many sick and injured men.

In November, 21 Liberators flew low over the camp. The sight of the bombers put all ranks in very good heart but when they dropped a few bombs on a bridge a few miles away, some fell on Tamakan camp and caused casualties. Tamakan was later evacuated and the nearby large girder bridge on concrete piles was soon destroyed by Allied bombing. Christmas 1944 was spent at Chunki in much the same style as the festivities of the previous year.

In February 1945, all officers were taken away from the men and put in Kanburi camp, about six miles distant. When the end finally came the battalions were scattered in small parties on different parts of the railway, some also on the Japanese mainland as forced labour down the salt mines. The parties on the railway were taken to either Bangkok or Petburi aerodromes and as they arrived were flown to Rangoon. Petburi had been built by prisoners of war but, ironically, the first planes to use it were Allied C-47 'Dakotas' sent by the Americans who were magnificent in evacuating the camp – even in monsoon.

The end itself is remembered as coming with dramatic suddenness. It had been heard over the secret wireless sets hidden around the camp that Germany had gone down to total defeat in May 1945, and all realised that now the Allies could concentrate all their energies on the war in the Far East, and by that token, the days of the Japanese were numbered. By early August there was a distinct change in the attitude from the Japanese prison guards and their former brutality changed to a cringing servility.

On 15 August all camps were buzzing with rumours, and it could hardly be believed that Japan had surrendered. But within a few days relieving officers and supplies from Burma were parachuted on to the camps bringing vivid reality to the fact of freedom. Gradually all prisoners were brought down to centres where they could be re-equipped with clothing and properly housed, preparatory to a return to England. The long months of captivity had at last come to an end.

The first 140 soldiers of the Royal Norfolk Regiment liberated from the hands of their Japanese captors landed at Southampton aboard RMS *Corfu* on 13 October 1945. Representatives of the Army Council and local civil authority greeted the men with the local British Legion parading their banners in a salute while WVS ladies and other civilian organisations gave the disembarking men cigarettes and chocolates. At the landing the regiment was represented by Brigadier Willian John O'Brien Daunt, CBE, Lieutenant-Colonel D. C. Buxton (late 6 Royal Norfolk) and Major J. G. Steward, OC Depot Party, Britannia Barracks, and messages of greeting expressing pride in the returning men were sent from General Peter Strickland, Colonel of the Regiment, and Councillor Edward Williamson, Lord Mayor of Norwich.

Colonel 'Flicker' Knights was later to record a fine tribute to the Royal Norfolk Regiment soldiers who survived captivity:

> In spite of all the Japanese could do, the brutality of the guards, frequent beatings, humiliation and torture suffered, the men of the 4th, 5th and 6th Battalions of The Royal Norfolk Regiment never forgot they were soldiers. It was their steady discipline, inflexible courage through adversity and native dignity that could withstand every provocation and comradeship unique to Norfolk men that brought them through their horrific ordeal.

The regimental history states: 'It was at a heavy cost in death and disablement, but their fine bearing in adversity will assuredly be remembered as one of the proudest glories of the Regiment.' Theirs was a triumph through death and disablement, may they never be forgotten and those who are left with their legacy remember the motto of Far East Prisoners of War (FEPOW) and 'keep going the spirit that kept them going'.

In the years after the war the men of B Company, 6 Royal Norfolk formed their own old comrades' association, which held regular meetings in Norwich, first at the Windsor Castle pub on Barrack Street, then The Leopard on Bull Close Road, The Artichoke on Magdalen Road and finally at The Magpie on Magpie Road until the group disbanded in 1990. Wherever they met a framed picture of the regimental badge and past and present uniforms were displayed. Beneath the picture was a verse by the artist Derek Page, and although written for the B Company Old Comrades, it could apply equally to all men of the Norfolk Territorial Battalions who fell at Singapore:

To the Men of The Royal Norfolk Regiment who fell at
The Battle of Malay

Under the burning tropic sky,
On lonely hill and plain,
Lie the lads that fell in their glory,
Never to rise again.

Lads from town and countryside
Stout Norfolk chaps and true,
The finest that ever the county gave,
They died for me and you.

Dear lads I knew steadfast and true,
You have not died in vain,
God keeps your memory ever green,
Until we meet again.

Chapter 6

7th Battalion

*Based on the accounts by Lieutenant-Colonel C. A. Debenham
TD (1939–42) and Lieutenant-Colonel Ian Freeland
DSO (1943–45)*

When the TA was ordered to double in size in the spring of 1939, 5 Royal Norfolk recruited up to double strength, with the intention of splitting into two battalions at some point at summer camp, 5 Royal Norfolk to take the eastern portion of the battalion area and 7 Royal Norfolk the western portion that covered the area of King's Lynn and district.

The new battalion began to take shape and attended the 163 TA Brigade summer camp at Falmer near Brighton for the second fortnight in July. Recruits had been joining almost up to the time they left, so for training purposes the battalion was divided into two halves: one of trained men under CO Lieutenant-Colonel C. A. Debenham and the other made up of recruits under Lieutenant-Colonel G. N. Scott-Chad.

The conditions at camp were far from ideal; it rained almost every day and many of the recruits had only one uniform, no issue greatcoat and no issue army boots – they had to provide their own. Not the most inspiring start but the men slogged on and on the return of the battalion to Norfolk the battalion area was separated geographically so that each battalion would be approximately the same strength. Parties were sent to the Massingham fuel dump and the Bircham, Feltwell, Marham and Raynham aerodromes for guard duties and to man anti-aircraft positions.

The order for embodiment was received at 1930 hrs on 1 September 1939 and 7 Royal Norfolk truly started its existence as a separate unit from that moment forward. Battalion Headquarters was at HQ Company at the Drill Hall, King's Lynn. Battalion strength was twenty-three officers and 621 ORs. Companies and officers were distributed as follows:

CO: Lt-Col C. A. Debenham
2ic: Maj Hon. J. J. Stourton MP
Adj: Capt C. B. K. Jickling
QM: Lt Qmr T. W. Reynolds, MM

Capts
E. W. O'F. Wilson
T. M. Wilkin
R. P Kershaw

Lts
P. L. Hawkins
E. V. M. Allen
A. D. Colley

2Lts
N. M. Thorneycroft
F. D. Gill
R. Brand
B. W. Rought-Rought
F. J. A. Smith
H. B. I. Bett
H. J. Walker
R. S. Gibson
J. H. Barrett
Hon. J. McDonnell
D. A. Jamieson
J. A. King
B. J. H. Wood

HQ and HQ Company: Drill Hall, King's Lynn
A and B companies: Swaffham
C and D companies: Dersingham

Soon after embodiment the battalion was joined by Second Lieutenant J. D. McKenzie, Lieutenant George Stephenson Hoghton and Lieutenant Norman Everard Monteuuis RAMC. A large number of medically unfits were drafted out and their places taken by 142 Militiamen from Norwich ITC.

HQ Company was initially billeted in King's Lynn, A and B companies at Swaffham and C and D companies at Dersingham. On 6 September a detachment under Captain Kershaw was sent over to the Cranwich Internment Camp and as there were no internees this camp became an invaluable training ground for the battalion.

During September and October complete companies were moved to the aerodromes for guard duties. Several warrant officers and NCOs who could not really be spared were also sent to the depot and No. 11 Internment Camp at Brandon.

On 1 November 1939 the battalion entrained for Aldershot and was accommodated in Talavera Barracks. The move away from the East Anglian Division was not received well but the men soon rallied when upon arrival the battalion took over a complete complement of carriers. Only to have them taken away after just a week and the battalion's role changed to 'Infantry Battalion Trained in Engineering Duties' – more or less a revival of the divisional pioneer battalions of the First World War.

The combination of the move away from Norfolk, the removal of the carriers and the change in role of the battalion were very unpopular and morale suffered. While at Aldershot the battalion received much help from the Royal Engineers by way of courses, lectures, demonstrations and digging exercises, which they put into practice in a twenty-four-hour digging exercise as pioneer battalion to 51 Highland Division.

At the end of November 7 Royal Norfolk received a draft of eighty-five reservists from the West Yorkshire Regiment and thirty-five reservists from Norwich Infantry Training Centre (ITC). These two drafts provided several much-needed NCOs. It was learned soon afterwards that the battalion would be proceeding overseas in the New Year. The battalion went through its weapons training course in December in dreadful weather and then began embarkation and

Christmas leave that was somewhat marred by the men receiving a violent form of reaction to the TAB inoculations they were being given and an outbreak of influenza.

On 30 December 1939 an advance part of the battalion was sent to Southampton to prepare for embarkation. On 3 January Brigadier C. A. Howard. DSO, the honorary colonel of the battalion, inspected the men and wished them good fortune in the coming months. The battalion motor transport then proceeded to Southampton on 7 January and the remainder of the battalion followed on 13 January.

An epidemic of German measles broke out at the time of sailing, which caused great consternation when the battalion arrived at Cherbourg and sick men were evacuated at every stopping place. The journey had been bitterly cold but, thankfully, uneventful and the battalion arrived at the concentration area of Saint-Rémy-du-Plain (Sarthe) on 15 January 1940 and would remain there in billets until 19 January.

The weather had not improved when four days later the battalion entrained for another bitterly cold and uncomfortable journey through ice and snow to Boisleux, about five miles from Arras, and was conveyed to the billeting areas by RASC transport. Battalion Headquarters, HQ Company and A Company moved to Fontaine with C and B companies at Croisilles. The MT (under Captain Hoghton, Lieutenant Thornycroft and Second Lieutenant Smith) put up a sterling show, driving all the way from Cherbourg to Saint-Rémy and Fontaine in bad weather without mishap. Here the battalion guarded the I Corps ammunition railhead and dump at Ecouest and Mory. Recesses and gun pits were required here but progress was very slow because the ground was frozen solid. When the state of the road permitted, trips were arranged to visit the First World War battlefields of Arras and Vimy Ridge.

In early March the battalion marched to Rouex to be concentrated and prepared for an imminent move. Arriving there on 8 March, they were joined by reinforcements on 9 March and the battalion establishment lifted to four rifle companies. At this time war had broken out between Finland and Russia and some excitement was caused when the battalion learned it had been earmarked as a pioneer battalion to 5 Division in this campaign. But this was not to emerge. The battalion remained at Rieux and had its first serious period of training under the wing of CE (Chief Engineer) I Corps and made considerable progress. At this time the battalion was joined by the padre, Captain C. King (CF).

On 1 April 7 Royal Norfolk entrained for Metz to begin their tour of duty with the British Brigade (144 Infantry Brigade, 48 Division) on the Saar and were seen off as they departed by none other than General Sir John Dill. Upon arrival the battalion was billeted in the Quartier de Vallières Barracks. The medical officer in charge of sanitation informed the CO that he expected the battalion to clean up the billets and forward villages and improve their sanitation after they had got into a filthy state during the hard winter. Again, an unpopular order so the CO gave a sigh of relief when the following day the brigadier of 144 Infantry Brigade countermanded the order and saw the reconstruction of the Ligne de Contact or Forward Defensive Line as far more pressing, especially as many of the fire bays were not even bulletproof. The French sappers also staked their claim on 7 Royal Norfolk to wire and dig some of the Ligne d'Arret d'Armée, the line on which any forces breaking through the Maginot forts were to be held pending a counterattack.

On 3 April advance parties of companies took up their new positions: C Company under Captain Colley at Bizing and D Company under Major Wilson to Halstroff, abandoned villages immediately behind the Ligne de Contact where the reserve platoons of the forward infantry companies were billeted. C Company was prevented from reaching Bizing that night as the Germans were engaging one of the outposts with intense artillery fire but the company came through after the attack ended at dawn. C and D companies then set to building proper section posts and platoon and company headquarters and wiring them under supervision of Royal Engineers.

A Company under Second Lieutenant Gill moved up to Metzeresche in the main Maginot defences where everyone was struck by the fact that the main street was lined with middens on both sides. There was a complete lack of piped sanitation. Thus, A Company was employed cleaning up the village and erecting latrines. While cleaning up brigade headquarters at Monneren even a dead cow was found in the midden outside the brigadier's billet. B Company under Captain Hawkins remained at Metz cleaning up the barracks, erecting blast walls and doing garrison fatigues. The Pioneer Battalion also remained there making latrines, latrine boxes, ablution benches and incinerators in the Ligne de Contact. B Company and HQ Company under Captain Wilkin and the remainder of the battalion were at Kédange.

At this juncture in the campaign there was much talk of a 'phoney war' as there appeared to be a gentleman's agreement not to shell each other's billets or MT on the roads but poor old C and D companies did not see much of that in evidence as they were constantly under artillery and mortar fire in the Grossenwald, Grindorf and Hartbusch woods and on Point 301. Fortunately, very few casualties were suffered. The sticky, waterlogged clay prevalent in the area made digging a slow and arduous job. In most areas they could not dig deeper than two and a half to three feet and had to erect sandbag breastworks. They worked by daylight to reinforce, build and rebuild defences; movement at night was prohibited because the Germans were keen on night patrols and raids in this area.

On the night of 14 April the 'general alarm' signal was received and remained in force for several days. To remain at such a heightened state of alert takes its toll and just as many thought, it was another night of alarm but no action. The enemy raided an infantry post in the Grossenwald Wood on the night of 16/17 April, killing six and capturing several men. D Company had to search the Lohwald Wood, in front of the forward defence localities, before work could commence the following morning. During the remainder of the month several attacks were suffered by the British troops occupying this sector.

On 1 May 51 (Highland) Division took over a complete divisional front from the French, including the sector already held by 154 Brigade. This included the area already occupied by the battalion; however, the divisional commander found himself short of two platoons for front-line duty. The following day, two platoons took over posts in the Ligne de Contact, which meant much borrowing of extra Bren guns, AT rifles and equipment. Training in the use of the Mills bomb also had to be done, as it was not on the war establishment of an infantry pioneer battalion.

On 2 May a platoon of C Company moved to Dalstein under Second Lieutenant Jim Walker and took over the international post outpost on the right flank of the division in the Bois de Filstroff and had an uneventful tour of duty until 7 May, when he was relieved by 13 Platoon, D Company, under Second Lieutenant J. H. King. The post was held by three British sections and one larger French detachment and was under command of a French officer. From 11 to 13 May there was much enemy activity and patrolling and counter-patrolling by 13 Platoon.

Private Arthur Gathergood (21), the only son of Albert and Mabel Gathergood of Tilney St Lawrence, was killed by enemy fire on 12 May 1940, making him the first fatality of 7 Royal Norfolk during the Second World War, and two others were wounded. On 13 May the enemy put down a heavy concentration of fire on the post, scoring direct hits on three dugouts, killing four and wounding four, at the same time attacking and capturing a neighbouring post from the French, who retook it the same day. During the night of 13/14 May, 7 Platoon under Second Lieutenant McKenzie took over and had a very lively tour with considerable artillery fire and enemy patrolling all round this very isolated post.

Meanwhile, on 5 May Battalion HQ and HQ Company were moved back to Metz. On 10 May the Luftwaffe bombed Metz aerodrome and several other targets in the sector. It was now very clear the war on the Western Front had begun in earnest. Hitler had unleashed the blitzkrieg. Between 3 and 11 May the forward platoons were engaged in a few patrols and counter-patrol actions and suffered periods of intense artillery fire but, as yet, no direct action.

13 Platoon, D Company, under Second Lieutenant Bett occupied the other front-line post situated in the Bois de Grossenwald on the left of the divisional front. They were relieved by Second Lieutenant McDonnell's platoon from C Company on 7 May. This platoon exchanged small-arms fire with a German patrol and came under shell fire that wounded two men, followed by a determined attack. The attack was successfully repulsed. They were relieved on 12 May by Sergeant William Bunkle's C Company platoon, temporarily commanded by Second Lieutenant Wood. For their brave actions Second Lieutenant Wood was mentioned

in despatches and Sergeant William Bunkle of C Company was awarded the Military Medal.

The main attack came at first light on 13 May when the enemy bombarded the entire front with artillery and mortars, destroying the forward posts. The majority of the battalion (less D Company) took over a sector of the Ligne de Recueil, the third line of outpost defences, in the Saint-François-Lacroix area from 6 Royal Scots Fusiliers. There would be yet more borrowing of Brens, AT guns and small arms along with hasty acquisition of signalling equipment before the battalion could function effectively in these positions.

Lieutenant-Colonel Debenham pointed out in his account of 7 Royal Norfolk: 'This shortage of weapons and signallers and complete lack of carriers and mortars really made a pioneer battalion unfit to fight as an Infantry battalion.' It was fortunate, in this instance, they were not to see action and were withdrawn to Kédange after the Ligne de Contact was evacuated.

On the evening of 20 May all British troops forward of the Maginot Line were withdrawn and moved by RASC transport to Jouaville, west of the Moselle River. The whole of 51 Division was now in reserve, and to the north the enemy had broken through the Allied lines and the BEF was beginning a fighting retreat to the Channel ports and ultimately Dunkirk. On 22 May the battalion suffered a great loss as RSM Swingler was evacuated sick; he was lucky to get home. CSM Jolly was then promoted to RSM. On 24 May the battalion undertook a night march of fifteen miles to Mars-la-Tour. Despite illuminating flares being dropped by the Luftwaffe searching for troop movements the battalion was not spotted and thus not attacked. They arrived at their destination severely fatigued, after little or no sleep over the previous four or five days.

Early on 25 May the battalion entrained for Rouen. The journey passing through Troyse and Orléans took over 50 hours. Upon arrival the battalion marched to Infantry Base Depot No. 1 Rest Camp, to find it deserted and it was obvious those who had been in the camp had left it in a great hurry a short time before. During the morning contact was made with five other battalions of 51 Division, all of whom were wondering what was going on and why brigade and divisional headquarters had not arrived from the move yet.

51 Division was now the last British division in France, holding the line of the River Somme in the Abbeville area with French troops on the right flank. In the early hours of 29 May contact was made with 51 Division again and it received orders to embus on French buses at 0900 hrs, arriving at Clais in the Seine-Maritime department in Normandy about an hour later. B echelon had arrived the previous day after a long and arduous drive in convoy. It was obvious the enemy would soon turn his attentions from Dunkirk to the Somme. The front against the German onslaught here was a thin one. Troops were tired and sparse, there were no defence lines, they had no armoured support and little or no or cover in the air. The enemy attack was not a matter of if but when. And when it did come all concerned knew the battle would be a bloody one. A decision was made to split up 7 Royal Norfolk, attaching one company to each brigade in 51 Division. Their duty was to provide each Brigade HQ with local defence and undertake fieldwork defences and roadblocks where required. B Company and Battalion HQ went with Divisional HQ and provided AA protection with LMGs.

On 30/31 May Battalion Headquarters and HQ Company under Captain Wilkin were at Clais, then moved to Harcelaines over 1–5 June. On 6 June they were at Guerville and Canehan on 7 June; on 8 June at Saint-Germaine after a very long march as bridges had been blown prematurely. On 10 June orders were received at breakfast to get out quickly as enemy tanks had broken through on the right of the division and then move to Saint-Denis.

A Company under Captain Allen was attached to 154 Brigade on 30 May less 8 Platoon who were attached to 8 Argyll & Sutherland Highlanders at Escarbotin. On 31 May 8 Platoon were sent to Saint-Blimont and 9 Platoon attached to 7 Argyll & Sutherland Highlanders at Quesnoy working on the banks of the Somme canal.

By 3 June the Dunkirk evacuation was over and German forces freed up to finish the conquest of France. On this day 51 Division with French armour and artillery mounted an attack on Abbeville to retake the town and push back the bridgehead the enemy had gained across the Somme. The attack was unsuccessful and several men from C Company lost their lives.

In the early hours of 5 June, the enemy was probing 8 Argyll & Sutherland Highlanders. Corporal Grimes's section of 8 Platoon was given a roadblock to piquet; the remainder of the platoon under Second Lieutenant Townsend being attached to D Company, 8 Argyll & Sutherland Highlanders, had withdrawn to a position east of Saint-Blimont. At about 1400 hrs a withdrawal was made to an orchard in Belloy where they were subjected to intermittent mortar fire and attacks by mobile troops. On the morning of 6 June, a position was taken up in the grounds of the château where many attacks by a motorcycle unit, supported by heavy mortar fire, were repulsed. At approximately 1800 hrs on 7 June D Company, 8 Argyll & Sutherland Highlanders was forced to surrender owing to shortage of ammunition and food, having been cut off for twenty-four hours. The roadblock piquet eventually rejoined company headquarters.

Also, in the early hours of 5 June 9 Platoon under PSM Parker with A Company, 7 Argyll & Sutherland Highlanders were ordered back in defence of Battalion HQ at Franleu but finding the headquarters surrounded took up positions in an orchard east of the village where several attacks supported by mortar fire were beaten off during 6 June. By the evening, however, they had run out of ammunition, food and water and OC A Company, 7 Argyll & Sutherland Highlanders had no other option than to surrender. That said, a small party of 9 Platoon that had become detached fought on for some time longer.

Company HQ and 7 Platoon withdrew on 5 June to woods south of Dargnies and on 6 June what remained of the company moved to Melleville in the morning and to Millebosc later in the defence of 154 Brigade HQ. On 8 June brigade moved again to Tourville and on the night of 9/10 June 154 Brigade was sent back to Line Fécamp–Bolbec to cover the embarkation of the division at Le Havre. Unfortunately A Company was missed off the operation orders to rejoin the battalion at Saint-Denis on 10 June. 154 Brigade made it home with A Company left to another fate.

B Company under Captain Hawkins, less one platoon, was sent to Harcelaine. The one detached platoon under Second Lieutenant Barrett was sent to Martainville in defence of advanced divisional headquarters for an attack on Abbeville. The Martainville platoon returned to Harcelaine on 5 June in high spirits claiming to have shot down an enemy dive-bomber. On 6 June B Company proceeded to Guerville less Lieutenant Barrett's platoon who were sent to defend Divisional HQ at La Grande Vallée and Second Lieutenant Rought-Rought's platoon joined a mixed force in defence of a bridgehead at Beauchamp. On 7 June B Company moved to Le Coudray and on 8 June to La Chausse. On 9 June Lieutenant Rought-Rought's platoon moved again to cover a crossroads at Totes and the rest of the battalion moved to Orvilliers.

C Company under Captain Colley was attached to 152 Brigade at Saint-Maxent on 4 June where 10 and 11 platoons took part in the attack on Abbeville and suffered several casualties. On 5 June they moved to Biencourt where they also claimed to have shot down an enemy aircraft with LMG fire. On 7 June the company moved to Sept-Meule in the Fort d'Eu. On 8 June they were in Criel-sur-Mer to cover the withdrawal of 6 Royal Scots Fusiliers from Le Treport and dug positions for them at Balleville. On 9 June they headed to Saint-Denis.

D Company under Major Wilson was attached to 153 Brigade at Réalcamp and then moved through Vismes-au-Val and Tours-en-Vimeu, arriving at Toeufles on 4 June. On 5 June D Company took part in the defence of Toeufles supported by artillery and later moved to Boillancourt. On 6 June they moved to Millebosc and Saint-Nicholas on 8 June and on 9 June were at the woods at Acheux and later to Tourville.

B echelon under Captain Hoghton MTO and Lieutenant Quartermaster Reynolds were at Foresters Hut in Forêt D'Eu. After a move south on 6 June they then moved to Bethincourt on 7 June, Caneham and Siant-Germaine on 8 June. On 10 June they were ordered to Melleville but almost ran into enemy tanks on the way so joined the battalion at Saint-Denis.

The position on 10 June was A and C companies were again under command with B Company (less the platoon at Totes) guarding Divisional HQ in the next village with D Company still attached to 153 Brigade.

Two naval officers had been spotted at Divisional HQ and hopes were raised of embarkation at Le Havre but these were dashed by the MTO's report of enemy tanks on the coast.

In a comment that was deleted from the original text of the regimental history one officer remarked: 'Actually, this embarkation was quite on the cards a few days earlier and would probably have been carried out if it had not meant the last British division on the continent abandoning our allies – a quite impossible decision.'

The only embarkation point left for 51 Division now was Saint-Valery-en-Caux. At about 1800 hrs, orders were received to destroy all kit not essential for fighting. The MT officer and quartermaster were choked to see their stores and spares that they had taken such trouble to maintain and acquire disappearing into the fast-flowing stream where they were dumped. All battalion MT was to be released for troop-carrying and to proceed to Saint-Riquier at dusk. This left just fifty men to be carried on RASC vehicles and together they set out via the choked roads around Saint-Valery-en-Caux, reaching Saint-Riquier at 0300 hrs on 11 June. No trace of Divisional HQ could be found and a horde of demoralised and mostly unarmed French troops attached themselves to the battalion.

Come the dawn artillery and small-arms fire were heard at close range but the enemy was not located. At about 0500 hrs the CO was informed Divisional HQ had settled at Cailleville instead of Saint-Riquier and an immediate move was made there. The B Company platoon from Totes rejoined the battalion here as did Captain Thornycroft, 2ic D Company, along with his company advance party; the rest of D Company had not reached their RV the previous night and were 'lost to the battalion'.

In fact, D Company had been unable to reach their target and Major Wilson placed himself under the orders of the nearby 1 Gordon Highlanders and was given a line to hold northwest of Nivelle. On the afternoon of 11 June, they suffered a heavy attack when enemy tanks had passed straight through their position, inflicting about thirty casualties. On the night of 10/11 June D Company was ordered to a point two miles west of Cagny but being unable to reach there, Major Wilson placed himself under orders of 1 Gordon Highlanders and was given a line to hold on the right of this battalion at Nivelle with 2 Seaforth Highlanders on their right. On the afternoon of 11 June, the company was heavily attacked by some twenty enemy tanks which passed straight through their positions inflicting about thirty casualties. D Company then reformed as an amalgamate unit with the survivors of B Company of 1 Gordons in a disused quarry and acquitted themselves gallantly holding out against an infantry attack at 0330 hrs on 12 June. The wounded were evacuated, and rations were brought up. In the evening enemy infantry commenced an attack on 1 Gordon Highlanders supported by machine guns and mortar fire but meeting with effective semi-automatic fire, they did not press it but kept up the mortaring and machine-gun fire through the night. At 0600 hrs orders were received to retire with Major Wilson covering the retirement with rifle fire from the upper window of a cottage. However, what remained of the company soon encountered enemy tanks and were captured.

Back to the main body of 7 Royal Norfolk and a reconnaissance was made for a position south of Nivelle and Cailleville but on return to Divisional HQ the CO was ordered to reconnoitre a 'Corunna Line' some two miles outside Saint-Valery with both flanks on the cliffs to cover the embarkation of the division. The prospects of any embarkation looked very black.

At 1400 hrs Divisional HQ moved to Saint-Valery, at the same time the CO and second-in-command set out on reconnaissance. At this time the enemy commenced bombing and shelling Saint-Valery and the battalion was moved to the outskirts of the town; as the reconnaissance party left the cliffs small-arms fire was heard in the vicinity and a few moments later about fifteen enemy tanks appeared on the cliffs. The CO set up a roadblock formed by a Bofors gun and a detachment to hold the enemy back and as soon as other troops arrived, he handed over and set off in search of Divisional HQ, eventually contacting the GOC, Major-General Victor Fortune, at Cailleville. En route he had come across a D Company CSM at Company HQ who informed him of their fate.

In the CO's absence Captain Jickling, the adjutant, sent A, B, C and HQ companies to their previously allotted area along the 'Corunna Line' but during the evening the fighting became confused; the men bravely held their positions and most of the division passed safely through.

During the night a large part of 51 Division and thousands of French troops in tow concentrated in Saint-Valery for evacuation. 7 Royal Norfolk was given orders to take up position for embarkation at 2345 hrs. A, B and HQ companies were assembled in a sunken road outside the railway station. C Company had lost touch with the rest of the battalion and would spend the night on the beach. There was no further firing on the town although many houses were still burning because of an earlier shelling.

All guns and vehicles were then rendered useless in readiness, but no boats arrived. At 0200 on 12 June the divisional commander ordered the battered remnants of 51 Division, including the battalion, to lie up in a wood about a mile and a half outside the town while he went to consult with French command about the possibilities of an embarkation that night, or the alternative of surrendering.

7 Royal Norfolk was ordered to defend Divisional HQ from the rear, but the situation was hopeless with practically no guns, no ammunition and no food. The white flag had gone up in surrounding villages and there was no other option than to surrender, which the battalion did at 1030 hours on 12 June.

Earlier that day, as dawn was breaking at about 0230 hrs on 12 June Captain Anthony Colley was convinced the navy were lying off the coast and, not having received any orders, showed great initiative and split C Company into parties of about eighteen, with the idea of trying to reach the naval ships by means of a few fishing boats moored in the river. After a hazardous walk parties led by Captain Colley and Second Lieutenant Jim Walker managed to secure boats but not finding any oars they improvised with spades and the butts of rifles. The progress of Captain Colley's boat was hampered because its mast would not pass under a low swing-bridge at the mouth of the harbour and was forced to return to the beach where Captain Colley was killed trying to get further parties off at Veules-les-Roses.

Second Lieutenant Walker and his crew passed under the bridge in their boat and assisted by the tide, made for the open sea. As they passed the end of the jetty they were hit by shell fire. Everyone escaped injury but the Germans machine-gunned the boat and hit it, but again, no one was hurt. By a stroke of luck, a heavy downpour obscured visibility and they got away and were eventually picked up by the destroyer HMS *Harvester* at Veules-les-Roses about one and a half miles to the north of Saint-Valery.

Jim and his crew landed at Southampton the following day. Out of the entire 7 Royal Norfolk just twenty-nine other ranks and one officer returned and for his resourcefulness and the achievement of this remarkable escape Jim Walker was mentioned in despatches.

For those left in France, after capture, men of the battalion and the division were marched over fifteen to twenty-five miles each day on pitiful rations. It took a fortnight to cover the 220 miles to Scheldt, where they were loaded into barges bound for prison camps in Germany. Initially, although the food was scant and poor quality, the men were treated reasonably by their captors. Later in the war many men of the battalion were shipped to so-called 'reprisal' camps in Poland where their treatment could, at best, be described as 'harsh and rigorous'.

The regimental history records:

> The campaign had been a tragic experience for the battalion. Newly raised and only partly trained, it had, by necessity, been thrown into a desperately hard battle for which it was not fitted, and its first experience of fighting had been one of the most disastrous campaigns of the war. Yet it acquitted itself beyond all expectation.

This was not to be the last we hear of 7 Royal Norfolk in the Second World War. The following account is based on the account compiled by Lieutenant-Colonel Ian Freeland, DSO, which was originally published in book form and presented to members of his old battalion in 1946.

Initially there was confusion. The few returned members of the battalion were sent from Southampton to Bordon and after five days' sorting out the small party moved to Paignton, Devon, then Sheffield and Leeds, for a day, then back to Sheffield where they were attached to 1/6 Battalion, South Staffordshire Regiment. Then orders came for the men to proceed to Dumfries where the battalion was said to be reforming. On arrival on 1 July, they were told nobody knew anything about a 7 Battalion, Royal Norfolk Regiment. Second Lieutenant Walker reported to HQ 51 Brigade and obtained permission to return the party to their depot at Norwich. Upon the welcome arrival at their home turf the reformation of 7 Royal Norfolk began.

On 8 July the cadre of eighteen officers and 150 other ranks arrived at Colwick Park, Nottingham, where the battalion was to be assembled and undergo initial training. The senior command structure was:

CO: Lt-Col. F. W. Clowes
2ic: Maj L. A. Villiers
Adj: Capt J. K. Forte
QM: Capt W. Carter
RSM: WOI Jewson
RQMS: WOII Kerridge

Although there was one final glitch – Colwick Park was found insanitary, so they promptly moved to Wollaton Park where the first intake arrived direct from civilian life on 17 July and was followed at fortnightly intervals by similar intakes of about 200 men. By 26 July the new battalion was up to full strength of 1,000 men but with almost every man coming direct from civvy street and supplied with little or no equipment until October, the battalion training officers and NCOs certainly had their work cut out for them.

In October the battalion moved to Grimsby, forming part of 205 Infantry Brigade of the Lincolnshire Division undertaking its operational duties guarding Grimsby Docks. The battalion remained in Lincolnshire throughout 1941 but, again, training was hampered with the loss of troops for drafts overseas and to operational commitments. During August 1941 the battalion constructed defences at Hemswell aerodrome and undertook the training of RAF ground defence personnel, many of whom were Polish. Language may have been a problem at times but great patience and teaching by 'see and do' led to good training and the formation of many friendships. In the October the cohesion of the new battalion was proved again when it took part in its first full-scale exercise in the North of England using requisitioned transport.

In December 1941 the battalion made a welcome return to Norfolk where it was given coastal defence duties with Battalion Headquarters situated, in turn, at North Walsham, Stalham, Happisburgh and Sheringham where they were visited by General Peter Strickland, the Colonel of the Regiment.

Early on the morning of 18 December 1941, when the Battalion HQ was at Happisburgh, a low-flying German aircraft dropped two bombs which hit the HQ, killing Privates Don Ramsey and George Faux, both members of the mess staff and slightly injuring the CO. The other officers had not yet assembled for breakfast, otherwise casualties would have been far higher.

The opening months of 1942 found the battalion badly weakened through drafting, which necessitated the establishment of a recruit company training ground and assault course at Bacton Holiday Camp under Major Peter Barclay, MC. Shortly after its formation Major Barclay formed 76 Battle School at Holkham and Captain Walker took over the recruit company. In mid-July the battalion concentrated at the King's Lynn training area for battalion and brigade training exercises. Four of them, codenamed *Teaser*, *Prickles*, *Bender* and *Savage*, were carried out successfully, followed in early August by a combined exercise at Sheringham in which the cooperation of infantry with armoured fighting vehicles was practised. At this time Lieutenant-Colonel Clowes relinquished command on attending a course at Senior Staff College and was succeeded by Lieutenant-Colonel H. Long, MC.

The battalion next proceeded by train to Stranraer and crossed to Northern Ireland aboard the *Royal Daffodil* (the same vessel that had taken 2 Royal Norfolk over to France in 1940) for a six-month period of full-scale training at Drumilly Camp, Loughgall, north of Armagh, where they joined 176 Brigade of 59 Division. Training was reinvigorated and more rigorous, and here the battalion had its first real opportunity to train properly without any static operational commitment. The men were being readied for active service in the field and good liaison with supporting arms quickly grew, especially with 116 Field Regiment, Royal Artillery, which would prove of inestimable value in Normandy. Just before the battalion was due to leave Lieutenant-Colonel Long was posted to the Middle East and was succeeded by Lieutenant-Colonel D. M. Fitzgerald. RSM Jewson was also medically downgraded and CSM Saunders was promoted to RSM.

In March 1943 the battalion along with the rest of 59 Division moved to Kent to join XII Corps. Their role was to train as a 'follow-up' division in the wake of the initial Normandy landings. The battalion was at Hawkhurst, Rye and Winchelsea and under canvas at Northam. Here Lieutenant-Colonel Fitzgerald relinquished his command and was succeeded by Lieutenant-Colonel T. G. L. Charles. RSM Swingler rejoined the battalion having been evacuated sick from France after a term getting the 70 (Young Soldiers) Battalion into shape.

The period from March to July was spent in battalion and brigade training with plenty of field firing on the downs around Lewes. In October the battalion mobilised and took part in Operation *Harlequin*, a launching rehearsal to test the marshalling area and administrative organisation for the Normandy landings. Many men did not know right up to the last minute that *Harlequin* was not the real thing but an exercise and sighed a heavy sigh of disappointment and relief as the battalion reached the quay at Dover where they were told the exercise was over. After the exercise the battalion moved to Margate where training continued through the winter, culminating in the spring with much sleeping out in the lovely Kentish countryside.

In mid-April 1944 Lieutenant-Colonel Charles was appointed General Staff Officer 50 Division, one of the assault divisions, and Lieutenant-Colonel Ian Freeland took over command; he would remain with the battalion into Normandy. Over the next six weeks training was intense and the battalion was forged into a strong unit ready for its operational duties. In May 1944 the battalion was joined by seven Canadian loan (CANLOAN) officers, but sadly only two, Lieutenant D. J. Smith, whose father had served with the regiment, and Lieutenant A. F. Bushell, could be absorbed into the battalion; the rest became first reinforcements and eventually served with other units.

On 5 June 1944, while 176 Brigade was holding a rifle drill, large convoys passing close inshore and considerable air activity proclaimed the start of the Second Front and it came as no surprise when D-Day was announced the following day, 6 June 1944. On this same day, by pure coincidence, a divisional commemoration service was held at Canterbury Cathedral. Those sent to represent the battalion would never forget this deeply moving and poignant service. 59 Division was due to land on D+16; the men stood ready but at the eleventh hour the battalion lost its 2ic, Major D. L. A. Gibbs, after just a month, appointed to command 2 Royal Warwickshire on D+1.

RSM Swingler, the man described as 'a tower of strength', an ex-Coldstream Guardsman and the man very largely responsible for the high standard of discipline and bearing in the battalion, had contracted pneumonia on the final divisional exercise, and had to leave the battalion. Lieutenant-Colonel Freeland wrote of RSM Swingler, 'a great debt of gratitude is due to him for his magnificent work at an age when the physical effort must have been great' but the battalion had to move on to meet its new challenges. Major G. M. Allen was appointed the new second-in-command and RSM Valentine the new regimental sergeant-major.

Before departure a service of dedication attended by the entire battalion was held at Margate Church before the battalion moved to the marshalling areas. Training continued and all vehicles were waterproofed. The battalion was divided into four parties for the move to Normandy; Captain Walker was to lead the advance party and was given the task of reconnoitring the area where the battalion was to concentrate and lead them there after the landing was made. The marching party under the CO Lieutenant-Colonel Freeland was to cross by LSI (landing ship infantry) from Camp J.2 at Stanmere Park near Brighton. The advance and marching parties both departed from Newhaven. The vehicle party under Major G. M. Allen were to cross in LSTs (landing ship tank/transport) from Camp 51 to sail from Tilbury on 20 June. A residue party under Captain Gibson remained in Margate and set off when the high-priority formations and units had been landed.

The nominal roll of officers and warrant officers who proceeded to Normandy with 7 Royal Norfolk:

Battalion Headquarters
CO: Lt-Col I. H. Freeland
2ic: Maj G. M. Allen
Adj: Capt N. T. Hardy
QM: Capt W. Carter
RSM: WOI Valentine
RQMS: WOII Benton

HQ Company
OC: Capt. R S Gibson
SIGO: Lt E. H. T. Ridger
IO: Lt N. S. Marsh
MTO: Lt T. G. Duxbury
MO: Capt A. D. Payne RAMC
Padre: Rev. N. Carter
CSM: WOII Brown

A Company
Maj H. P. Durant
Capt W. A. Adderson
Lt B. C. Carroll
Lt W. E. Morris
Lt L. D. Paul
CSM: WOII Jay

B Company
Maj A. G. Ellis
Capt N. G. Pettefar
Lt P. A. McCunn
Lt R. J. Manton
Lt A. A. Hammond
CSM: WOII Roberts

C Company
Major F. J. A. Smith
Capt D. W. Glass
Lt D. J. Smith (CANLOAN)
Lt D. A. Hill
Lt E. T. Gibbons
CSM: WOII Saunders

D Company
Maj F. H. Crocker
Capt D. A. Jamieson
Lt G. T. Bartlett
Lt A. F. Bushell (CANLOAN)
Lt D. W. Hague
CSM: WOII Jones

Support Company
OC: Capt H. J. Walker
Mortar Platoon Capt A. M. Alexander
Carrier Platoon: Capt W. J. Smart/Lt P. W. Buckerfield
Anti-Tank Platoon: Capt W. A. Redfern/ Lt T. P. K. Oakley
Pioneer Platoon: Lt A. E. F. Searanke
CSM: WOII Fuller

The strong gales and stormy weather over the channel held up the crossing of 59 Division for six days. The men, poised and ready for action, were frustrated to the extreme by this delay but the welfare arrangements in the marshalling area were excellent, particularly in the marching party marshalling area near Brighton and the fine weather on land made the enforced stay quite pleasant. The battalion certainly got a good view of the new German 'flying bombs' or 'doodle-bugs'.

When they eventually set off, the advance party had a very trying voyage with many delays, and in the end only reached the concentration area in Normandy at the same time as the marching party. The latter embarked at Newhaven on 27 June and had an uneventful voyage but were disembarked by their landing craft at the wrong beach at Bernières-sur-Mer instead of Courselles. After a hot and tiring march with a short halt at Ranville, the marching party was picked up by troop-carrying vehicles and reached the concentration area at Le Manoir at 1900 hrs on 28 June. The vehicle party arrived the next day after a good voyage and waded ashore without losing a vehicle, demonstrating how thoroughly their drivers had waterproofed them. The vehicle party crossed without incident and landed near Le Hamel on 29 June. Wading ashore without loss or damage to a single vehicle, the party arrived at the concentration area at 1500 hrs on 30 June.

Le Manoir was an attractive village situated about seven miles northeast of Bayeaux. The battalion spent their first week here busy de-waterproofing vehicles and getting ready for battle. Some training was carried out and the local river afforded reasonable bathing. Battalion HQ was established in a nearby farmhouse occupied by the charming old housekeeper of the owner, a high court judge in Paris. This kindly old lady soon became the adopted mother of many officers and men.

The battalion was bivouacked in nearby open fields but it was 'welcomed' in France by cold and heavy rainfall for their first two days. They then dried out their battle dress over the days afterwards when the weather cleared. Colonel Charles paid a visit to his old battalion; his division (50 Division) had been fighting since the landings and he was able to assure the men that their training in England had been 'on absolutely the right lines' and they had nothing to fear. Visits were also made by officers and senior NCOs of 1 Royal Norfolk who were holding the extreme left of 3 Division near Biéville and on the west bank of the Orne. This meeting imparted many very useful tips.

By 1 July 21 Army Group was firmly established in the bridgehead, and the build-up programme was progressing satisfactorily, but the lodgement area was heavily congested and any attempts to drive southeast to encircle Caen from the west faced fierce opposition from enemy armour concentrated in this area. Caen was the main objective of 3 Division but the enemy had reacted strongly and was now in a well-organised defensive position north of Caen and astride the Orne. The early capture of Caen was essential to enable the successful development of future operations and therefore I Corps was given this task with 59 Division under command for its first battle with 3 Canadian Division on their right and British 3 Division on their left.

The battalion was still at Le Manoir when warning of the attack came. Their objective was the village of Epron, which lay astride the main road into Caen from Saint-Aubin-sur-Mer. The success of the battalion's mission was entirely dependent on the battalions in the first phase of the battle obtaining their objectives for 7 Royal Norfolk to pass between them. The battalion assembled just north of Anguerny on 2 July behind 3 Division. Desultory shelling here gave the men of the battalion their first experience of fire in anger. Reconnaissance carried out on 4 and 5 July were followed by orders on 6 July and every man of the battalion was briefed on a model made by the intelligence section laid out on the ground in front of them.

The order of attack was C Company (Major Smith) directing on the right, A Company (Major Durant) left, B Company (Captain Pettefar) following and 'mopping-up' any stubborn enemy pockets and D Company (Major Crocker) in reserve. The Carrier Platoon (Captain Smart), less two sections left guarding tactical Battalion HQ, was dismounted to provide protection for the left flank from a small copse east of Epron.

A heavy bomber attack at 2150 on 7 July by some 400 Lancasters on Caen heralded the opening of the battle for Epron and raised the morale and confidence of the men for the fight. British artillery was active, but the enemy was eerily quiet. Breakfast was brought up on Jeeps before first light and at 0620 hrs orders were received by wireless for the second phase of the battle to commence at 0730 hrs. It was therefore assumed that phase 1 had been successful. As soon as the companies crossed the start line, they came under shell fire. One early casualty was the CO's bodyguard, Lance-Corporal Don Dawson (24), a stalwart of the battalion and the 18 set radio was put out of action.

As the forward companies came into the open on the left of 1 Suffolk, heavy machine-gun fire raked over from the high ground west of Lebisey, instantly causing casualties, particularly in A Company, and caused the men to go to ground among the corn where the enemy mortars and artillery took their toll. Many acts of gallantry were displayed; Bren gunners stood up from the crops and fired from the hip at the enemy who were by then pouring fire from the hedged banks around and to the east of La Bijude. But being enfiladed from both flanks and without cover A and C companies did not stand a chance. Visibility had been reduced to about 300 yards by the results of the preliminary bombardment, so the tanks could neither see the enemy nor friendly forward troops from so far back.

In the smoke and haze C Company was misdirected on to La Bijude from which fire was coming. In A Company every officer and the CSM were all soon casualties; CSM Len Saunders of C Company was killed by a sniper. Here intensive fire of all kinds was brought down by the enemy, and it was a most unpleasant place to be, several casualties being suffered. After a lapse of 30 minutes and no news from the forward companies it was obvious that the main effort was in trouble. B Company was therefore launched on the C Company axis, helped by the tanks firing smoke to mask the enemy machine guns on the left flank. B Company soon came under heavy fire and sustained heavy casualties. Captain Pettefar with a small party managed to join up with the remnants of C Company under Major Smith and Lieutenant Gibbons on the southeastern side of La Bijude. Captain Pettefar sent back a written message with a runner to the CO stating the enemy still held La Bijude. Due to the destruction of the 18 set radios this was the only message to reach the commanding officer during the attack. This message confirmed the fear that the enemy and not 6 North Stafford held La Bijude. Until the arrival of this message at about 1045 hrs the situation was very confused and alarming rumours reached Battalion HQ from various sources.

In the process of clearing the enemy from the hedgerows near La Bijude, Major Smith, Captain Pettefar and Lieutenant Gibbons were all wounded. The remnants of their two companies, now without their leaders, withdrew to the defended area around Château de la Lande and the attack petered out. B Company waiting to do the mopping up suffered several casualties.

Lieutenant-Colonel Freeland appreciated that future attacks around the left flank would be futile and that the only hope of retrieving the situation lay in the early capture of La Bijude, so he ordered D Company and the tank squadron to assemble at the château area with the object of attacking La Bijude up the axis of the road.

At that moment the brigade commander Brigadier Fryer came forward and approved the plan for the attack by D Company on La Bijude supported by Major Cotter's Sherman tanks of the 13/18 Hussars. Meanwhile the remnants of A, D and C companies were being collected and reorganised in the château area by the 2ic who had come forward to assess the situation and collected fifty men, forming a composite company to be held in reserve.

The attack on La Bijude commenced and at 1400 hrs on 8 July. D Company closely supported by the tanks attacked with one platoon each side of the road. Considerable small-arms fire was encountered chiefly from hedgerows on the right and heavy mortaring fire continued throughout. Major Cotter's tank was 'brewed up' by a Panzerfaust almost at once but he continued to direct the fire of his tanks by walking from one to the other. It was hard fighting for an hour. Major Frederick Crocker who personally led D Company throughout the operation was exposed to heavy close-range sniper, machine-gun, mortar and artillery fire, but drove the enemy out and firmly established his company on the southern side of the village as anti-tank guns were brought forward.

C Company was fortunate to have battalion sniper Corporal Ted Barleycorn attached to them for this action. The leading troops of the company had been held up behind a bank by heavy fire from an enemy tank as Barleycorn managed to get into a firing position from which he was able to engage the vision slits of the tank and caused it to withdraw. Barleycorn then worked his way toward the enemy, and crossed the village covered by a Bren gun and took out a sniper who had been inflicting casualties. In fact, one of C Company was acting as observer and confirmed Barleycorn had killed at least seven enemy during the action despite Barleycorn himself being twice wounded.

This, however, was not without a toll of casualties that included Lieutenant Gilbert Bartlett (23) who went forward alone to silence a Spandau machine-gun post and destroyed the entire crew but was killed in the action. With support from the tanks, the village was taken and anti-tank guns brought forward but casualties sustained by D Company saw it reduced to two officers and sixty-five men – to hold their gains the composite company could not be considered a suitable attacking force. After communication with Brigade HQ, A Company, 7 South Stafford, was placed under command of 7 Royal Norfolk, and given two troops of tanks with the order to capture Epron by nightfall at all costs.

The brigade plan was for 7 South Stafford to attack the earthworks to the west of La Bijude, where the enemy was strongly entrenched, while 7 Royal Norfolk captured Epron. The two attacks were not to be coordinated. The battalion attack was planned astride the road with A Company, 7 South Stafford, supported by two troops of tanks on the left and D Company supported by one troop of tanks. Artillery and mortars were to stonk Auberge, a small farmstead on the rising ground south of Epron, which was D Company's objective, and to neutralise the right flank. The composite company was to remain in reserve.

At H-Hour, 2030 hrs, the tanks opened a devastating fire against the hedges and buildings in Epron. Major Crocker's D Company took the left-hand flank in the attack; he led from the front again despite being slightly wounded in the face. He remained in command until the objective was gained and D Company had been reorganised and he was then temporarily relieved by Major Ellis.

D Company's left flank in the attack on Epron was bravely defended by the Carrier Platoon. Carrier Corporal Philip Harley was conspicuous in his provision of covering fire and going out into the open fields on three occasions to bring in wounded men and weapons under heavy machine-gun, sniper and mortar fire. Later, when Carrier Platoon was held up in front of a small copse, Harley kept a cool head and moved his carrier to a close range under heavy fire to provide them with cover for them to advance and achieve their objective.

7 Royal Norfolk achieved their objective by 2200 hrs and they were soon joined by 7 South Staffordshire who only took slightly longer to take the right flank. By last light the battalion was firmly established and reorganised in Epron with anti-tank and medium machine guns in position against counterattack. Recce patrols in the darkness brought

back news that the enemy had withdrawn out of contact, leaving many of their dead behind.

Major Crocker was awarded a Military Cross and battalion sniper Corporal Barleycorn and Corporal Harley of Carriers would receive Military Medals. Lieutenant Gilbert Bartlett was posthumously mentioned in despatches.

The enemy had taken a hammering, but the action had also taken its toll among 7 Royal Norfolk. Stretcher-bearers had been magnificent enacting many 'long carries' to the regimental aid post but still three officers and thirty men had been killed and seven officers and 111 men wounded.

Next morning, as no counterattack developed, A Company advanced to Couvre-Chef and found it clear of enemy. The only excitement in the day occurred at Auberge where Major Ellis, Sergeant Wingrove and Lance-Sergeant Furr captured a sniper who had been troublesome and was hiding in a house. A very nasty moment occurred when a squadron of tanks supporting 3 Division on the left thought Auberge was still in enemy hands. Luckily no casualties were suffered in D Company despite many 75mm shells fired before the tanks realised their mistake. At 1500 hrs A Company reverted to 7 South Stafford. On the left the attack on Caen was developing, the enemy having withdrawn to the north of the town.

7 Royal Norfolk remained another 36 hours at Epron during which the battlefield was cleared up and a memorial service held for the dead. On 11 July the division moved back to Ryes near Arromanches to rest and reequip. To reconstitute the battalion, the following promotions were made:

OCs
A Company Maj W. A. Adderson
C Company Maj H. J. Walker
S Company Capt W. J. Smart

To captain
Duxbury
Ridger
Searanke

To CSM
Beattie
Brown (from HQ to B Coy)

The following joined the battalion (their companies noted in brackets):

Lt L. Dawson (B)
Lt F. C. Bell (CANLOAN)
Lt A. J. M. Maybank (C)
2/Lt D. H. Wood (C)
G. R. Holt (B)
P. G. O'Connell (B)
L. Williams (D)
D. W. Coleman (D)

On 14 July the whole of 59 Division passed to XXX Corps. 21 Army Group was now to deliver a series of southward thrusts to make progress toward Thury-Harcourt and maintain pressure on a broad front in order to keep the main German forces in the east and away from the intended breakout area at the base of the Cherbourg Peninsular. 59 Division was concentrated north of Fontenay-le-Pesnil and was ordered to capture the Noyers area on the road from Caen to Villers Bocage.

The Noyers area was strongly held and 49 Division, through which the division would attack, had experienced heavy fighting two weeks before when capturing Fonteney and Rauray. 176 Brigade was to be in reserve for this attack and concentrated at Audrieu, three miles northeast of Tilly on 14 July. After 36 hours the brigade moved forward to an assembly area southeast of recently captured Fontenay, and in the middle of the gun area.

There, 7 Royal Norfolk dug in among the guns in the cornfields and waited while the other two brigades attacked Noyers. At night the Luftwaffe came over regularly and bombed the guns. The battalion was well dispersed and dug in but was still fortunate not to sustain any casualties, though several vehicles were peppered by fragmentation bombs.

The enemy opposition at Noyers was so strong that the attack was only a limited success. On 17 July 59 Division was ordered to halt the attack and take up a defensive position on a wide front with all three brigades up. 176 Brigade was to take over from Vendes to opposite Noyers, with 7 Royal Norfolk being on the right and 6 North Stafford on the left.

On the night of 18/19 July the battalion relieved 7 Royal Warwickshire south of Tessel-Bretteville without opposition but at dawn stand-to an enemy patrol was engaged by D Company, during which Second Lieutenant Harry Rosco Williams (29), one of the young officers who had only just joined the battalion, was killed.

The ground 7 Royal Norfolk had to defend was typical Normandy bocage of small fields, high hedges and enclosed lanes, and therefore short fields of fire. Such ground makes for concealment and good patrolling, and an alert defence is essential to prevent infiltration and surprise attacks.

The battalion was disposed with D and C companies forward astride a crossroads and hamlet, B Company covering the right flank, which was echeloned back behind Vendes, and A Company and Carriers in reserve, the former having a counterattack role. Battalion Headquarters was dug in in an open field and the regimental aid post was set up in a large bomb crater.

Several successful patrols were carried out both day and night under the centralised direction of the 2ic and a comprehensive picture of the enemy positions was established. The opponents appeared to be 986 Grenadier Regiment. The most successful patrol was a daylight recce from C Company under Lance-Sergeant Clarke. Coming upon enemy positions suddenly in the thick country this patrol killed three enemy without loss to themselves and gained much accurate information.

The Mortar Platoon and Vickers guns carried out many harassing shoots, the former gaining much useful experience and the counter-mortar methods of the battalion were greatly improved during this time. The enemy paid most attention to the area held by 6 North Stafford and several casualties were suffered in 7 Royal Norfolk from artillery or mortar fire.

On 25 July the battalion was relieved and moved back into divisional reserve just north of Tessel-Bretteville. The battalion had put in a week of such excellent aggressive defiance that the divisional commander congratulated the battalion on good patrolling and domination of the enemy, adding it was very satisfactory to be able to hand over the area to another battalion with the enemy well under control.

Plans were now made for the destruction of 5 Panzer Division and 7th Germany Army, who were to be kept away from the American operations in the Cherbourg region. The task for 59 Division as part of XII Corps was to destroy the enemy covering Villiers Bocage and then exploit to the area of Thury-Harcourt. For their part 7 Royal Norfolk's actual tasks would consist of five counterattacks supported by 9 Royal Tank Regiment. When the necessary recces had been carried out and the plans formulated, both units got down to infantry and tank cooperation training. As a result, an excellent liaison was formed and both units were confident in each other, especially as they had been told to expect to fight the next battle together when the attack on Villers Bocage took place. While the battalion was in reserve plans for the breakout were being made. On 2 August 7 Royal Norfolk moved to an assembly area west of Vendes in readiness for the attack.

The task of 59 Division as part of XII Corps was to destroy the enemy covering Villers Bocage and then to exploit toward the Orne around Thury-Harcourt, forcing a crossing if possible. 50 Division was on the right and 53 Division on the left. VIII Corps was at the time thrusting south toward Caumont and Mont Pinçon. When XII Corps attack had made itself felt, First Canadian Army was then to attack Falaise from the north. The army group plan was therefore to pivot on First Canadian Army, which would attack south and east.

The 59 Division plan was for 197 Brigade to capture the high ground immediately north of Villers Bocage from the direction of Vendes. 177 Brigade was to hold the present line north of Noyers. 176 Brigade, initially in reserve, was then to pass through, capture Villers and exploit to the Orne.

The battle went according to plan and after some initial hard fighting 197 Brigade's attack went quickly. On 3 August, 176 Brigade passed through with the men of 7 Royal Norfolk riding on the Churchill tanks of their friends. 9 Royal Tank Regiment led the brigade through the northern outskirts of Villers Bocage which Royal Armoured Corps fire and RAF bombing had reduced to powder. By last light the battalion had seized high ground southeast of the town without opposition.

Here 107 Royal Armoured Corps took over, which necessitated some regrouping. There would be little sleep for the battalion that night for orders for the advance next day had to be given out. On 4 August the Churchills of 107 RAC took Major Ellis's B Company forward with Westminster Dragoons flail tanks in case of mines and one troop of AVREs (Armoured Vehicles Royal Engineers) led the brigade on the right route down to the Orne at Ouffières. It was a strange sensation to be advancing so far without opposition after the hemmed-in feeling of the bridgehead, and so it was no surprise when the advanced guard came under heavy fire.

On approaching the river the leading infantry and tanks met Spandau and mortar fire and two Churchills were hit by 88mm shells from the right and far bank. B Company proceeded to clear the near bank while the remainder of the battalion took up a firm base position around Ouffières. The ground was very close and the riverbanks so steep and in places wooded, that no view of the river could be gained except from the bank itself. The enemy realised this too and had turned a group of houses near the bank into a strongpoint and B Company had difficulty in trying to clear it without tank support. When the AVRE tanks were brought forward the entire enemy post was destroyed. B Company lost Lieutenants O'Connell and Hague and had two sergeants wounded. Major Ellis showed great qualities of leadership and with Lance-Corporal Smith, brought in the wounded Lieutenant O'Connell and two badly wounded men who were lying in an exposed position.

By last light no enemy remained on the near bank, but a close watch had to be kept on the right flank which was completely open. C Company was brought up on the left of B Company and D Company positioned behind C Company. A Company guarded the right flank. That evening a brigade O group was held and plans were made for crossing the Orne. The brigadier decided that the assault would be carried out on the night of 6/7 August. The night of 5/6 August was used for reconnaissance of possible crossing places and for resting the troops who had had little sleep for 48 hours.

Two patrols were sent out during the night of 5/6 August. A fighting patrol from A Company under Lieutenant Paul covered a reconnaissance by a Royal Engineers officer to find the most likely crossing place where the banks were not as steep as elsewhere. Farther upstream C Company provided a covering patrol for a Royal Engineers sergeant. This patrol was commanded by Major Walker, the company commander, whose task also included guiding Captain Jamieson, commanding D Company, on a reconnaissance of the approaches. D Company was to lead the battalion across.

Finding fordable places and a site for a class 40 bridge involved elaborate and difficult patrolling; the RE sergeant was unsuccessful in his recce and here Captain Jamieson came into prominence, for with his height of 6 feet 5 inches, he hung over the bank held by the ankles by Major Walker, and was unable to reach the surface of the stream, thus proving that the banks there were too steep for an assault crossing or bridge at that point.

Major Adderson commanding A Company was ordered to take out a patrol himself and find a fordable place using the early morning mist as cover. As the patrol reached the river the mist lifted, but in spite of this Major Adderson, leaving his patrol to cover him, took a man with him, and waded across the river in three foot of water in full view of the enemy; he then penetrated 150 yards from the water into enemy territory and was able to find evidence of a panzer division in a house. He then retuned without any noticeable reaction from the enemy.

Farther downstream 7 South Staffordshire had found a fordable place two miles north of Ouffières and it was there the brigade commander decided the crossing would be made. The plan was to form a bridgehead with the battalions west of Grimbosq Forest and south of the village. The plan depended for its success on speed and surprise and for the use of darkness for the reorganisation and bridge building. A class 9 bridge was to be completed by first light on 7 August over which essential vehicles and 6-pounders were to pass. The tanks were to wade the river at a ford after the banks had been bulldozed. 17-pounders, medium machine guns and mortars were to remain in position on the near bank and make use of their range to support the troops in the bridgehead, which would be in full view of the steeply sloping ground.

The battalion plan was for companies to wade the river in order D, A, C, B, dismounted Carrier Platoon, Battalion HQ and move to the start line of the road running south from Grimbosq to Brieux, then on orders given over the radio to advance to their objective by compass bearing and dig in by first light. Essential vehicles and 6-pounders under the command of Captain Redfern (Anti-Tank Platoon) were to join the battalion at first light when the bridge was open. The battalion would be carrying everything it would want immediately, e.g. radio sets, rations, 150 rounds per rifleman, etc. Rear Battalion HQ and non-essential vehicles were to remain under the 2ic in the assembly area on the near bank. B Squadron, 107 RAC, and one troop AVRE were to join the battalion as soon as possible in daylight. The mortar platoon was to position itself on the near bank and fire by observation or on call.

The initial crossing achieved surprise, and 7 South Stafford and 6 North Stafford captured their objectives without heavy fighting. The latter battalion took longer than expected to cross with the result it was getting dark before 7 Royal Norfolk moved off from the assembly area. The arrangements by brigade for marking the route went through thick woods on the steep hillsides and the battalion took a long time to reach the river and then only after some subunits had got lost in the pitch darkness and thick undergrowth.

After three hours of difficult marching in single file and carrying heavy loads the battalion led by D Company reached the river. By this time the initial surprise had worn off and the crossing was under heavy shell and mortar fire. An alternative place was found 600 yards away by Captain Jamieson, and the companies waded through three feet of water. The actual crossing was quickly carried out and although a heavy Nebelwerfer concentration came down just after the last man was across, no casualties were suffered. By 0100 hrs the whole battalion was across, and as it was only a short time before first light and the enemy did not appear to be opposing the bridgehead in any strength, companies were ordered to advance straight to their objective by compass bearing and dig in as fast as possible.

A Company had advanced from the start lines without incident but on getting within fifty yards of their objective, heavy fire was opened by the enemy. 9 Platoon under Lieutenant Bell on the right attacked immediately, drove the enemy back and started to dig in. 7 Platoon under Lieutenant Paul and the platoon sergeant, with Major Adderson, led the platoon forward again. 8 Platoon under Sergeant Rayner and Company Headquarters took up their allotted positions.

At 0340 hrs the enemy counterattacked from the orchards to the left, but the attack was smashed by well-controlled fire and the enemy withdrew in disorder. A patrol was now sent out to try to contact D Company on the left, but it ran into strong enemy positions and had to return after suffering casualties. For the rest of the night the company's position was under continuous, heavy, close-range fire and it was impossible to dig in.

At 0445 hrs the enemy attempted to work round to the right flank of 8 Platoon but were again forced back by accurate 2-inch mortar and Bren fire. As soon as dawn broke the enemy made a determined counterattack from the front. This was driven off with heavy loss, but not before A Company had themselves suffered severely. Major Adderson was with 9 Platoon, which had only eight men left, while Captain Searanke was with 8 Platoon. The enemy now proceeded to subject the position to intense mortar and Spandau fire.

The casualties mounted and by 0815 hrs, while the early morning mists were rising, the enemy subjected the remnants of A Company to intense mortar and Spandau fire then launched an overwhelming attack from the right and the rear. Major Adderson took over the 2-inch mortar and kept firing until all his bombs were expended and he was knocked out by a grenade. Lieutenant Bell, although wounded, opened fire with the PIAT gun until he too was laid out.

The last remaining Bren of 9 Platoon was kept in action to the end through the devotion of Corporal Vasey, who although three times wounded kept the gun supplied with ammunition, inflicting heavy casualties on the enemy. But as their ammunition was now exhausted the remnants of the company were soon overrun and taken prisoner. Sixteen dead were left on that battlefield and 75 per cent of A Company were wounded. The enemy also suffered severely. Two companies of infantry had opposed A Company, and a German doctor told Major Adderson when he was brought into a German field dressing station that sixty-seven wounded had been evacuated from the battlefield during the morning and many had been killed.

Immediately after first light on 7 August a patrol from C Company tried again to contact A Company but only encountered enemy machine-gun fire from the area where A Company should have been. By 0900 hrs on 7 August the noise of battle had died down on the right, A Company's 18 set radio was no longer on the air, and it was feared that the company must have been overrun. Hopes that they might still be holding out persisted and further attempts were made throughout the day to gain contact.

Soon after 0900 hrs the battalion's fighting vehicles and 6-pounders began to arrive after fighting through from the bridge. Private Herbert Wright was aboard the first carrier to cross the Orne in the battalion group of essential vehicles and was sitting high up on the back of the carrier. On reaching a point about 600 yards over the bridge, the road was heavily mortared and one man on the carrier was wounded. Private Wright immediately dressed this man's wounds, refusing to take cover from the mortaring. Then five German soldiers opened fire from the roadside. Private Wright, still sitting on the carrier, immediately returned fire, killing at least one of the enemy and the rest withdrew.

The vehicles next came under heavy Spandau and rifle fire from forty yards away. Private Wright again returned fire from the top of the carrier until the wireless operator was wounded. Wright dressed the man's wounds while still exposed to heavy fire. He then manned the wireless set and kept the vehicle group in touch with Battalion HQ until the vehicles arrived at the bridgehead.

Wright showed a degree of courage and devotion to duty which has rarely been surpassed. His actions were largely instrumental in getting the vehicles through to the battalion.

On arrival the 6-pounders quickly got into their pre-allotted positions. Shortly afterwards the Churchills arrived and were positioned one troop with D Company on the left, one troop watching the open right flank and the remainder of the squadron in reserve just behind Battalion Headquarters. Battalion HQ was dug in in an orchard just east of the road, the pioneers having worked hard to dig a command post. The RAP was in a farmhouse nearby.

During the morning D Company was ordered to clear some houses immediately south of Grimbosq and was given a troop of AVREs to help them. Twelve German soldiers were captured from 271 Infantry Division including an officer. Apart from this there was little enemy activity except constant shelling of the riverbank and approaches. Taking the morning to prepare for the next phase, by 1200 hrs Battalion HQ was dug in, and two sections of the Carrier Platoon under Lieutenant Buckerfield were positioned in the gap between C and D companies where they were occasionally under Spandau fire. Contact was established with 6 North Stafford to the right rear and with 7 South Stafford to the left rear. At 1400 hrs a brigade O group was held at 6 North Stafford headquarters at which the brigade commander gave orders for enlarging the bridgehead the next day, an order that seemed optimistic even at that time.

At 1600 hrs a hot meal was brought over in Jeeps from rear Battalion Headquarters and as a result everybody was feeling in good form although tired. This was the last hot meal the battalion would have until after the battle on 8 August. At 1730 hrs C Company made a final attempt to see what had happened to A Company and sent a patrol commanded by Sergeant Smith, supported by a troop of tanks. Almost immediately the patrol ran into the enemy who were forming up to attack, and about twenty enemy were killed.

At 1830 hrs the first enemy counterattack came in the form of tanks rumbling down the track from the forest directly opposite D and C companies and Battalion HQ. The ground was thick and the fields of fire were short. Heavy mortar and artillery fire came down and tanks suddenly appeared at close range.

Sergeant Arthur Courtman's section of 6-pounders was sited in D Company's right forward platoon. The guns were forty yards apart, and as the crews had already suffered heavy casualties crossing the bridge in the morning, Sergeant Courtman fired the guns himself, running from one to another under fire to do so. He blew up his first tank at sixty yards with his first shot. Next, a Panther approached. Courtman ran to his second gun and with his first shot, at over 100 yards knocked it out too and the crew bailed out. Shortly afterwards he knocked out a second Panther at 200 yards These successes achieved under intense fire so raised the morale of D Company, the enemy meeting with such stiff opposition that they did not succeed in penetrating D Company's position.

Throughout this action Captain Jamieson's company gave a magnificent account of itself under heavy fire. Despite the fierce fighting and several anxious moments the battalion was still in firm possession of its positions at last light. Everyone was feeling pleased with how they had accounted for themselves during the day but knew there was still plenty more fighting to come. With the enemy dominating the bridge there could be no evacuation.

The fighting at the Orne was conducted at close range and was ferocious. The situation was confused and the enemy attack began to tell. In the centre the enemy infiltrated buildings around fifty yards from Battalion HQ from which Captain Ernest Ridger and Lieutenants Oakey and Hammond and a few men made a counterattack with the support of a platoon from Major Ellis's B Company. C Company was not so heavily engaged thanks to a successful patrol by Sergeant Smith an hour earlier.

On the right, however, enemy tanks got far too near the bridge and shelled the Battalion HQ area. Captain Rodney Gibson, OC HQ Company, was killed and Captain Redfern of the Anti-Tank Platoon was wounded by 88 shells. Churchill tanks in the brigade area were knocked out. With the enemy dominating the bridge no evacuation was possible, except for walking wounded who could get back over the river and the RAP soon filled up with fifty or so wounded.

After dark, standing patrols were put out near the exits of the forest and with the bright moonlight and burning houses, it made standing patrols necessary against tank attack. Lieutenant Hamond (Intelligence) was going back to brigade to report but on reaching the Brieux road junction, he and his party were shot up and taken prisoner.

At 0800 hrs on the morning of 8 August the enemy began its second counterattack. This time special attention was paid by the enemy to Sergeant Courtman's guns and one was soon knocked out along with two of the three Churchill tanks with D Company taking the full brunt of the attack. A strong enemy force had worked its way around the north of Grimbosq and attacked D Company from two sides. Rapidly, they overran the forward platoon and CANLOAN Lieutenant Andrew Fraser Bushell was killed while Sergeant Courtman was firing his last remaining gun alone and under intense fire of all kinds. Courtman was finally killed by a tank shell.

Lieutenant-Colonel Freeland wrote of Sergeant Courtman: 'So died one of the bravest men of all times, who by his magnificent example had inspired the men of the D Company around him to superhuman efforts.' Sergeant Arthur Courtman (31) was a King's Lynn man; he was mourned by his wife and parents and of course his comrades in the battalion – they never forgot him or his bravery. In the light of his valour many were disappointed to learn Sergeant Courtman was only recognised with a posthumous mention in despatches.

Captain Jamieson was the only officer from D Company left alive but kept his cool and reorganised the remnants of his two forward platoons round Company HQ, his reserve platoon and the single remaining Churchill tank. But to Jamieson's dismay they manoeuvred directly into the line of fire of a concealed enemy tank. A fierce fight now ensued at close range, and Jamieson tried desperately to attract the tank commander's attention toward an important target but to no avail. He then ran and tried to use the phone at the back of the tank but could not get through. Ignoring incoming fire, he clambered on to the tank. As he did so an armour-piercing shell drilled a hole through the driver's compartment. Jamieson was thrown off, peppered with shrapnel and badly shaken, receiving wounds near his right eye and in his left forearm. CSM Jones took command while Captain Jamieson was having his wounds dressed.

At the regimental aid post the MO Captain Payne and his staff were under extreme pressure and despite at one stage of the battle having seventy-five wounded, performed a 'miraculous' evacuation of wounded men to the safety of a stable. After directing the battle with skill for some time, CSM Jones was also badly wounded and had to be evacuated. It appeared the position would be overrun but the 18 set radio operators, Privates Pennington and Nicholson, although without a company commander, continued to relay accurate and essential information to their CO, Lieutenant-Colonel Freeland.

Despite being in great pain Captain Jamieson, his eye dressed and his arm in a sling, returned and took command again and walked about among his men, encouraging them to greater efforts and sent back targets for the artillery over the radio. At one stage the position was so serious the fire had to be brought down on the company itself. Luckily, they were well dug in as the accuracy of the guns of 116 Field Regiment was outstanding. It was later recorded each gun fired about 1,000 shells during the thirty-six-hour battle. Lieutenant-Colonel Freeland wrote:

> So successful was Captain Jamieson in his direction of the battle and so magnificently did D Company fight that the enemy was held and heavy casualties inflicted upon him. There was constant fire, the enemy had attacked several times but each time they were repulsed … Capt Jamieson's outstanding leadership and personal bravery was largely responsible for the defeat of these determined attacks. He refused to be evacuated and stayed with his company until the company were relieved in the evening.

Jamieson's VC citation concludes:

> Throughout this 36 hours of bitter and close fighting, and despite the pain of his wounds, Captain Jamieson showed superb qualities of leadership and great personal bravery. There were times when the position appeared hopeless, but on each occasion, it was restored by his coolness and determination. He personally was largely responsible for the holding of this important bridgehead over the river

Orne and the repulse of seven German counter-attacks with great loss to the enemy. … D Company had fought magnificently and every man had done more than his duty. Lance Sergeant Kay had particularly distinguished himself in command of the remnants of his platoon. Captain Jamieson, throughout the whole 36 hours of fighting, showed superb qualities of leadership and personal bravery. Largely through his actions on August 7–8 the important Orne Bridgehead was successfully held. The Victoria Cross which rewarded his great gallantry can seldom have been more courageously won.

Captain David Jamieson was to be the only one of the five Royal Norfolk Regiment recipients of the Victoria Cross during the Second World War to live to receive it personally. Of his award of the Victoria Cross he once modestly said: 'It was certainly not personally deserved. It was won by a group of men in a tight position.' The author had the pleasure to meet him on a number of occasions, and he thinks that sums up the dignified, unassuming hero and upright gentleman who was Major David Jamieson, VC.

For some hours the fate of the bridgehead hung in the balance and largely on the individual gallantry of D Company. C Company was also closely engaged but artillery defensive fire was very effective. The RAP was set on fire, but Captain Payne and his assistants succeeded in transferring their seventy-five wounded cases to a stable.

By 1400 hrs brigade was able to send over 7 Royal Warwickshire who drove the enemy back and opened up the road to the bridge. This made it possible to evacuate wounded who had been in the RAP since the previous evening.

B Company now only had five tanks left, and the battalion was very reduced and exhausted after three days' continuous fighting. Enemy tanks could be heard in the forest and medium artillery engaged them, and at length two companies of 7 South Staffordshire under Major A. J. C. Prickett recrossed the river, one relieving D Company and the other clearing Grimbosq village.

A new squadron of Churchill tanks came up and in the evening the brigade commander arranged for 7 Royal Welch Fusiliers to relieve the battalion, which was thus withdrawn. It was later discovered the enemy engaged consisted of 12 SS Hitlerjugend Panzer Division using the 25 and 26 Panzer Grenadier Regiments supported by tanks. The former was reduced from a strength of 400 men to thirty.

This was one of a series of desperate counterattacks by the German 5 Panzer Army and 7 Army and showed that troops of the quality of the Royal Norfolk Regiment could fight it out in defensive positions against such odds, provided the fire plan was well laid on and ammunition did not run out. The brigade was congratulated by Major-General Lyne, divisional commander. The magnificent support given by 59 and 56 Divisional artillery was the subject of friendly exchanges between Lieutenant-Colonel Freeland and Brigadier Paddy Boylan, commanding the 59 Divisional Artillery:

My Dear Freeland
Your kind letter was most gratifying. I am glad indeed that we were of assistance in your gallant stand, but I am satisfied in my own mind that you would have held the ground without us. What a grand show your battalion put up, it will undoubtedly add to the finest traditions of your Regiment. … I do congratulate you most heartily and am proud that some of the Royal Regiment were able to merit such generous praise as you give. … Good luck and I hope to see you when you get a little respite.

Lieutenant-Colonel Freeland would be decorated for his gallantry at the Orne with a Distinguished Service Order, his citation stating:

At Grimbosq on 7 and 8 August 7 Royal Norfolk commanded by Lieut Col I. H. Freeland were holding the eastern apex of a bridgehead over the River Orne. During the 48 hour period the Germans launched no less than nine determined counter attacks with the object of destroying our bridgehead, the first two with infantry from 271 Division, the remainder with tanks and infantry from both battle groups and 12 SS Division. The Norfolks stood their ground. They repulsed each counter attack with heavy losses to the enemy after grim hand to hand fighting and showed such fine spirit that at the end of this prolonged and bitter fighting they were themselves attacking the withdrawing Germans.

During this operation Lieutenant Colonel Freeland showed the highest qualities of leadership and the magnificent example of coolness and personal bravery which he set was an inspiration to all ranks of the Battalion. ... Despite almost continuous heavy artillery and mortar fire he was continually visiting his forward companies and moving about in the open to encourage and steady his men. ... At the height of the battle his one thought was how to go over to the offensive and he ordered up flame throwers in order to be able to attack the Germans as soon as the opportune moment arrives. ... Lieutenant Colonel Freeland's whole conduct of this operation was an absolute model of what personal command of a battalion by an outstanding officer can achieve. There is no doubt that his great gallantry and inspiring example had much to do with the magnificent stand made by his battalion.

Major Wilfred Alfred Adderson also received a DSO. CSM Ernest George Jones of D Company, Sergeant Robert Charles Smith of C Company, Lance-Sergeant Ellis Kay, Corporal Harry Vasey of A Company, Private Herbert Cecil Wright of Intelligence Section and Private Geoffrey Stephen Pennington of Signals Platoon all received Military Medals.

It is this last recipient that so much was owed to the successful outcome of this dramatic action. Private Geoff Pennington manned his radio set throughout the action under heavy fire from enemy mortars, Spandau, rifles, MGs and enemy tanks firing HE at Company HQ, his citation stating:

The wireless never failed and it was through this set that the Company Commander was able to bring down intense artillery fire which broke up the enemy's first attack. Next morning the enemy attacked D Company again shortly after first light using a fresh battle group. The forward platoons of D Company were over run and enemy infantry penetrated to within a short distance of Company HQ on three sides. … During this attack the Company Commander and CSM were wounded and Private Pennington with his fellow operator were left alone but he did not flinch and kept his set going through which he passed information to Battalion HQ on the situation. The Commanding Officer was then able to direct the artillery on to targets passed through by Private Pennington. … The enemy were finally driven out of D Company's position but during the day attacked three more times, each time being repulsed. Throughout the whole day the set manned by Private Pennington never failed, if it had done so the artillery should not have been directed onto the important targets, there being no FOO with the company. … With complete disregard for his own safety and with a coolness of action that has rarely been surpassed, Private Pennington was largely responsible for the successful repulse of all attacks made on the bridgehead at Grimbosq on 7 and 8 August 1944.

Mention should also be made of the 481 Battery commander Major P. Pettitt and Captain B. Johnson who directed the massed artillery 59 and 53 Division (six field regiments and one medium regiment supporting the bridgehead) as requested over the 18 set by Lieutenant-Colonel Lywood. A devastating fire was brought down in minutes and it was primarily this that broke up the enemy attacks time and again and inflicted heavy casualties. During the thirty-six hours of the bridgehead battle the 25-pounders alone fired 1,000 rounds per gun.

7 Royal Norfolk had three days in a quiet village to rest and reequip. A Company, 7 South Staffordshire, came to replace A Company under

Major R. Webb. Even so the shortage of officers remained acute. Sergeants commanded the Pioneers and Mortars. Lieutenant T. P. K. Oakley was promoted to captain to command the Anti-Tank Platoon. Captain E. Mercer of 7 South Staffordshire became OC HQ Company and Captain Hughes Intelligence Officer.

Owing to the shortage of reinforcements and the heavy casualties suffered by 21 Army Group during the first ten weeks of fighting 176 Brigade headquarters was disbanded and one battalion in each brigade was reshuffled between 177 and 197 brigades. 7 Royal Norfolk joined 177 Brigade when opposite Thury-Harcourt and after two uneventful days motored to a concentration area ten miles northwest of Falaise, arriving at the high ground at Ouilly on the main road running west from Falaise at 0300 hrs on 17 August. Movement light was used and was of the greatest help as it was very dark.

7 Royal Norfolk was to act as an advanced guard for their brigade in an attack on Les Isles-Bardel. The battalion marched through beautiful countryside and for a while the enemy was not obvious. The battalion had just marched down a long open road, and crossed a tributary of the River Orne at the bottom of the valley with C Company under Major Walker in the vanguard. When they reached the high ground west of Les Isles-Bardel, suddenly all hell broke loose as they were met by a hail of machine-gun fire, mortar shells and enemy artillery raining shells onto the road. Enemy positions were difficult to pinpoint, and any battalion attack would have been a difficult undertaking but attack they did.

C Company fought their way slowly to a sunken road and incurred some casualties. The enemy was on dominating ground which overlooked all the approaches, and it was difficult to locate all the positions and select objectives while under such an attack. A complete battalion attack would be required to dislodge the enemy from such a strong position. Preparations, however, were made and once the Churchill tanks were up, the attack went in with 5 South Stafford on the left and a squadron of Churchill tanks. A Company led these to the attack while D Company followed and took care of the flank. C Company was fire company with B Company and Carriers in reserve. The artillery smoked a feature on the right of the objective as well as fire concentrations on to likely enemy positions.

A Company captured their objective with only six casualties, and the enemy withdrew. D Company met no opposition and reorganised guarding the right flank. This small but valiant action saw Private Eric Bird awarded the Military Medal for his gallantry. Bird's Bren team had been knocked out and he had been wounded. Despite the wound bleeding badly and blood pouring over his face, Bird continued firing his gun and gave covering fire to the remainder of his section and another section of his platoon, enabling them to close with and assault the enemy. By this time Private Bird had run out of ammunition but refused to leave his gun until his platoon commander ordered him to the regimental aid post.

Next morning the battalion was ordered to clear some large woods about 1,500 yards in front of their position. A Company accomplished this without incident and the rest of the battalion closed up, but 5 South Stafford encountered enemy two miles ahead and were held up all day.

Early on the following morning the commanding officer went over to meet the brigadier at 6 South Stafford for a recce. As the advanced guard was held up on the axis the brigadier was considering the opposition by passing the battalion through 6 South Stafford on the left. It was eventually decided that the ground was not suitable, and the battalion remained where it was, although ready to move at short notice. That afternoon D Company and the Carriers were moved up close behind 5 South Stafford as a counterattack was feared.

Next day 5 South Stafford made slow progress and 7 Royal Norfolk was directed to seize the high ground west of Bazoches, overlooking the main road from Falaise to Putanges. There was no opposition to this advance of six miles. The enemy retired in disorder, leaving equipment and several ammunition dumps behind. A patrol of C Company captured the intelligence officer of 374 Division who had been asleep and left behind.

The battalion now began its last operation, the mopping up of an area full of rejoicing French civilians. The best capture was a German main dressing station with staff and some wounded British prisoners. The MO was particularly pleased to have these immaculately dressed German doctors. In all 107 prisoners were taken.

At the end of this day Lieutenant-Colonel Freeland was informed by the brigadier that 59 Division, being the junior division of 21 Army Group, was to be disbanded and all the infantry battalions dispersed to provide reinforcements for other divisions. 59 Division concentrated for dispersal at the scene of its greatest triumph, on the banks of the Orne, north of Thury-Harcourt. 7 Royal Norfolk was accommodated in tents on the site where B Company had fought on 5 August. Ironically, when the battalion arrived in France, it rained and now as it was being dispersed, it rained again.

The rifle companies were moved off to their new battalions on 26 August. Lieutenant-Colonel Bellamy came over personally to arrange reinforcements from this dispersal for 1 Royal Norfolk and so the entire D Company joined 1 Royal Norfolk along with some personnel from S and HQ companies. B Company and the remainder of HQ Company joined 1 Suffolk, C Company went to 1 Ox and Bucks Light Infantry and A Company joined 2 Monmouth. Lieutenant-Colonel Freeland was appointed to command of 5 Queens in 7 Armoured Division.

The following officers and senior NCOs of 7 Royal Norfolk transferred to 1 Royal Norfolk Regiment:

Maj F. H. Crocker, MC
Capt D. W. Glass
Capt T. P. K Oakey
Capt E. H. T. Ridger
Capt W. J .Smart
Lt P. W Buckerfield
Lt L. Dawson

WOII L. W. Brown
WOII R. Fuller
WOII S. Flint
WOII E. J. L. Langford
C/Sgt E. Lacey
Sgt J. Moore
Sgt W. Paskell

The final winding up of the affairs of the battalion was carried out by the quartermaster who then returned to England. At the end of the Normandy campaign not one of the original rifle company subalterns of 7 Royal Norfolk was left. Of the rifle company commanders only Majors Ellis and Walker had come through unscathed. Caister man Major Arthur Ellis was later killed in action on 12 October 1944 during fighting in Holland while commanding a company of 1 Suffolk. Of the officers who left England with the battalion in 1944 only fifteen (including the MO and the padre) remained at the end of the Normandy fighting. The only CSMs to come through were CSM Brown and CSM Fuller. CSM Len Brown was killed while serving with 1 Royal Norfolk on 16 October 1944. On VE Day 1945 only six of the original officers of 7 Royal Norfolk still serving in 21 Army Group remained unscathed.

Lieutenant-Colonel Freeland wrote in conclusion of his battalion:

> During its short active service career for the second time in the war 7 Royal Norfolk had made a name for itself which was in keeping with the highest traditions of the Regiment. At the time of its dispersal, in spite of severe casualties, its morale and fighting record was of such high order that it was singled out for special praise by not only the Divisional Commander, but the Commander-in-Chief himself. In the two months fighting the battalion had been awarded one VC, two DSOs, one MC, ten MMs and five Mentions in Despatches. Many more deserved decorations … The breaking up of a good battalion at the height of its success was a very bitter blow to all ranks. In spite of this all members felt that they had done their duty and contributed a little toward the superb war record of The Royal Norfolk Regiment.

Selected Bibliography

Bates, Thomas J., *Normandy: The Search for Sidney* (Bates, 2000).

Battalion, The, *The History of the 1st Battalion, The Royal Norfolk Regiment during the World War 1939–1945* (Jarrold, 1947).

Beith, Major General John Hay, *The Citizen Soldier* (Hutchinson, 1939).

Brough, Arthur, *My Wasted Years 1940–1945* (Brough, 2003).

Carew, Tim, *The Royal Norfolk Regiment* (Leo Cooper, 1967).

Delaforce, Patrick, *Monty's Iron Sides: From the Normandy Beaches to Bremen with the 3rd Division* (Sutton, 2002).

Freeland, Lieutenant Colonel I. H., DSO, *A History of 7th Battalion, The Royal Norfolk Regiment in World War II (July 1940-August 1944)* (privately published for the battalion, 1946).

Hart, Peter, *At the Sharp End: From Le Paradis to Kohima* (Pen & Sword, 1998).

Jolly, Cyril, *The Vengeance of Private Pooley* (Heinemann, 1956).

Jolly, Cyril, *The Man Who Missed the Massacre* (Jolly, 1986).

Keegan, John and Holmes, Richard, *Soldiers: A History of Men in Battle* (Hamish Hamilton, 1985).

Kemp, Lieut-Commander P. K., RN, *History of The Royal Norfolk Regiment 1919–1951 Volume III* (Regimental Association of The Royal Norfolk Regiment, 1953).

Lincoln, John, *Thank God and the Infantry: From D-Day to VE Day with the 1st Battalion The Royal Norfolk Regiment* (Sutton, 1994).

McNish, Robin, *Iron Division: The History of the 3rd Division* (Allan, 1978).

Montgomery, Field Marshal Bernard, *El Alamein to the River Sangro* (Arrow, 1960).

Pratt, Jack, *Jack's Memories: The Life of a Norfolk Boy* (Pratt, 2000).

Scarfe, Norman, *Assault Division: A History of the 3rd Division from the Invasion of Normandy to the Surrender of Germany* (Collins, 1947).

Storey, Neil R., *Britain's Coast at War: Invasion Threat, Coastal Forces, Bombardment and Training for D-Day* (Pen & Sword, 2021).

Storey, Neil R., *The Pride of Norfolk: A History of the Norfolk Regiment Territorials* (Halsgrove, 2009).

Troup, Jack, *The Life that Jack Lived: Experiences of a Norfolk Soldier and Policeman* (Larks Press, 1997).

Battalion war diaries, newspapers and *The Britannia: The Journal of The Royal Norfolk Regiment,* unpublished memoirs and interviews are annotated accordingly in the text.

Acknowledgements

The author would like to express his thanks to the following: The National Archives, Imperial War Museum, BBC Radio Norfolk, The Royal Norfolk Regimental Museum, Norfolk Heritage Centre, Norfolk Record Office, 1st Battalion Royal Norfolk Regiment D-Day Veterans' Association, Dunkirk Veterans' Association, Far Eastern Prisoners of War Association, The Burma Star Association, Norwich & District Normandy Veterans' Association, Royal British Legion Industries, The Tommy Club, Norfolk Record Office, The Le Paradis Commemoration Group, *Britain at War* magazine, Lieutenant-Colonel Alan B. Cubitt, Major Tom Eaton, OBE, TD, DL, Major Harry Schulman, MBE, Major Bob Hamond, Major J. Monty Smythe, Major John Raybould, TD, Major Gilly Banthorpe, Captain John Lincoln, MC, Tommy Catlin, MM, Ted Shepherd, MM, Ernie Seaman, MM, John Slaughter, Paul Buckerfield, Verdun Storey, Joan Way, Jack Forrest, Herbert Lines, Ernie Leggett, Ernie 'Strips' Farrow, Arthur Brough, Ivor Self, Harold Cooke, Bertie Perkins, George Clapham, Arthur Hewitt, Jack Pratt, Lucy Best, Nigel Gant, Aaron Gant, Wilf Morter, George Brodie, Dennis O'Callaghan, John Head, Tim Bennett, Terry Davy, Vic Brown, Chris Reeve, Ian McCallum, Thomas Williamson, Vic Sharman and my dear family for all their love and support. The author also would like to place on record his sincere gratitude to the many Second World War veterans and their families who have shared and entrusted their wartime stories, letters, memoirs and photographs to him over the years.

Index

Dear Reader,

We hope you have enjoyed this book, but why not share your views on social media? You can also follow our pages to see more about our other products: facebook.com/penandswordbooks or follow us on X @penswordbooks

You can also view our products at www.pen-and-sword.co.uk (UK and ROW) or www.penandswordbooks.com (North America).

To keep up to date with our latest releases and online catalogues, please sign up to our newsletter at: www.pen-and-sword.co.uk/newsletter

If you would like a printed catalogue with our latest books, then please email: enquiries@pen-and-sword.co.uk or telephone: 01226 734555 (UK and ROW) or email: uspen-and-sword@casematepublishers.com or telephone: (610) 853-9131 (North America).

We respect your privacy and we will only use personal information to send you information about our products.

Thank you!